Something to   .....
Travelling: Thailand

Robert A Webster and Contributing Authors

Acknowledgements

Contributing authors:

A big thanks to: Captain Bob Pipinich, Stuart Duncan, Kerry Eggleton, Anthony Shambrook, Somasak Meesili, and Somchai Piluk; for their writings and research.

Colin (Ginge) Hardiman for his endless supply of jokes

Michael C Smith http://beezeebooks.com/

Christine Sherborne http://www.colourstory.com/

For their tireless efforts with promoting books.

Contents

Quiz Answers

Bibliography

Introduction

Something to Read While Travelling is an informative and entertaining companion to accompany you on your travels.

Something to Read While Travelling- THAILAND. Contains useful information about Thailand, some of which you won't find in travel guidebooks. Comprehensive travel guides will go into more detail on specific areas of Thailand. This publication only deals with the popular tourist hotspots, giving you plenty of time to read and enjoy the, Useful Tips: Thai Language Made Simple: Popular Thai Recipes: Fun Quizzes and Brainteasers: Hilarious Jokes: Short Stories: and the full comedy adventure novel, SIAM STORM – A Thailand Adventure.

Leave your cares and woes at the arrivals section of the airport. Make sure you pack a big smile and this travelling companion in your suitcase. Open your heart and mind, and enjoy your wonderful time in the Land of Smiles.

http://www.buddhasauthor.com/

http://stormwriter.weebly.com/

About Thailand

The Kingdom of Thailand is the most popular South East Asian holiday destination, where. you can find almost anything: thick green lush jungles, crystal blue waters that feel more like a warm bath than a swim in the ocean. Exotic, yet safe and cheap, Thailand is equipped with every modern amenity you need. There is something for every interest and every price bracket, from beach front backpacker bungalows to some of the best luxury hotels in the world. The Thai people are known for their friendly (**Sanuk**, happy) demeanour and with delicious taste bud tingling array of fresh foods, tropical climate, fascinating culture and spectacular temples, Thailand is a tourists dream destination.

Geography

Thailand is a country in Southeast Asia with coasts on the Andaman Sea and the Gulf of Thailand. It borders Myanmar (Burma) to the northwest, Laos to the northeast, Cambodia to the southeast and Malaysia to the south.

Cities

Bangkok — Thailand's bustling, frenetic capital, known among the Thai as Krung Thep

Ayutthaya — a historical city, UNESCO World Heritage Site and old capital of Siam

Chiang Mai— de facto capital of Northern Thailand and the heart of Lanna culture

Chumphon— gateway to the Chumphon Archipelago, Pathio's unspoilt beaches & Ko TaoIsland

Chiang Rai — gateway to the Golden Triangle, ethnic minorities and mountain trekking

Kanchanaburi — home of the bridge over the River Kwai and numerous World War II museums

Nakhon Ratchasima — largest city of the Isaan region

Pattaya — one of the main tourist destinations, known for its nightlife

Sukhothai — Thailand's first capital, with amazing ruins still

Surat Thani — home of the Srivijaya Empire, gateway to Koh Samui

Other destinations

Koh Chang — once a quiet island, now undergoing major tourism development

Koh Lipe — small island in the middle of Tarutao National Park, amazingly unspoiled with great reefs and beaches

Koh Pha Ngan — site of the famous Full Moon Party with miles of quiet coastline

Koh Samet — the nearest island beach escape from Bangkok

Koh Samui — comfortable, nature, and entertainment hippie hangout gone upmarket

Koh Tao — known for its diving and nature, easily reached from Chumphon by high speed catamaran

Khao Lak — gateway to the Similan Islands, hard hit by the 2004 tsunami, but vibrant once more

Khao Sok National Park — one of the most beautiful wildlife reserves in Thailand

Khao Yai National Park — take a night time 4x4 safari spotting deer or visit the spectacular waterfalls

Krabi Province — beach and watersports hub in the south, includes Ao Nang, Rai Leh, Ko Phi Phi and Ko Lanta

Phuket — the original Thai paradise island, now very developed, but still with some beautiful beaches

Khon Kaen — in the heart of Esaan (Isan) known for their silk and dinosaur sites.

Mae Sot — a thriving multi-cultural border town, with lots of national parks around to explore

Mae Sariang — small town life at the Thai Burmese border with trecking and Salween National Park

With the exception of Phuket; Koh precedes all Island names

Thailand can be conveniently divided into five geographic and cultural regions:

Regions of Thailand

Northern Thailand : Chiang Mai, hill tribes, and the Golden Triangle.

Isaan: The great northeast region. Get off the beaten track and discover back country Thailand, mouth watering food, and some magnificent Khmer ruins.

9

Central Thailand : Bangkok, lowlands and historic Thailand.

Eastern Thailand: Beaches and islands within easy reach of Bangkok, like Pattaya, Koh Samet and Koh Chang.

Southern Thailand - Lush rainforest, hundreds of km of coastline and countless islands on both the Andaman Sea and the Gulf of Thailand: Phuket, Chumphon, Krabi, Koh Samui, Koh Tao and more of Thailand's famous beach spots.

History

Known as Siam until 1939, Thailand is the only Southeast Asian country never to have been colonised by a foreign power, and is fiercely proud of that fact. A bloodless revolution in 1932 led to a constitutional monarchy. During World War II, while Japan conquered the rest of Southeast Asia, only Thailand was not conquered by the Japanese, due to smart political moves. In alliance with Japan during World War II, Thailand became a US ally following the conflict.

Politics in Thailand

Thailand is a constitutional monarchy, with the king as a very highly respected and revered Head of State. The Thai parliament is bicameral, consisting of a Senate, of which about half are directly elected with each province electing one member, and the other half being appointed by a committee, as well as a lower house which is directly elected by the people. The Prime Minister is the Head of Government, and is usually the leader of the party with the most seats in the lower house.

Thailand is presided over by King Bhumipol Adulyadej (Rama IX), the world's longest-reigning monarch, who has dedicated his life to his people, with his innovations and edicts, leading Thailand into the modern day society we have today. King Bhumipol is a deeply loved and respected figure by the Thai people. With that being said, do not disrespect the King or the royal family. Even though the king's role is largely ceremonial, with the Prime Minister holding the most authority in government, the king and the royal family are still protected by strict lèse majesté laws, which stipulate long jail terms for anybody convicted of insulting the king or any other members of the royal family.

Climate

Thailand is largely tropical, so it's hot and humid all year around with temperatures in the 28-35°C range (82-95°F), a degree of relief provided only in the mountains in the far north of Thailand.

Cool: From November to the end of February, it doesn't rain much and temperatures are at their lowest, although you will barely notice the difference in the south and will only need to pack a sweater if hiking in the northern mountains, where temperatures can fall as low as 5°C. This is the most popular time to visit and, especially around Christmas and New Year's or at Chinese New Year a few weeks later, finding flights and accommodation can be expensive and difficult.

Hot: From March to June, Thailand swelters in temperatures as high as 40°C (104°F). Pleasant enough when sitting on the beach with a drink in hand, but not the best time of year to go temple-tramping in Bangkok.

Rainy: From July to October, although it only really gets under way in September, tropical monsoons hit most of the country. This doesn't mean it rains non-stop, but when it does it pours, flooding is not uncommon.

There are local deviations to these general patterns. In particular, the south-east coast of Thailand (including Koh Samui) has the rains reversed, with the peak season being May-October and the rainy off season in November-February.

Culture

Thai culture is heavily influenced by Buddhism. However, unlike the Buddhist countries of East Asia, Thailand's Buddhists follow the Theravada school, which is arguably closer to its Indian roots and places a heavier emphasis on monasticism. Thai temples known as Wats, resplendent with gold and easily identifiable with their ornate, multicoloured, pointy roofs are ubiquitous and becoming an orange-robed monk for a short period, typically the three-month rainy season, is a common rite of passage for young Thai boys and men. Some of the main temples are spectacular sights to behold.

One pre-Buddhist tradition that still survives is the spirit house (saan phraphuum), usually found at the corner of any house or business, which houses spirits so they don't enter the house and cause trouble. The grander the building, the larger the spirit house, and buildings placed in particularly unlucky spots may have very large ones. Perhaps the most famous spirit house in Thailand is the Erawan Shrine in Bangkok, which protects the Erawan Hotel (now the Grand Hyatt Erawan) - built in 1956 on a former execution ground - and is now one of the busiest and most popular shrines in the city.

Some traditional arts popular in Thailand include traditional Thai dancing and music, based on religious rituals and court entertainment. Famously brutal Thai boxing (muay Thai), derived from the military training of Thai warriors, is undoubtedly the country's best known indigenous sport.

In addition to the mainland Thai culture, there are many other cultures in Thailand including those of the "hill tribes" in the northern mountainous regions of Thailand (e.g., Hmong, Karen, Lisu, Lahu, Akha), the southern Muslims, and indigenous island peoples of the Andaman Sea.

Calendar: In addition to the Gregorian calendar, Thailand also uses the Thai solar calendar, which is 543 years ahead. Thus, Thai year 2558 corresponds to the Western year 2015. Thai dates in English are often written as B.E., short for "Buddhist Era".

Some Thai holidays are still calculated with the older Thai lunar calendar, so their dates change every year.

Holidays and Festivals: Thailand has many holidays, mostly related to Buddhism and the monarchy. Nobody celebrates all of them, except for banks, which seem to be closed a lot.

Wisakha Bucha — falls on a full moon in the sixth lunar month, which is usually in May or sometimes June. It commemorates the birth, enlightenment, and death of the Lord Buddha that all happened on the same day in Buddha period. Wisakha Bucha Day is recognized as the most important day in Buddhism and also recognized as "World Heritage Day" by UNESCO. On this day, Thai Buddhists visit a temple to make merit in the morning and listen to sermons (Dhamma) by monks. After sunset, candle-lit processions (Wian-Tian) take place at most temples across the country. Buddhists carry lighted candles, three incense sticks and flowers, usually lotus flowers and walk around the central Wat three times in clockwise direction among smoke from the candles and incense sticks.

Makha Bucha — falls on the full moon in of the fourth Lunar month, which usually falls in February or March, and commemorates the spontaneous gathering of 1,250 people before the Buddha, which led to their ordination and subsequent enlightenment. At temples in Bangkok and throughout Thailand, Buddhists carry candles and walk around the main shrine three times in a clockwise direction.

Asanha Bucha — falls on a full moon in the eighth lunar month, usually in July. It commemorates the first sermon of the Lord Buddha and the first monk of Buddhism. Many Thai Buddhists make merit, give food to monks, donate offering to temples and listen to sermons given by monks. Ceremonies are held in Buddhist temples throughout Thailand. In the evening, Buddhists perform candle-lit processions (Wian-Tian) by walking around the main chapel together with carrying candles, three incense sticks and lotus flowers. This day is also marked as the beginning of Buddhist lent period (Vassa) that neat

13

wax candles are lit and kept burning during this period. In Ubon Ratchathani province, a Candle Festival is held which there is a parade of candles that each candle is enormous and made up very elaborately and creatively in many different figures. In Saraburi, monks will walk through the town with their bowls, on this day, to let Buddhists put flowers into their bowls instead of food.

Chinese New Year, usually February depending on Lunar calendar — Chinese Thais, who are numerous in Bangkok, celebrate by cleaning their houses and offering food to their ancestors. This is mainly a time of abundant feasting. Visit Bangkok's Chinatown or Yaowarat to fully embrace the festivity.

Songkran — Thai New Year, sometime in April (officially April 13th to 15th, but the date varies in some locations). What started off as polite ritual to wash away the sins of the prior year has evolved into the world's largest water fight, which lasts for three full days. Water pistols and Super Soakers are advised and are on sale everywhere. The best places to participate are Chiang Mai, the Khao San Road area in Bangkok and holiday resorts like Pattaya, Koh Samui and Phuket. Be advised that you will get very wet, this is not a spectator sport. In recent years, the water-throwing has been getting more and more unpleasant as people have started splashing iced water onto each other. It is advisable to wear dark clothing, as light colours may become transparent when wet.

Loy Krathong — falls on the first full moon day in the twelfth month of the Lunar calendar, usually in November, when people head to rivers, lakes and even hotel swimming pools to float flower and candle-laden banana-leaf (or, these days, styrofoam) floats called krathong(กระทง). The krathong is meant as an offering to thank the river goddess who gives life to the people. Thais also believe that this is a good time to float away your bad luck and many will place a few strands of hair or finger nail clippings in the krathong. According to tradition, if you make a wish when you set down your krathong and it floats out of sight before the candle burns out, your wish will come true. Some provinces have their own version of Loy Krathong, such as Sukhothai where a spectacular show takes place. To the North, Chiang Mai and Chiang Rai, have their own unique tradition of floating Kom or lit lantern balloons. This sight can be breath-taking as the sky is suddenly filled with lights, rivalling the full moon.

Coronation Day, 5 May — Commemorates the crowning of the current King in 1950 (although his reign actually began on 9 June 1946 - making him not only the longest-serving monarch in Thai history, but also the world's longest-serving current Head of State).

The King's Birthday (5 December) — is the country's National Day and celebrated as Father's Day, when Thais pay respect to and show their love for His Majesty the King. Buildings and homes are decorated with the King's flag (yellow with his insignia in the middle) and his portrait. Government buildings, as well as commercial buildings, are decorated with lights. In Old Bangkok (Rattanakosin) in particular, around the Royal Palace, you will see lavish light displays on trees, buildings, and the roads. The Queen's Birthday (12 August) is Mother's Day, and is celebrated similarly if with a little less pomp.

Royal Ploughing Ceremony — The old rite since ancient times to enhance the morale of farmers. To commemorate the importance of agriculture to the economy of Thailand. Ceremonies are conducted at Sanam Luang.

Queen's Birthday/ Mother's Day is on 12 Aug, — the birthday of HM Queen Sirikit.

Children's Day — The second Saturday of January in each year and has a motto for children by the Prime Minister of Thailand. Many organizations have celebrations and events for children to get a gift and toy.

Visas

(A) Countries/territories that do not require a visa for stay up to 90 days:-Argentina, Brazil, Chile, Peru and South Korea.

(B) Countries/territories that do not require a visa for stay up to 30 days: (30 days when entering by air; by land border only 14 days)-Australia, Austria, Belgium, Bahrain, Brunei, Canada, Czech Republic, Denmark, Estonia, Finland, France, Germany, Greece, Hong Kong, Hungary, Iceland, Indonesia, Ireland, Israel, Italy, Japan, Kuwait, Laos, Liechtenstein, Luxembourg, Macau, Malaysia, Monaco, Mongolia, Netherlands, New Zealand, Norway, Oman, Philippines, Poland, Portugal, Qatar, Russia, Singapore, Slovakia, Slovenia, Spain, South Africa, Sweden, Switzerland, Turkey, United Arab Emirates, United Kingdom, United States and Vietnam.

(C) Countries/territories that do not require a visa for stay up to 14 days or others (if indicated):- Cambodia, Ukraine.

Those with passports from countries not widely known, including European city-states, or have problems with document forgery, should obtain a visa in advance from the nearest Thai embassy. This is true even if visa on arrival is technically permitted. There are reports of tourists being detained using valid passports not commonly presented in Thailand. In addition, ask for a business card from the person or embassy which granted the visa, so they may be contacted on arrival, if necessary. Anyone whose nationality does not have its own embassy in Bangkok, should find out which third country represents your interests there, along with local contact information.

Proof of onward transit:- long happily ignored by Thai immigration, has been known to be strictly applied in some instances (Indian passport holders beware). The requirement is for an international flight itinerary - NOT train, ferry, or other departure type.

Airlines, who have to pay for your return flight if Thai immigration doesn't let you into the country, also check this and often will not let you board your flight for Thailand without it.) A print-out of an international e-ticket on a budget airline is sufficient to convince the enforcers, but those planning on continuing by land may have to get a little creative. Buying a fully refundable ticket and getting it refunded once in Thailand is also an option. Land crossings, on the other hand, are a very straightforward process and proof of onward journey is generally not required (Indian passport holders beware again... or anyone, if the border officials simply decide to uphold the bureaucracy).

Starting 29 August 2014, 30-day visa exemption and tourist visas can be extended for 30 days once at the nearest immigration office. According to immigration, you should bring with you an onward flight ticket, THB10,000 or 20,000 (some have reported the money has not been asked for), hotel booking confirmation/itinerary, passport sized photo, and application fee of THB1,900 before expiry of the initial 30 day period. Get there early, they start handing out numbers usually at 08:00.

Overstaying:- Overstaying in Thailand is possible with a 500 baht fine per day. Earlier it was fairly simple to avoid overstaying by doing a visa run to a neighbouring country overland or via a cheap flight, but since 12 August 2014 this will not be possible according to latest developments.

Stricter regulations introduced on 22 July 2014 now impose harsher penalties as a means of curbing overstaying. As can be seen from the tables, a distinction is made regarding an overstayer's circumstances. Overstayers presenting themselves to immigration officials at an airport or other border control are subject to the regulations in the first table.

In all other circumstances, overstayers will incur the much harsher penalties of being banned from re-entering Thailand for at least five years even if they overstay by just one or two days.

More information can be found on the Thai Immigration website.

The Tourism Authority of Thailand (TAT) ((TAT)), Tourism Authority of Thailand 1600 New Phetchaburi Road, Makkasan, Ratchathewi, Bangkok 10400, THAILAND (Suvarnabhumi Airport), ☎ +66 02 250 5500 (120 automatic lines), Suvarnabhumi Airport Arrival Floor, Domestic Tel: (66)2134 0040 Open 24 hours Arrival Floor, International Tel: (66)2134 0041 Open 24 hours for all TAT Local Offices see their web page edit.

Useful Information and Tips

All information is current at the time of publication.

Nationality: THAI

Currency : THAI BAHT (THB)

You will get a far better rate for your currency or travellers cheques if you exchange in Thailand. Banks, ATM's, and currency exchanges are commonplace around towns and cities. There are plenty at the arrivals section of airports, so you can easily change money on arrival

Language : THAI

See also section Thai Language Made Simple.

Thais address each other with their first names prefixed with "Khun", which stands equally for Ms, Mrs or Mr. It's polite to learn the most common greeting in any language: in Thai males say, "**khap**," and females say," **kah.**"

A Thai will meet and greet you with a *Wai and "**Sawadee (hello) Khap/ Kah**" It is polite to return the greeting.

*Wai -. Bring your open palms together at chest height, then bow slightly.

Most Thai's in the tourist areas speak English, so making yourself understood is usually not a problem (.**Mai Pen Rai**.) However, learning a few essentials doesn't hurt and Thai's consider it respectful if you try to communicate in their language, besides it's fun and part of your holiday experience and although it seems confusing, have a go by using **Thai Language made simple** section. You will soon get the hang of it and maybe pick up a few Thai friends along the way. If you go to areas were English isn't used or understood, remember your big smile and "**Mai Khow Chai Khap/Kah** (polite: - I don't understand) this will get you assistance.

Communication and Power supply

Free high-speed internet connection is easily available in most places. Using a Thai Sim-card is the easiest way to call around Thailand and abroad, with calls being relatively inexpensive. You can buy a Sim card in the many phone shops or minimarkets. At the time of publication, foreigners are required to show their passport or some form of ID to obtain one.

The electricity in Thailand is 220 volts, 50 cycles/sec.

Most wall sockets in Thailand are two prong, missing the third grounding/earth prong at the bottom. However, the newest office and condominium dwellings usually offer the third prong due to increased awareness of the importance of grounding for both safety and equipment damage reasons. Adapters are readily available in most shops and Mini marts.

Medical/Health

Certain vaccinations are required/recommended for Thailand. Consult your GP or medical practitioner for the current WHO requirements

Malaria prevention — Unless you are travelling to remote islands or areas of jungle known and clearly marked to have the anopheles malaria-carrying mosquitoes; preventative medicines for malaria are unnecessary and the side effects from these medicines can be unpleasant.

Pharmacies

Medicines: Leave your pharmacy at home. There are a Plethora of pharmacies everywhere, with most well stocked with inexpensive, modern medicines that are far cheaper than most places. Most are available without a prescription. The pharmacists usually speak good English and if you relay your symptoms, they will give you the best remedies. They are used to the ailments that the foreigners succumb too.

Clinics

If you want to see a doctor there are small clinics doctors and medical staff are there to help you. These small clinics are inexpensive and there are several open 24 hours a day

Pharmacies signs - Green Cross.   **Clinics** - Blue Cross

Hospitals

Thailand has some state of the art hospitals. They can cope with any emergency, and arrange anything to meet your needs. It is always advisable to take out medical insurance while you are travelling and every major hospital will accept this. The hospitals are far more expensive than the clinics, but the care and facilities are of world class standard.

Simple remedies and precautions

Mosquito stings can be irritating and become infected, so apply a good repellent. The most effective ones can be bought in Thailand. If a sting becomes infected, consult a doctor or pharmacist for antihistamine and or antibiotics

Minor, cuts, stings and abrasions.

To avoid risk of infections, keeping small cuts and abrasions dry and clean is a priority, especially during rainy season. The simplest and most effective way to do this is:

If going outside: Clean wound with hydrogen peroxide (available at pharmacies) dry thoroughly and apply band-aid or dressing. If staying indoors: Clean thoroughly and dry. Apply 'PISES' powder (available at all pharmacies and some minimarts) and leave open to dry.

PISES POWDER   TIFFY

Coughs and colds: Although it sounds strange, coughs and colds do occur in Thailand. The locals take, **TIFFY**, which is available in tablet form in pharmacies, Minimarts, and supermarkets.

Diarrhoea and Vomiting: With the change in climate, food, and water, Diarrhoea and vomiting can occur. It is usually a symptom of something that your body is trying to expel, or a stomach infection, Imodium is usually the anti-diarrhoea drug of choice, but if you have a stomach infection, taking anti diarrhoea medicine may lead to stomach cramps, were antibiotics such as Ciprofloxacin and an antispasmodic such as Spasfon may be required. Consult a pharmacist or clinic doctor if you start getting stomach cramps as they are very unpleasant. If diarrhoea is mild, take nothing and let nature run its course. Stay hydrated.

Dehydration

Thailand is hot and you quickly lose fluids and salts, Drink plenty of fluids during your stay, at least 3+ litres per day. As well as water; fruits, some foods and beverages also contribute to fluid intake. Alcohol will not hydrate you

Electrolytes: take a daily sachet of electrolyte replacing powder in water. The most popular brand is ROYAL D, which is available in pharmacies, minimarts, and supermarkets. It gives you your daily salt and vitamin requirements and it tastes good (orange). Note: If in doubt, urine colour is a good indicator. If you are well- hydrated your urine should be light yellow or colourless. Dark urine usually denotes dehydration, so drink more.

Warning: If your tongue feels dry and you suddenly feel dizzy with a headache, you are severely dehydrated. Most tourist facilitators know this as it is a common occurrence. Sit down and sip a glass of ROYAL D in water. Keep taking sips of water until the symptoms subside, usually around 30 minutes. Remember, prevention is better than cure, so keep hydrated.

Jellyfish stings and Urchin spines: The allure of the ocean in Thailand is irresistible, especially in the Andaman coast region, where the water is clear with a tremendous amount of colourful and amazing sea life, which you must explore. Nothing in this wonderful undersea kingdom is out to hurt you. However, several times of the year jellyfish and its larvae can become an encumbrance. Most are not venomous but if you swim into one, they will give you a painful sting and leave irritation on your skin. If stung: get out of the water, remove any tentacles and wash in sea water to neutralise the sting. Seek medical attention.

Sea Urchins are commonplace especially around rocks. If you stand on one or brush against one the spines easily dislodge, go into your skin and become infected Trying to remove the spines is fruitless as they are brittle. Take a bottle or hard object and roll and hit the spines until they appear crushed under your skin, Rub on a fresh lemon or lime, repeat this process over the next few days until traces of the spine have gone. Urchin spines are calcium so they will dissolve with the citric acid from the fruit.

Stone fish, lion fish and weaver fish can be found around the seas of Thailand. If stung by one of the above, the sting cannot only be painful but venomous. The suggested treatment for these stings is to immerse the area in hot water and scrub with soap and water. Seek immediate medical attention.

Snake bites. Snakes: venomous and non-venomous are found in many areas of Thailand usually in the jungle areas It is unlikely you will see one, let alone be bitten by one. In the unlikely event you are bitten, there are anti-venom units based in Thailand in many of the hospitals. Common sense will dictate your actions. You must seek immediate medical attention, to help with anti-venom needed, try to note as much detail about the snake as possible colour, markings, etc.

Animal Bites

Thailand does have Rabies, so any bites that break the skin from dogs, cats or other animals, seek immediate medical advice

Getting Around

(Also see specific areas)

Buses and coaches: An inexpensive and scenic way to travel from town to town. The buses are usually to schedule and go regularly. Each town has a bus station with the main tourist areas and cities having main bus stations that are foreigner friendly and easy to use.

Trains: Thailand has an extensive railway network, reaching to the furthest extremities of the kingdom, and to the borders of Burma, Laos, Cambodia and Malaysia. Thailand's railways are comfortable and inexpensive, safer than travel by road, cheaper and more relaxed than travel by air. You can check timetables and destinations on line at http://www.railway.co.th/checktime/checktime.asp?lenguage=Eng

Planes: Most tourist destinations and major towns and cities have airports, either international or Domestic. Check local guide or on line at your nearest airport for destinations and times.

Boats: Around Bangkok there is a boat taxi service that travels around the Chao Phraya river system This is a great way to miss all the traffic, but like a bus, you need to know the routes and times. These are only small Thai long-tail craft so getting on and off can be tricky, and you don't travel around crystal clear water, The river can smell in some places, but it is an experience. (read more in Bangkok section)

Tourist boat trips are easily available to and from all t islands. These can be luxury speedboats, car ferries, passenger ferries and long-tails. Check a local guides for times, alternatively seek out a rep and book There are many walking around the tourist hotspots.

Metered Taxi : These are usually only found in major towns and cities. They are a cheap and comfortable way to get around. Taxis are usually well marked as such. If you see one with the taxi sign on they are available to hire, They can be hailed from the roadside. Ensure that the meter is set to zero before you set off.

Baht Bus or songthaew: These are passenger vehicles in Thailand adapted from a pick-up or a larger truck and used as a shared taxi or bus. Most have roofs high enough to accommodate standing passengers within the vehicle. More typically, standing passengers occupy a platform attached to the rear. They are mainly found in towns and cities, mainly along the Eastern seaboard, with Pattaya having the most. These buses drive around the one way systems taking on passengers.

Tuk-tuks -- the sputtering, three-wheeled motorcycle taxis can be found jockeying for position in the clogged streets of Bangkok, Chiang Mai, and other towns and cities in Thailand. While riding in a tuk-tuk can be described as more chaotic than comfortable, taking at least one ride is mandatory for a true, Thailand experience!

Tuk-tuks are abundant in many tourist resorts and towns mainly on the south coast for travelling short distances. The same rules apply here as in Bangkok, with most now displaying a price list. However, confirm the price. If they say "up to you." don't get on that tuk-tuk,

25

because when you pay 'up to you,' it is not enough, they will demand more.

Tuk-tuks found in Thailand are open-air, three-wheeled carriages attached to a motorcycle chassis. Drivers are fond of decorating their rides with lights, colourful paint, and dangling trinkets to get attention. The typical capacity for a tuk-tuk in Thailand would be two people, although the driver will always find a way to squeeze in an entire family if necessary!

Mototaxi's: Usually 125 cc, mopeds are found everywhere in towns and cities. These are the cheapest way to get short distances to a direct route, although you are limited to one passenger. The drivers usually wear coloured jackets. These are hailed or are usually found in groups sat around on streets. Find out the price first, which is usually a standard fair.

Renting motorbikes and cars/jeeps: Is a fun and inexpensive way to get around. However, it does have pitfalls

Rules of the road - There doesn't seem to be any. Although it seems hectic there is an order to the chaos Concentrate on the road ahead, don't worry what's behind you as they are concentrating on you. Drive on the right hand side. Motorbikes can be dangerous, with many drunken foreigners killed annually, so take extra care, and use common sense. Drink driving rules are in force. Always wear a crash helmet and do not run red lights — IT'S THE LAW. and you will be stopped and fined. If you have an accident it is your fault, you are a foreigner. The Thais train of thought being 'if you wasn't in their country it would never have happened.' Don't get road rage or angry....you will lose. If the accident is small with no injury, do not get police involved unless absolutely necessary. Most things will go away with a few 100 baht. If the police become involved this will be more expensive. However, you will get a police report and you will be able to claim on your insurance for any expenses incurred.

Theft and prevention

Punishment in Thailand for thieves is harsh; however, there are still petty thieves around in the tourist hotspots. Be vigilant and take simple precautions to avoid becoming a victim. Lock valuables in the hotel safe. Don't take out more than you need, this includes iPones iPads etc. Bag snatching by motorbikes is a problem, so ladies, if you go out with a handbag, wear it on the inside shoulder. If renting a motorbike ensure it is well-locked when you leave it anywhere.

Tourist police are usually out in force in tourist hotspots, so if you are unfortunate enough to get robbed, report it to them immediately

Traditional Thai Music and Dance

Thais love to sing and dance. Music plays a large part in their culture. There are many places where you can hear and see Thais perform their Traditional Music and dance. Although some songs sounds like a constipated cat, the majority are enchanting and melodic, especially when combined with their rhythmic and hypnotic dances. Each song and dance tells a story, which any Thai will happily explain the meaning to you.

Shopping

Thailand is a shoppers paradise, which hosts a myriad of large shopping malls with brand name goods many times cheaper than most countries.

Market stalls: small open markets and stalls are commonplace in towns and cities You won't need to venture far to find one selling most things.

Street sellers walk the streets trying to sell copy watches, DVD's, toys and games etc. These items can usually be bought cheaper at the market stalls, although if you want something specific these traders will get it for you.

The fun of haggling.

Products that you find in the shopping mall's and supermarkets will already be marked with the prices. The market stall traders will haggle. When haggling remembers, you are a foreigner so the price will start high. Your aim is to get to a price that makes you and the stall owner happy. This is fun.

You - **"Tow Lie khap/ Kah** (how much is it?)

The trader will give you the price and show you on a calculator.

Look shocked, smile and say **"Pang** (expensive) What is your best price?"

The trader will then give you a better price.

Shake your head and offer them slightly less.

If you are happy with the price, buy. If not, thank them and walk away, they will usually call you back and accept Please bear in mind the mark up on items are small and the Thai market traders work on very little profit, so be fair with your price.

Street Vendors

Tuk-tuks, moto- taxis, tailors, massage and girlie show touts, and street vendors will pester you in some area. If approached by a any, unless you want their services, then just say **"Mai Aow (Khap/Kah)"** I don't want it. (smile when you say this, it is polite, yet will dissuade any street seller from pursuing you further).

Jewellery and Gemstones are a popular purchase, with Thai Rubies and Sapphires being very sought after. However, unless you know what you are doing this is a risky purchase as the vast majority of gems being sold are fake. Thai gold is of a high carat, so it is softer deeper in colour than the western standard and isn't hallmarked. The same applies to silver and many shops sell plated. If buying gold or silver as an investment them seek out a reputable jeweller who will used a test kit to show you the carat and weigh the item. They will give you a price based on the current trend. Gemstones are a lot trickier, so be careful and use a main jeweller, gem shop, or gallery. Make sure they give you a receipt and offer a money back guarantee. If they do not, then don't buy.

If you just want a nice piece of fashion jewellery with gemstones that looks like they are worth a million dollars, but aren't, then a good rule of thumb is: if you like it and it's cheap; buy it.

Even though the quality of all goods made in Thailand is usually excellent, make sure you thoroughly check your purchase before you pay, even in the shopping malls.

Dining Out

Thailand has everything to suit any palate, taste, or budget. Everything is fresh, from the seafood to the vegetables. Restaurants are scattered around towns and city as are fast food outlets and food stalls. There are too numerous to list and unnecessary as you will easily find a good place to eat, anytime of the day or night. Thai food is delicious (**Al – loy**) and aromatic. It can also be very spicy, if in doubt ask for something mild, (**Mai Pet** – not spicy)

Foreigners seem hesitant about eating at the small food stalls - don't be - you will find the best Thai food at these little stalls, Pad Thai noodles, fried rice, spicy Kah pow and delicious broths. Each stall will sell its own speciality, so look for the ones where the Thais are eating.

Thais like eating bugs, which come in all shapes and sizes. You will see food stalls cooking and selling these. They are full of protein and taste okay... try some.

Bars and restaurants restaurant opening and closing times are now regulated. Closing times for bars and restaurants at the time of this publication is officially 1:00 am...officially?

Muay Thai

Muay Thai is the national sport of Thailand. This combat sport uses stand-up striking along with various clinching techniques. This physical and mental discipline, which includes combat on shins is known as "the art of eight limbs" because it is characterised by the combined use of fists, elbows, knees, shins, being associated with a good physical preparation that makes a full-contact fighter very efficient. A Muay Thai fighter undergoes intense training from a very young age and champions of the sport are highly regarded in Thailand and around the world. Muay Thai became widespread internationally in the twentieth century, when practitioners defeated notable practitioners of other martial arts.

Ladyboys are part of life in Thailand – they can be lovely or they can be a menace, but they are a well-known fact about the country and are well accepted. Don't insult or abuse them, they can turn violent.

Prostitution

This has always been touchy subject in Thailand. Prostitution is Illegal. However, the words prostitute, brothel, and Pimp are is not in the Thai vocabulary and for good reason. As with most South East Asian countries, many Thai girls, especially ones from poor families, work in bars. This age-old tradition, highlighted in recent years in the tourist towns and cities, has seen many impoverished village girls coming to these areas in search of the foreigner's money to improve their family's lifestyles. They are just normal happy-go-lucky Thai girls, working in body massage parlours, go-go and lady bars and go with men or women who pay them for sex and, like lady boys, are an accepted part of the Thai culture, and a euphoric adventure for the single man, with many having Thai bar girls for wives

Thai Etiquette

When visiting a temple

Most Thais practice Buddhism, and religion plays a very important part in everyday life. It is even protected by law. You can be arrested if you disrespect a Buddha image.

Don't touch a Buddha image, climb on top of it, or sit next to it, even for a picture. It is very disrespectful.

Dress conservatively. Cover your shoulders and knees. This applies to men and women. Remove your shoes upon entering a temple.

General

Don't perceive it as intrusive if a Thai asks you questions about your age, marital status or income. Questioning why you aren't married is considered suitable for small talk.

When interacting with a Thai don't touch their head, not even the cutest child's. You may mean well and see it as a form of caressing, but the head is considered to be the most superior and sacred part of the human body to Thais. They believe that the soul resides in the head. Only family members or monks are allowed to touch anyone's head.

Don't point your feet towards or show the soles of your feet to anyone, and never ever point your feet in the direction of a Buddha figure. In contrast to the head, the feet are considered the most inferior and filthiest part of a human body, so pointing your feet at someone is regarded as an insult.

Don't step on or tear anything that has the image of the king on it, such as money or stamps.

When out in public, don't shout, argue or lose your temper. In the eyes of a Thai only insane people or people of poor upbringing lose their temper in public. Loud voices and angry talk are counterproductive in Thailand. Shouters will lose face and Thais won't want to deal with someone who has lost face in public.

Smile as much as you can. A smiling face is a sign of respect toward surrounding people. It will get you what you want faster than any demonstration of anger.

Be discreet even if you are married. Kissing and displays of physical affection other than holding hands or walking with your arms around each other are considered very impolite in Thailand. Buddhism teaches to be modest and reserved, and Thais will feel embarrassed if you kiss in their presence.

In a restaurant, don't call a waiter by waving your index finger. This is considered just as rude as giving somebody the finger in a Western country. Before entering a Thai's home, always remove your shoes.

In case of emergency.

Tourist towns and cities have free pocket tour guide publications listing emergency numbers in that specific area. Grab a copy of one of these and keep it with you.

Keep details of your nearest embassy on your phone or other mobile device.

DRUGS ARE ILLEGAL IN THAILAND

The Bangkok Hilton is not a 5 star hotel

Bangkok is the capital and the most populous city of Thailand. Known in Thai as Krung Thep Maha Nakhon, which roughly translates to City of Angels, over 14 million people live within the surrounding the Bangkok Metropolitan area. Bangkok is the Central region of the country.

Despite the civil unrest, military coups, devastating floods, and bombings that Bangkok has endured in recent years, it remains a popular tourist destination. The Thai capital is a city that never sleeps. Apart from it being stopover for other destinations in and around Thailand, there is plenty to do and see. From the spectacular temples and palaces, the high end retail malls, to the frantic open markets. The Thais take great pride in their capital and the main streets, gardens, and architecture us kept impeccably clean.

Bangkok began as a small trading centre and port community on the west bank of the Chao Phraya River some 200 years ago. Today, while the city is up to speed with modern times, the grandeur and glory of its illustrious past still prevails. Be it dazzling temples, spectacular palaces, a world-famous floating market or colourful Chinatown, each of these famous places has an intriguing story to tell.

Bangkok is a vibrant city and at night, it is alive with entertainment venues, shows, restaurants, fast food outlets, and an abundance of small food stalls, with each selling their fresh delicious Thai specialities.

Thai markets usually start around 6 pm and go until the early hours of the morning. Here you can buy almost anything for tourists and if you haggle, you will get a bargain.

Sakhumvit Road: In the capital, Sakhumvit Road serves as a main commercial street, and this section is often congested, even at late evening hours. It is the main area for tourists, boasting the most hotels, entertainment venues, bars, nightclubs, and restaurants per capita.

The area between Sakhumvit Soi 1 and Sakhumvit Soi 63 is popular as residential area for western expatriates. Japanese nationals tend to prefer from Soi 21 Asok intersection upwards, especially Soi Thong Lo. Rentals tend to be higher in the even numbered streets between Soi 8 and Soi 28 and in the odd numbered streets between Soi 15 and Soi 39.

The areas of Soi Cowboy (between Soi 21 Asok and Soi 23) and Nana Entertainment Plaza (Soi 4) are packed full of go bars and other places of prostitution. Restaurants of various levels of luxury exist all along the road, as well as hotels including famous names such as The Westin, JW Marriott, Sheraton, Ramada Hotel and Suites Bangkok Sakhumvit, and Four Points by Sheraton. Several shopping malls are found, like the upscale The Emporium shopping centre. It also harbours the eastern bus station at Soi 63 Ekkamai.

Sky-train – Runs the length of Sakhumvit Road. It is an easy and cheap way to avoid the traffic jams

Bars are now regulated and usually close around 1 am...usually?

Some places in Bangkok well worth a visit :

Grand Palace & Wat Prakeaw

Jim Thompson's House

Wat Arun - The Temple of Dawn

Khao San Road

Floating Market - Damnoen Saduak

Soi Cowboy - Sukhumvit

Grand Palace & Wat Prakeaw – Old City

The Grand Palace and Wat Prakaew command respect from all who have walked in their sacred grounds. Built in 1782 and for 150 years the home of Thai Kings and the Royal court, the Grand Palace continues to have visitors in awe with its beautiful architecture and intricate detail. Wat Pra Kaew enshrines Phra Kaew Morakot (the Emerald Buddha), the sacred Buddha image meticulously carved from a single block of emerald.

Wat Arun - The Temple of Dawn - Riverside

The impressive silhouette of Wat Arun's towering spires is one of the most recognised in Southeast Asia. Constructed during the first half of the 19th century in the ancient Khmer style, the stupa showcasing ornate floral pattern decked out in glazed porcelain is stunning up close. Apart from its beauty, Wat Arun symbolises the birth of the Rattanakosin Period and the founding of the new capital after Ayutthaya fell.

Floating Market - Damnoen Saduak

The pioneer of all floating markets, Damnoen Saduak continues to offer an authentic experience despite its increasingly touristy atmosphere. Imagine dozens of wooden row boats floating by, each

35

laden to the brim with farm-fresh fruits, vegetables or flowers. Food vendors fill their vessels with cauldrons and charcoal grills, ready to whip up a bowl of 'boat noodle' or seafood skewers upon request.

Chinatown (Yaowarat) - Chinatown

Chinatown is a colourful, exotic, and pleasingly chaotic area, packed with market stalls and probably the highest concentration of gold shops in the city. During major festivities like Chinese New Year and the Vegetarian Festival, the dynamism and spirit of celebration spreads across town like wildfire, and if you happen to be around, don't miss an opportunity to witness Bangkok Chinatown at its best.

Wat Pho - Old City

There is more to Wat Pho than the gigantic reclining Buddha and traditional Thai massage. Wat Pho harbours a fascinating collection of murals, inscriptions, and sculptures that delve into various subjects, from warfare to astronomy to archaeology. The vast temple complex contains a landscaped garden with stone sculptures, stupas adorned with glazed porcelain, a souvenir shop, and the College of Traditional Medicine.

Chao Phraya River & Waterways - Riverside

One of the most scenic areas, the riverside reflects a constantly changing scene day and night: water-taxis and heavily laden rice barges chugging upstream, set against a backdrop of glittering temples and luxury hotels. The areas from Wat Arun to Phra Sumeru Fortress are home to some of the oldest settlements in Bangkok, particularly Bangkok Noi and its charming ambience of stilt houses flanking the complex waterways.

Chatuchak Weekend Market - Chatuchak

Once only popular among wholesalers and traders, Chatuchak Weekend Market has reached a landmark status as a must-visit place for tourists. Its sheer size and diverse collections of merchandise will bring any seasoned shoppers to their knees. The market is home to more than 8,000 market stalls. On a typical weekend, more than 200,000 visitors come here to sift through the goods on offer.

Khao San Road - Old City

If Bangkok is a city where East greets West, then Khao San Road is the scene of their collision, the place where they jostle for superiority and poke one another in the eye. With travellers from every corner of the modern world, sleek clubs playing sophisticated sounds, eclectic market stalls, converted VW cocktail bars, and foods tamed to suit the Western palate.

Soi Cowboy - Sakhumvit (Asoke)

Soi Cowboy Named after the cowboy hat-wearing African-American who opened the first bar here in the early 1970s. This red-light district has a more laid-back, carnival-like feel to it than Patpong or Nana Plaza. Flashing neon lights up a colourful streetscape comprised mainly of middle-aged expats, Japanese and western tourists, and of course a lot of sex girls with cries of 'hellooo, welcome!'

Jim Thompson's House - Siam

Jim Thompson's three decades of dedication to the revival of Thai silk, then a dying art, changed the industry forever. After he mysteriously disappeared into the jungles of Malaysia, he left a legacy behind, reflected through his vast collections of Thai art and antiques now on display at the Jim Thompson's House and Museum, itself a lovely complex of six Thai-style teakwood houses preserved to their original glory.

Hotels in Bangkok are plentiful; from the opulence of the 12000 THB per night, Mandarin Oriental, to the Khao San Rd budget backpacker from 200 THB per night, with everything in between to suit taste and budget.

Visiting a temple or Wat can be a moving experience. However, remember to dress accordingly, no vests, t-shirts, shorts, bikinis etc and observe the rules on the Useful Information and Tips page

Getting Around

Bangkok, as with other major towns and cities has a major problem with traffic congestion. Unless you know the Sub-way, Sky-train, or Boat-taxi around the river system, the only way to get around is by **metered taxi** or **tuk-tuk**. These are hailed on the street. **Metered Taxi** - Ensure that the meter is on and set to zero before departing.

Tuk-tuks Bangkok has pushy and fast-talking tuk-tuk drivers are experts at somehow convincing travellers to pay more than they normally would for an air-conditioned taxi ride the same distance. Prices for rides in Tuk-tuks must be negotiated in advance. While "Tuk" means "cheap" in Thai, the truth is that unless you are an expert haggler or the driver is having an off day, metered taxis are often cheaper than Tuk-tuks and offer a much more comfortable ride.

Safety Precautions

Pick pockets are at most large markets and they are good. Keep valuables tucked away and monitored. Only take out what is necessary.

Touts: during the day touts offering temple tours, jewellery markets and sightseeing tours may approach you although they are slick, you will find these tours are not as the tout advertises and if you take one you will undoubtedly be ripped off. Book your tours through a reputable company at your hotel or a tour office.

Nighttimes: Touts are around at night, mainly in the Sakhumvit Road area looking for drunken tourists. They mainly push go-go bars, nightclubs, and massages with happy-endings. If you go with these touts, you will certainly pay a lot more and there is every chance that you will end up in a clip joint. Remember, if approached by any tout, smile, and say **"Mai Aw Khap/ Kah"**

TOURIST MAP

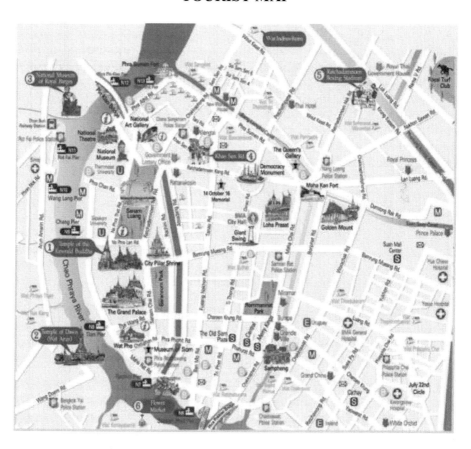

Pattaya. This once quiet fishing village in the Eastern seaboard region is now lined with resort hotels, high-rise condominiums, and large, modern shopping malls. Jet skiing and parasailing are popular activities on Pattaya's busy beaches. Once having the stigma of a sex tourist heaven, Pattaya has flourished, developing into a small modern metropolis, and becoming a mecca for tourists wanting to enjoy the orient in luxurious surrounds. Pattaya now offers something for everyone, with its large high-end 5 – star hotels such as the Hilton, Marriot, Royal Cliff etc., as well as Thailand's own high-end brand such as the Dusit group. For the majority of you, there are numerous mid range, comfortable, pristine hotels. For back packers and low budget tourists, Pattaya has some cheap rooms available; If you want to stay near the beach, you will find many hotels on the coast that extend along to Jomtien. Here the hotels overlook the ocean and islands.. Check out Booking.com.Agoda.com or other popular booking sites. From Pattaya, there are many other tourist destinations close by, The most popular ones are listed in this section.

GETTING AROUND

Finding your way around Pattaya is relatively simple. See map at the bottom of page. The main roads are: Beach Rd, Second Road and Third Rd. The smaller Roads are named, Pattaya Klang, Pattaya Thai, and Pattaya Nua. The streets are called Sois, some are numbered, and some are named.

Baht Bus or songthaew: are cheap and easy ways to get around Pattaya. They drive around all day and night picking up passengers. If you want one, just stick out your hand and they will stop. When you arrive at your destination, press the overhead buzzer, alight, and pay the driver 10 baht. Each Baht bus follows a set route, so make sure you know where you are going. They follow Pattaya's one-way system, so sometimes you have to go a long way around to get to your destination.

Moto taxi: Usually a set price, but check before you depart. This is for one person only, but sometimes the driver will squeeze on two if you ask.

Renting mopeds motorbikes jeeps and cars

A fun way to get around Pattaya is to rent a motor. Many shops, open pitches on the beach, and hotels rent out small 100 -125cc mopeds, most nowadays being automatic. Larger motorbike rental are mainly found along the Beach Rd area. Be careful when riding these machines, which range from 200cc to Superbikes. Do not be stupid and ride when drunk. Pattaya is notorious for foreign deaths on motorbikes. **Be warned:** most rental places will take your passport as security and you are not insured.

Cars and Jeeps; It is far safer to rent a car or jeep from a reputable dealer and not off the beach. There are several car rental businesses now in Pattaya (see a pocket guide or look on line.)

With the recent influx of tourists, there is major congestion on the roads in Pattaya. At the time of going publication there are major road works going on to try to alleviate this problem, leading to slow moving traffic in the city.

Swimming in Pattaya Bay is inadvisable. The sea in the Bay area is polluted; look at the amount of watercraft and you will understand why. Good clean beaches are a short distance north of the bay area and at Jomtien beach to the South.

SHOPPING

A shopper's paradise. Pattaya hosts a cornucopia of large and small shopping malls, with brand name goods many times cheaper than most countries. Haggling isn't usually done in the main malls with the prices being displayed. However, it never hurts to try. The malls usually open at 10am and close around 11pm.

Outdoor Market and stalls seem to be everywhere in Pattaya and **street sellers** walk the streets trying to sell copy watches, DVD's, toys, games etc. These items are cheaper at the market stalls, but if you want something specific, these traders will get it for you. Market opening times vary, as does their closing times, usually around 11pm. There is a plethora of market stall along beach road and their busiest times are between 7-10pm.

This is were your haggling technique comes in handy.

Touting isn't as much as a hassle in Pattaya as it is in Bangkok and you will seldom see a tout. Tailors and stall owners will speak to you if you pass their shops and girls will whoop at you to come into their bar. This is not a problem as they will not hassle you further, just go in, or walk on.

DINING OUT

With such a diverse mix of nationalities both residing and visiting Pattaya, it is no small claim that the city can boast to be the gateway of Asia for international cuisine catering for all pockets and tastes, be it Scandinavian, French, Italian, Mexican, German, Chinese, Korean, Japanese, Indian, British etc, and of course the wonderful Thai dishes. Pattaya has everything to suit any palate, taste, or budget. Everything is fresh, from the seafood to the vegetables. Restaurants are scattered around the city, as are fast food outlets and food stalls. There are too many to list and unnecessary because you will always find a good place to eat anytime of the day or night.

Small Thai food stalls and BBQ 's line most of the sois,' The food is cheap and usually delicious. Eat where the Thais are eating.

TOURS

Although Pattaya is mainly known as a lively night scene destination; apart from shopping and lazing on the beach, there are tours available and places that are well worth a visit.

Nong Nooch Gardens   Si Racha Tiger Zoo   Mini Siam

Million Year stone Park and crocodile Farm   Koh Larn

Nong Nooch Gardens: a sprawling recreational park in typical Thai settings. Groups of traditional Thai houses and gardens of different flowering plants are dotted around the beautifully landscaped site. Watch cultural and elephant shows, which attract delighted visitors. There is a miniature open zoo and aviary. During the entertaining elephant show, watch the animals perform various tricks such as riding bikes, playing football etc. Visit the orchid farm and beautifully landscaped gardens.

Si Racha Tiger Zoo is located between Pattaya and Bang Saen. Here a large number of Bengal tigers as well as crocodiles and other animals can be found. Watch the shows involving trainers with tigers and crocodiles. You may choose to hold and take photos with tiger cubs. You will be thrilled to see how friendship can be possible among tigers, pigs, and dogs, living together peacefully. View a large number of scorpions on ladies' bodies. Witness a crocodile wrestling

6

show by lady performers and visit a crocodile farm and see the amusing tiger show.

Mini Siam located north of Pattaya. This is a wonderland of miniature replicas of outstanding architectural works in Thailand and around the world, including Temple of the Emerald Buddha, Thailand House of Parliament, Tower Bridge, Eiffel Tower, the Statue of Liberty, and Great Wall of China on a scale of 1:25. More than 100 models are displayed, surrounded by different types of well-selected trees.

Million Year stone Park and crocodile Farm Established in 1989, this privately owned and operated park has numerous displays of strange, and oddly shaped rocks, petrified trees, and other rock anomalies. Laid out in a park-like setting, the garden is a wonderful place to spend an afternoon, and if visitors so feel, they can also pop over to the crocodile farm that is just around the corner and feed the hungry crocs.

Islands

You will see several small islands just off Pattaya. If you walk along the beach, there are plenty of agents who will sell you a speedboat ride for a day on **Koh Larn** However, you will spend the day on a packed beach with overpriced food and drink.

Don't despair. Walk to the end of walking street you will find the **Bali Hai Pier.** The Koh Larn ferry runs regularly and costs 20THB. The ferry will take 40 minutes and stops at a jetty on the island away from the main tourist hub. This is where the island Thais live. Catch a moto and ask to go to Samae beach. This tranquil beach is a well kept secret and idyllic. From there you can see Koh Sak and the tour submarines; you can swim in the clear still water. Restaurants on the beach sell fresh food at reasonable prices. **Koh Sak** is an interesting island not open to tourists, but if you can hire a boat from a local on Samae beach, go there and take a look. It was where the Thai Royal family vacationed, along with celebrities from the 60's. Small beach

7

bungalows have been untouched from that period, along with handprints from celebrities such as Bob Hope and Apollo astronauts adorn the walkways. In the bay, there is a pristine coral reef abundant in sea life...Amazing adventure.

Koh Si-chang is a small island situated in the Gulf of Thailand. Its proximity to shipping lanes has made it a convenient anchorage for dozens of barges which trans-ship their cargos to lighter barges for the trip up the Chao Phraya river to Bangkok. Koh Si-chang makes a nice weekend outing for local tourists and there are basic accommodations on the islands with a small ex pat community. While the beaches are not as enjoyable as those on islands further east and south, such as Koh Samet, tourists can explore the remains of a former royal palace, which was built as a summer retreat for King Chulalongkorn. The royal residence was abandoned in 1893 when the French occupied the island during a conflict with Thailand over who would control Laos. The island also has many places of religious interest and value. From Pattaya the Koh Si-chang ferry is in Sri Racha, approximately 20 minutes away. Upon arrival in Sri Racha, take a tuk-tuk for 50 baht to the pier. Boats to Koh Si-chang leave hourly (or every two hours in low season) from the pier on Koh Loy. The ferry takes about 40 minutes and is 50 baht per person each way.

Koh Samet is located in the Gulf of Thailand in Rayong province. There are 14 white sand beaches on the island, which are surrounded by colourful coral reefs providing such aquatic sports as swimming, snorkelling, and scuba diving. The most popular beach areas are: Saikaew Beach, Ao Phai and Ao Vong Duan.

From Pattaya - book at any tour office along with a hotel, this is the best way. Alternatively take a bus to Rayong port, about 40 minutes. Along the port, there are many small jetties with boats to Samet and hotel booking Kiosks.

Khao Laem Ya - Mu Koh Samet is a national park maintained and run by the "National Parks of Thailand," There are park rangers visible on the island, their job is to collect the park entrance fee & look after the up-keep of the island and wildlife protection. The park rangers' offices & park information centres are located on the entrance to Saikaew Beach & Ao Vongduen Beach Area.

Koh Samet being a national park, all foreign visitors must pay a park entrance fee on arrival of 200 Baht per adult. Koh Samet is approximately 13.1 km2 in size and shaped somewhat like the letter "T." From North to South the island is 7km in length and East to west measures 4km's at its widest point. The Island has only three roads, One links Saikaew area with Ao Noi Na, the other links Saikaew with the east and southern route.

Cars are very few; Motorbikes are many and are the best way to explore the Island. Songthaews are available all over the island.

Koh Chang (Elephant Island) is a tropical marine national park. Its hinterland consists of over 70% virgin rainforest and is the best-preserved tourist holiday destination in Thailand. Situated to the east of the country in Trat province, from Pattaya you can take the bus to Trat port and catch a ferry. These run frequently throughout the day and take around 40 minutes.

It has chain of white sandy coves and beaches, pristine rain forests and abundance of wildlife and marine life, coral reefs, high mountain peaks, several scenic waterfalls, with a rich variety of cuisine and great nightlife.

Accommodation on the island ranges from simple beach huts and bungalows to luxury villas, suites, and apartments. If you drive, you can hire motorbikes, jeeps, and cars to take you to any of the beaches along the coastal roads and, in the evening, there are plenty of restaurants, live music bars, and nightclubs to choose from to spice up your holiday.

PATTAYA NIGHT SCENE

Pattaya's night scene is vibrant and diverse, with most Sois lined with bars restaurants and shows. Finding something to do at night is as easy as walking out of your hotel. Pick up a Free Pattaya pocket guide. You will never be at a loss for something to do at night. Most of pubs, bars, beer bars, discotheques, transsexual cabarets, karaoke bars, go-go bars as well as restaurants line up along Pattaya Beach Road and along the connecting lanes or Sois, off the main street. Walking Street is the most populated with these venues. The street is closed for pedestrians only after 06.00 pm.

Walking Street

Glowing colourful neon signs illuminate this renowned street of Pattaya at night. Walking Street is an entertainment area that has 100 beer bars, more than 30 go-go bars, sport bars, discos, cabaret shows, massage parlours, and a wide range of ethnic restaurants as well as seafood line up in the main street and many more in the side-Soi leading towards Pratamnak Road. It starts from the south end of Beach Road to Bali Hai Pier. The street is free from vehicles from 06.00 pm. - 02.00 am. The legal closing time is 02.00 am.

Pattayaland - Central Pattaya

Soi Pattayaland 2 (Soi 13/4) is lit up with neon light of go-go bar signs. This Soi one of the discernible symbol of Pattaya. Yet, there are about 10 go-go bars, 6 bars, some restaurants, and grocery stores in this Soi. There is a mix of straight and gay bars in this Soi.

Soi Pattayaland 3 has no direct access from Beach Road. It runs from Soi Pattayaland 2 to Pattaya 2nd Road. The majority of the bars and go-go bars here feature male dancers but there are also a few female go-go bars, some restaurants, and a hotel in the Soi.

Soi L.K. Metro

Soi L.K. Metro lies between Soi Diana and Soi Buakhao. This Soi is quite new, features several go-go bars, restaurants, inexpensive guesthouses. A lot of bars and cafes are outdoors, which makes it a good spot for people watching. The Metropole Hotel and the Areca Lodge are located here.

Location: South Pattaya

These lively Sois are a cluster of beer bars in this area as well as some go-go bars. It is one of the places where there is always something happening around the clock. In the morning, there are places that serve breakfast. Those who like to start the early, bars and pubs are open for a warm-up of the fun night. Several large hotels, travel agencies, and convenient stores are also located here.

Soi Yodsak (Soi 6)

Location: North Pattaya

Soi Yodsak is one of the most colourful and notorious streets in Pattaya. It has a great number of bars that are open as early as 01.00 pm. and closed at 01.00 am. It is not a totally pedestrian street but walking here at the daytime can be a good experience. There are not only bars but also restaurants, dive centres and deep sea fishing store.

Second Road - around the Soi 2 & Soi 3 junctions

Location: North Pattaya

More than 35 beer bars are located on the west side of Pattaya 2ndRd opposite Central Festival Centre. The road becomes lively and flocked with tourists from 04.00pm. and stay open until 02.00 am. There is also a great option of restaurants as well as fast food chain opposite Second Rd.

Beer Bars: Pattaya has over 1,500 beer bars to choose from. Females to attract attentions from tourists normally staff the beer bars in Pattaya. Most of the bar features games such as pool, connect-four, shut-the-box, or dart and music is always played. The official closing time in entertainment zone is 01:00 Am., but often you can find those that stay open until 02:00 am. or 03:00 am.

Note: For those coming to Pattaya in pursuit of the hairy magnet or otherwise. It is recommended that you read the Pattaya survival guide 'Money Number One' By Neil Hutchison http://moneynumberone.net/

TOURIST MAP

Phuket and Koh Samui are the main tourist hot-spots located in the Southern region of Thailand. Phuket on the west coast and the Andaman Sea and Koh Samui on the east coast of the gulf of Thailand, with both having international airports Even though there are other amazing tourist destinations in this region, Phuket and Samui are the two detailed in this section. The distance between them by road and boat takes about 6 hours

Other popular destinations around Phuket include:

Koh Phi Phi – The setting for the Beach movie, which was devastated in the 2004 Tsunami. However, it now rebuilt and a popular tourist destination

Koh Racha:(Noi and Yai) - Two quiet tranquil islands about 40 minutes by speedboat Racha Yai has a large beach with restaurants and some great reefs

Krabi – A small town with a large ex pat community. More subdued than the touristy towns of Phuket and Samui it is a jump off point to most islands, including James Bond Island. Around Krabi there is some spectacular scenery.

Khoa Lak, and the Similan Islands – A few hours north of Phuket lies Khoa Lak. Another town decimated by the Tsunami, but now re built

15

with modern hotels and tourist attractions. A quiet alternative to Phuket. Similan Islands are further north and boasts one of the top ten dive spots in the world.

Please note: Reefs around Phuket and the islands do have Banded Sea Krait snakes. Although **highly venomous**; they are timid creatures and will usually swim away from you. There is no anti venom for this snake and the bite is lethal, so don't piss them off.

Around Koh Samui:

Koh Toa – A great place to learn to dive and well known for inexpensive dive courses

Koh Pangyang – A popular destination for back packers and partygoers with its famous full moon parties

You will find more details about these places in any good travel guide.

PHUKET

Phuket lies off the west coast of Southern Thailand in the Andaman Sea. It is Thailand's largest island at 550sq km, and surrounded by many smaller islands that add a further 70 sq km to its total land area. Phuket is separated from the mainland by the Chong Pak Phra channel at its northernmost point, where a causeway connects the island to the mainland at Phang Nga Province. Although an island and preceded by a Koh, it is better known as just, Phuket.

Phuket is a large island with a wide choice of beaches to suit every taste and requirement. Most of the beaches are located on the west coast of the island. The quieter beaches tend to be found towards the island's northwestern coastline, while the greatest concentration of hotels, shops and restaurants is located around Patong and stretches south towards Karon and Kata.

It is warm in Phuket all year round with temperatures ranging between 25 – 34°C (77 – 93°F). It is prone to torrential rainstorms in the rainy season July - October.

Although probably the most expensive place to visit in Thailand, Phuket has everything for a memorable holiday experience. During the day, you can spend relaxing on the beaches around the coast or take a boat to the many islands only a short distance away. Phuket is surrounded by lush green jungle and jungle trekking on an Elephants is a memorable experience. Although water-sports play a major draw in Phuket, there is also golf, go- karting, ATV's and other activities to fill your day.

Nighttimes, you can go to eat at one of the quiet restaurants in quiet areas such as Kata or Karon or take in a show such as Phuket Fantasy. Alternatively, you can head to Patong and the manic Bangor Rd. If you are travelling here for the first time, it is a good idea to familiarize yourself with the layout of the island and the location of the various towns and beaches.

| Stunning Islands | Boat Tours | Idyllic Beaches |
| Golf Courses | Go-Karts | Phuket Fantasy |

BEACHES

Bang Tao: A large open bay with one of Phukets longest beaches. The Laguna Phuket complex, containing five luxury hotels.

Cape Panwa Beach: Ideal for those seeking peace and relaxation. Cape Panwa is located to the south of Phuket City where lush hills provide.

Chalong: A large bay with a pier that is the main departure point for diving and fishing trips from Phuket. The pier is a good.

Kamala Beach: A beautiful and serene beach, Kamala is perfect for those looking for a relaxed and laid-back beach. Kamala is about 10 minutes drive from Patong.

Karon beach: A long stretch of powdery white sand just south of Patong. The beach is very long so it never feels overcrowded.

Kata Beach: Towards the southern end of Phuket is Kata Beach, which is divided into Kata Yai and Kata Noi.

Laem Singh Beach : A small, secluded beach that can get quite crowded during the high season.

Layan Beach : This is a small and relatively unknown beach, nestled in a shallow bay at the north end of Bang Tao.

Mai Khao Beach: Located just north of the airport is Mai Khao beach, an incredibly long and mostly deserted stretch of sand.

Nai Harn Beach: A picturesque, quiet beach near the southern tip of the island.

Nai Yang : A long curved bay fringed with tall casuarinas trees. The beach is a popular spot among locals who come to picnic on.

Nui Beach : Just south of the Kata viewpoint, Nui Beach offers the opportunity to enjoy a quiet idyllic beach.

Patong Beach: Phuket's busiest resort area, Patong has the greatest of shops, restaurants, and nightlife on the island.

Rawai Beach : Popular with locals and expats who come to enjoy seafood and the lovely view of the islands from the shore.

Surin Beach: just north of Kamala, is an undeveloped stretch of sand lined with casuarina trees.

Phuket City: Usually referred to as Phuket Town, is well worth taking time out from the beach for its shops and markets, its Sino-Portuguese buildings, its temples and its many restaurants. Most visitors to Phuket head straight for the beach and rightly so, but if you want to take a break from the sand and catch a peek of a more 'real' side of the island, then Phuket Town has much to offer. The town is about 30 minutes away from Patong by car and easily reached by Tuk-tuk if you don't have your own transportation.

GETTING AROUND

Travelling around the island is not as convenient or cheap as you might expect. Unless you are staying in a busy resort area such as Patong or Karon, it won't always be possible to just flag down a Tuk tuk and buses only run during the day and mostly do not connect the main beaches. Using the taxi service supplied by your hotel is probably the easiest option followed by renting a car or motorbike.

Tuk-tuks can be found all over Phuket, although they tend to be clustered in large numbers around Patong. Tuk-tuks are basically small red vans, which have open backs and sides, and can carry about five passengers. They are 4-wheeled as opposed to the 3-wheeled version found in Bangkok. The fare must be agreed beforehand depending on the distance. Do not let the driver try to charge per passenger as well. This is a scam. The current fares in Patong have been set at 200 Baht for any distance within Patong but many drivers will try to charge more. If you are going to a more distant location, you will need to agree a round trip fee or try to hire them by the hour. Otherwise, you might have difficulty getting a ride back. Make sure you insist that the driver does not take you anywhere other than your specified destination.

Motorcycles ranging from 100cc bikes to superbikes can be found for hire in most busy beach areas. Prices start at about 200 Baht per day for a 100cc Honda or Suzuki motorbike. The law is vague concerning tourists and motorbike licences. No one will stop you hiring one without a bike licence, or even bother to ask if you have one, and the police may or may not care if you have one. Often a car driving licence is enough. Insurance is often non-existent or of minimal value. In fact, there is no such thing as first-class insurance on motorbikes in Thailand, no matter what the rental shop may tell you. However, by law, they must have third-party insurance. This however, is very basic and doesn't cover theft.

Boats can be hired for trips to nearby islands or fishing sites. The main areas for hiring are Chalong Pier and Rawai with fares depending on the number of passengers, distance, length of time and type of vessel. Long tail boats are a lot cheaper than speedboats. However, they are slower and not as comfortable. On the plus side they do provide a more traditional Thai sea-going experience, which is by no means unpleasant. Whichever type of boat you choose, make sure you check with the driver that life vests are provided.

Koh Samui, is an island off the east coast of the Kra Isthmus in Thailand. Located close to the mainland town of Surat Thani it is blessed with natural beauty, with its beautiful white sand beaches, clear warm water, lush tropical gardens and gentle ocean breezes. You can enjoy a relaxed holiday amidst the beauty of nature or a fast-paced vacation. There is a great deal of variety available when it comes to Koh Samui activities. From the wild, mountainous interior to the tropical seas surrounding the little island, there is something to do at every step. For the thrill-seekers, pit yourself against the rocky cliff faces between Lamai and Chaweng or surf the waves on a kiteboard. Check out the local wildlife on a quad bike jungle safari or grab a snorkel and explore the reefs.

If you want more sedate activities on Koh Samui, be sure to try elephant trekking or check out the excellent selection of spas for a relaxing massage. You can also enjoy a round or two of golf, a relaxing sunset cruise or treat the people back home to something more than a cheap T-shirt by taking Thai cooking classes. In the unlikely event that lazing on the beach gets too much for you, rest assured that there are a host of options.

Climate : Koh Samui is warm/hot all year round. However, rainy season between July and November can have heavy rain and the odd shower.

Magnificent Temples

White Sandy Beaches

Lively Clubs

Shops and Malls

Jungle Trekking

Spectacular Statues

Chaweng Beach: The party central of Samui and the part of the island with the most hotels, other accommodation, and numerous restaurants located around the place. Nightlife is plentiful and Chaweng is known for its famous Green Mango strip, which is a horseshoe shaped road dotted by the town's favourite clubs. This strip is approximately 3 km length, with some landmarks like McDonalds and Murphy's Irish Pub speckled on the stretch.

The beach itself is of pristine white sands. There are also many shops selling souvenirs and tourist items. You can also enjoy water sports, horse riding, bungee jumping, mini golf, and other activities around the beach area.

Secret Buddha Garden : Baan Saket: Towards the mountains on Koh Samui's southern side, hidden behind a dense foliage of trees, is this stunning, almost mystical garden-created and carved over a period of 12 years by a local Samuian farmer, Nim Thongsuk. Intricately carved statues fill the landscape, depicting deities, animals, and humans in varied poses. There is one of the sculptor himself. Completing the mysticism of the place are the waterfalls and streams gurgling nearby. Figures are out of Buddhist folklore and in fact, each statue will have a story to tell. Be sure to explore around and peer down the hill where breathtaking views await you.

Silver Beach (Thong Takian): Silver beach in particular is one of the lesser-known beaches in Samui, tucked away in a world of its own. Named after its white sandy beach, it's nestled within a dense foliage of palm trees, with incredible granite boulders dotting the coastline.

Wat Phra Yai:: Sitting regally on a small, hilly island just north of Koh Samui, the huge golden meditating Buddha statute observes the daily life over the island. It has been one of the most popular tourist attractions since its construction finished in the 1970's and due to its size, it can be seen from very far away. It is believed that the posture of the Big Buddha, sitting with right hand facing down and the left palm resting on the lap, 'the Mara posture,' which reflects Buddha's journey, specifically where he learned to overcome temptations. The pose is representative of purity, enlightenment, and steadfastness. There are two other Buddha images encased in pavilions here. You can also find some food stalls over here, to enjoy a quick snack or a meal.

Bang Po Beach: This haven of silvery sands lined with palm fronds and skirted by the azure ocean lies on the calm and quiet northern coast of Koh Samui, looking towards the neighbour island, Koh Pangyang. Stretching on for about 4km from Ban Tai to Bang Po, the beach is lined with a few restaurants and makes for the perfect place for your evening time stroll. The shallow and calm ocean waters offer extraordinary snorkelling with the shallow coral reefs housing a plethora of colourful fish.

Lamai Beach: Samui's second-largest resort area after Chaweng. It is quieter and less bustling than its big sister, but still with plenty of accommodation, dining and shopping options, and some great spas and tourist sites to explore.

The general atmosphere is laid back and Lamai has slightly older, and by extension cheaper tourist facilities than Chaweng, although there is some indication that the area is slowly being rejuvenated. Along with the rest of Samui, there is a steady trend away from the 'cheap and cheerful' toward smarter, high-end accommodation and dining.

Hua Thanon:: Starts just beyond Hin Ta & Hin Yai, is similarly quiet and is home to a few long-stay backpacker resorts as well as one of Samui's last remaining traditional fishing fleets. The Muslim village has a charming atmosphere and is well worth a visit for a glimpse into island life before mass tourism.

The fishermen's elegantly painted kor lae boats are very photogenic, as is the village's fish market. There are a few decent seafood restaurants by the side of the sea, which give you a taste of true Samui cuisine at bargain basement prices.

Bang Kao: Home to Centara Villas Samui, which offers upscale accommodation that stretches down a steep hillside to the beach below.   There are also a couple of older mid-range bungalow operations and a few independent restaurants but little else in the area apart from the Samui Aquarium & Tiger Zoo, and the nearby Butterfly Garden, which showcases indigenous varieties in a well-managed environment.

GETTING AROUND

Baht Buses (songthaew) : circle the island on various fixed routes all day and fares start at around 20 baht for a short trip - this is paid at the end of the journey. There are no fixed stops, so flag one down anywhere and ring the bell or bang on the roof to get off. After dark, many songthaews' operate as private taxis, so it's necessary to negotiate a fare before getting aboard. Expect to pay several hundred baht to travel between beaches.

Motorbike and jeep rental is readily available everywhere on the island. Expect to pay around 200 Baht per day for a bike and around 800 Baht for a car. It is worth remembering that Samui has some of the highest accident rates in the country though, and has many steep, sandy roads. Honda Dreams are the most common bikes available, though Yamaha Nouvo's are becoming more widespread. Nouvo's cost about 50 Baht more, but are recommended because they are fully automatic and therefore much easier to ride. The local police are beginning to crack down on foreigners riding bikes without safety helmets and fining them accordingly. The 500-baht fine must be paid immediately at a nearby police station, whilst the police hold onto your bike, driving license or passport as insurance. Many people are caught at once, the process can take several hours.

Insurance does not exist in Thailand for motorbikes, so riders are liable for any danger and it's usually the foreigner's fault. Many jeep hire 'bargains' will come without insurance and are therefore a risky proposition. Any established company such as Budget or Avis will include comprehensive insurance in the rental.

Bicycles for hire: are increasingly common, though not recommended for long trips at night for safety reasons.

Both Phuket and Samui seem to be plagued with Tailors. Some are good, some are bad, but they are annoying and pester you along the street. The Majority of these are Indian, so "No Thank You will suffice"...unless you want a cheap suit.

Warning: The gemstones peddled by the street sellers are all fake.

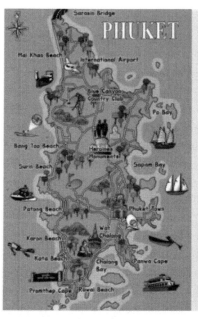

Chiang Mai is referred to as "The Rose of the North" Situated in the Northern region, 700km north of the capital city of Bangkok, Chiang Mai is the second largest city in Thailand, yet only has a population of around 200,000. Compare this to Bangkok which has about 9 million and it is easy to see why even the Thai people in Bangkok love to visit Chiang Mai for a holiday. The city is now becoming increasingly popular with overseas travellers as word spreads of this magnificent tourist location. In the last twenty-five-years, tourism has gradually transformed this once sleepy area into a traveller's paradise whilst still maintaining its provincial charm. The ever-friendly and polite Thai people are full of smiles. The food tastes sensational, and it is a shopper's paradise, even on a shoestring.

Chiang Mai was built in 1296 as a walled city surrounded by a moat. The old city was roughly 1.5km square. Whilst a good portion of the original city wall has collapsed the four corner bastions are still intact along with various other sections. The original moat is still in use to this day. Chiang Mai city is made up now of the old city (within the walled area) and the new city which has grown up around it. Grab a Tuk-tuk and go for a scenic visit to Chiang Mai's lovely moat and the ancient walls of the old city. If you like ancient temples (Wats) and buildings, then visit Chiang Mai and the surrounding areas, have several hundred. Most of these ancient temples are still in use today by Buddhist monks.

Awe inspiring Temples

Spectacular Views

Elephant Treks

Jungle Adventures

Tiger Zoo

Relaxing Thai Massage

ACTIVITIES

There are more things to See and Do in Chiang Mai and Northern Thailand than most tourists have the time to experience.

Abseiling

Bungy Jump: Jungle Bungy Jump: Mae Rim area)

Butterfly Farms: Mae Sa Butterfly Farm & Sai Nam Butterfly/Orchid Farm

Caves: Chiang Dao Cave & Muang-On Cave

Cooking Schools: Thai Farm Cooking School, Gap's Thai Culinary Art School, Chiang Mai Thai Cookery School, Baan Thai Cookery School.

Cycling: hire a bicycle on the Chaiyaphum Road, also try near the Tha Phae Gate

Elephant Farms: Numerous elephant camps have been established to help protect the numerous elephants in the area. The camps put on elephant shows and activities for tourists where the elephants display their various skills. Most of the camps have elephant rides where tourists ride the elephants for an hour or two through the jungle surrounding the camps. There is the Mae Ping Elephant Camp, Patara Elephant Farm, Mae Sa Elephant Camp, Thai Elephant Conservation Center (near Lampang)

Elephant Nature Park: This is a sanctuary and rescue centre for elephants. You can visit or volunteer to stay for days/weeks looking after the elephants.

Golf: 10 golf courses in the area.

Hash House Harriers: Five hashes in Chiang Mai,

Language Schools: Pro Language School and the AUA Language Centre

Muay Thai Boxing: Clubs - Lanna Muay Thai & Muay Thai Sangha - regular Friday night matches at the Kawila Boxing Stadium.

Museums: National Museum, Tribal Museum, City Arts, & Cultural Centre

Para gliding: Chiang Mai Paramotor Club for a glide with a difference

River Cruises: day cruises or night dinner cruises on Mae Ping River, Scorpion Tail

Rock climbing: and other outdoor adrenaline rushes

Snake Farm: Mae Sa Snake Farm (Mae Rim area)

Tennis: The Anantasiri Tennis Courts & Chiang Mai Land and Lanna Sports club

Thai Massage Schools: Are numerous, and the Blind Institute massage is popular with tourists

Treetop Zip Lining : "Flight of the Gibbon" - includes 3 hours of exhilarating rides through the rainforest canopy on zip lines and sky bridges high above the forest floor, have lunch and then spend time exploring an amazing 7 level waterfall.

Tiger Kingdom : Get up close and personal playing with the tigers. Ultimate experience for lovers of the big cats.

Trekking: Chiang Mai province was originally populated by many different hill tribe peoples. Many are still there today. Many tourists/travellers go on organized treks through the mountain regions to visit and even stay in the various hill tribe villages. You can see various hill tribe people around Chiang Mai daily, often at the markets selling their locally produced goods to support the families in the villages. See a tour operator for the different types of trekking activities available as trek lengths can vary from half a day to several weeks.

Wood Handicrafts : Hang Dong & Baan Tawai villages (15klms south west of Chiang Mai)

Zoos - Chiang Mai Zoo, Night Safari

TEMPLES (Wats)

There are over 200 Temples in and around Chiang Mai. The following is only an overview of the most well known Temples, all of which are easily accessible.

Wat Chiang Man: situated in the northeast corner of the old walled city was the first Temple in Chiang Mai, built by King Mengrai in 1296 as part of the original city construction. Housed within are two rare Buddha statues, the Crystal Buddha and the Marble Buddha. At the rear of the main Temple stands an ancient Chedi decorated with elephants.

Wat Phra Singh: located in the western side of the old walled city is a classic example of Northern Thai architecture built in 1345. It houses the Phra Singh Buddha, a highly revered statue. Housed within the Temple complex is a learning centre for young boys and men studying to become Buddhist monks. It is one of the most important Temples in the city.

Wat Suan Dok: located 1km west of the old walled city, built in 1371. The grounds were initially a royal flower garden that was offered by King Keuna to a very revered monk from Sukhothai. A holy Buddhist relic that was transported to the new Temple of Wat Suan Dok inexplicably split in two. One part of the relic remained at Suan Dok and the other was the relic that caused Wat Phra That Doi Suthep to come into being. Located at Wat Suan Dok you will find a huge 500-year-old Bronze Buddha, one of the largest in Thailand. In the grounds are a large number of white chedis some of which house the ashes of members of the former royal family of Chiang Mai. The Temple is currently the site of a Buddhist University.

Wat Phra That Doi Suthep: The most famous Temple in the area, standing near the top of Mount Suthep to the north-west of the city. This Temple was built around 1383. King Keuna of Chiang Mai selected a white elephant to carry a holy relic of the Lord Buddha to what would be its resting place. The elephant wandered up Mount Suthep until it came to a place where it finally laid down. A Temple was built on the spot to house the holy relic, and both remain there to this day. Housed there as well is a stunning larger than life replica of the famous Emerald Buddha, the original of which is in Bangkok.

Wat U-Mong: Located some 2km to the west of the old city on Suthep Road in the forested foothills of Mount Suthep, is one of the most unusual of all the Temples because it is mostly underground, beneath a large hill with a flattened top. The under-hill complex contains many brick lined tunnels, which are easily navigated. Built in the 14th century for a revered monk it was later abandoned for six centuries. A large chedi sits on the flat hilltop and nearby are the quarters of the monks who live there. If you look at the many trees throughout the complex, you will see them decorated with hundreds of short Buddhist proverbs in both English and Thai.

Wat Chedi Luang: Built around 1400 and with several later additions stood some 90 meters tall, it was reduced to around 60 meters in height when the upper section fell because of an earthquake in the 16th century. The Emerald Buddha was once housed here but it was removed after the earthquake for safety reasons. A replica of the Emerald Buddha made of black jade has recently been placed where the original once stood. At only a few of the many Temples you visit, you may find an amazing life like statue of a venerated monk who had been associated with that particular Temple. A fine example of this is to be found in the Library Temple behind the main Chedi at Wat Chedi Luang.

Wat Jet Yot: Located in the north-west outskirts of the city on the Super Highway, The Temple, built in 1455, was the host place for the Eighth World Buddhist Council in 1977.

Wat Bupparam: Located some 500 meters east of Tha Phae Gate, and built around 15th century, it houses beautiful statues and ornamentation including three major Buddha images, one in painted wood, one covered in gold leaf, and one of a green gemstone. The gardens surrounding the main building are crowded with flowers and statues, including some recently added statues of a few famous Disney characters.

You are allowed to enter the Temples, but you must remove your shoes before you go inside and as mentioned previously, wear something appropriate.

GETTING AROUND

Red Songthaews: Continually drive around the city It is cheaper to take a Songthaew because they will pick up several parties at once. You may not take the most direct route to your destination if someone else jumps in. They are the best option for larger parties because they can take up to 8-12 people. Most trips around the city will cost 20baht per person per trip. If you make the mistake of asking how much it will cost, then the driver will assume you are a tourist and that you do not know this, so they will increase the price. Often times they will double it. What you need to do is this: tell the driver where you want to go and if they nod yes, just jump in. If they nod no, then they are headed in a different direction than your destination, so you will have to wait for the next truck. If they want to charge you more than the customary 20baht, they will tell you. However, there will usually be some room to negotiate. To tell the driver to stop while you are in the truck, push the button overhead.

Tuk-tuks: Taking a Tuk-tuk is the more expensive option, however, you get the convenience of a more direct route, and they will take you to your exact location. At night, from far locations, and busy tourist areas, the price per trip for Tuk-tuk and Songthaew will be anywhere from 80-180baht per person per trip

Mototaxi: Same as everywhere for a single passenger, check price first.

Trips from the airport are usually 250-350baht by metered taxi. If you arrive in Chiang mai during the day, you can ask the taxi driver to put on the meter instead of negotiating a price, and your trip may be cheaper. If you get in late or are not staying at a very large hotel, make SURE to bring the Thai phone number of the place you are staying so that the taxi can call the location for directions. The driver will NOT be able to follow an address, find a location on a map, or know where smaller hotels are located. You can also request that the hotel arrange for your pick up, and the driver will be waiting for you with a sign that has your name on it.

Renting motorbikes: 100-125 cc mopeds are 200baht/day.

SHOPPING

Shopping is one of the great pleasures in Chiang Mai. There is the famous night bazaar, Baan Tawai wood carving village, Bosang Sa paper and umbrella village and Sankampang with its many handicraft factories.

Night Bazaar: The night bazaar has some excellent bargains but be careful. The night bazaar is great for t-shirts, fake designer clothes and watches but not handicrafts. Lacquer-ware and wood products purchased here will split and crack after a year or so. It is not real lacquer-ware but only painted with a couple coats of sprayed-on lacquer paint. Wood products are not treated correctly unless you are from a hot and humid climate like Thailand. For wood and lacquer-ware, go to the factories in Sankhampang. Sudaluck is excellent for wood products and Lai Thai for lacquer=ware. Here the wood is treated properly and the lacquer-ware is treated with real gum lacquer with seven coats. Every coat is dried and polished.

Silk: Is another great bargain in Chiang Mai. If you don't know much about silk then make purchases from a reputable shop such as Jollie Femme. Most of the silk at the night bazaar is partially polyester or made by machine in Chinese factories. Real Thai silk is handmade so the weave is very tight and will stay together after many years of wear and hand washing. It is longer than Chinese machine made silk.

Tailor made suits: Clothes are well made if you go to the right tailor. Be careful of these, 'one coat, two pants, tie and shirt' deals for 3300THB. The material is very low quality and one sleeve may be longer than the other. The biggest complaint is the pockets are excessively shallow.

Open Markets of Chiang Mai: Most new foreigners are steered directly either by guidebooks, travel agencies, hotel desk clerks, and even tuk-tuk drivers to the Night Bazaar on Changklan Road between Tha Phae and Loi Kroh Roads. This sizeable market, with a gigantic, well lit sign in English and surrounded by many familiar food chains of the West. It is where most Western visitors get their first taste of a traditional Northern Thai shopping experience. Once amongst the tightly packed stalls, visitors very soon become acquainted with the bargaining game.

Weekend Bazaars: While the Night Bazaar has its flashing neon signs advertising the western food chains and merchandise, crowded narrow walkways crammed with hawkers and tourists; the Weekend Bazaars offer a more relaxing experience. Large wide avenues are blocked off from vehicle traffic at 5 PM until 11 PM. Talented craft persons and northern Thai fresh food vendors politely sell their wares along the sidewalks and on colourful temple grounds. Both weekend walking markets are excellent however, each is different in the types of wares sold, atmosphere, and experiences.

The Saturday Bazaar - Wualai Road: The old city silver-making district and even today you can still hear the tapping of hammers as the silversmiths sculpture beautiful designs on bowls, cups, bracelets, rings and wall murals. You can watch them make their beautiful creations as they sit on the street in front of their shops.

There are several silver shops on Wualai Road so look at all of them before deciding on a purchase. There are plenty of food and drink vendors along the street, with small restaurants where you can rest and take in the surroundings.

The Sunday Bazaar - Rajdumnern Road: Begins at Thapae Gate and ends at the city police station about six blocks west. About half way up, at Prapokklao Road, the Bazaar continues south past Wat Chedi Luang for another block and north to the three kings statue and the old Provincial Hall, which is now the Chiang Mai City Museum. A stage is set up on the grounds of the museum where northern Thai musicians and dancers in traditional costumes give live performances starting around 7 PM.

Both Bazaars are lots of fun and several hours can be spent here enjoying the culture, food, people, and atmosphere. Unlike the Night

Bazaar with its copied brand products, fake jewellery and handicrafts made in China or Burma, both weekend markets have real handcraft persons selling their goods.

The real fun is not the shopping but the ambience. Every block has traditional Thai Music being played by elders and children. The rich colours of the surrounding temples, the smell of garlic, grilled fish, sausages, and chillies being cooked and roasted. People are eating, smiling, and just having a good time.

Tip: get your snack and cold drink, then take it to one of the many foot massage operators and get your feet pampered after a hot day of shopping.

TOURIST MAP

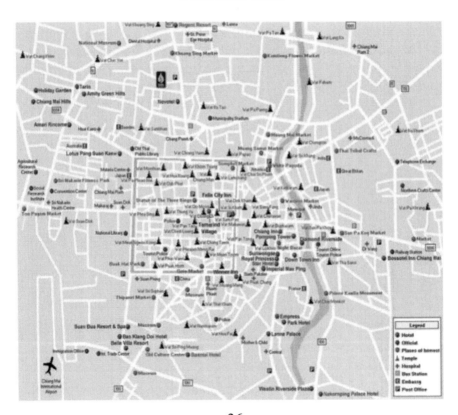

Thai Language Made Simple

The Thai dialect varies from region to region. This simple guide will help in all the tourist areas of Thailand.

Thai language is tonal, and as in English, has many words that sound the same but have a different meaning, for example: No, know, there, their, were, where etc. As this is not a Thai grammar lesson, just a simple guide to have fun with and get you through. The words will be spelt for you as you need to say them. The tones are not essential at this stage, as you will soon improve with practice...have fun.

Khap or Kah You will hear thus a lot in Thai conversation. Men say "Khap" women say "Kah" it is the polite end to a sentence as well as a commonly used form of **Yes** or **Okay.**

Mai, is used at the end of a sentence to make it a question. **Sabai dee Mai** - How are you?

Mai is also used at the beginning of a sentence to make a negative.

Mai Sabai – I am not fine / don't feel well.

Mai Pen Rai (Khap or Kah) - this is a useful phrase that you will hear a lot with the Thai's laid back attitude. It can mean several things like no problem or never mind.

Chai is a formal **Yes - Mai Chai is No.**

Aow (Khap or Kah) – want/need (please) - **Mai Aow (Khap or Kah)** – don't want/ need. (thanks)

Maak enlarges a statement (very): **Pang-** expensive − **Pang Maak -** very expensive

Pai : go/ to go **Pai duai**; go together. **Pai con diaw-**.go alone. **Pai lei-aw-kwa** - go/turn right. **Pai lei-aw-sai** - go left. **Pai trong pie** - go straight. **Aow pai** .... **Khap/ Kap** I would like to go.to,........ please.

When translating from the English, think simple: Want, Like. No want, No like, Water hot, Water cold, and remember to end sentences with **Khap or Kah.**

Numbers

0	SOONG	6	HOK	20	YI SIB	80	PAD SIB
1	NEUNG	7	JET	30	SAAM SIB	90	GOA SIB
2	SONG	8	PAD	40	SEE SIB	100	ROI
3	SAAM	9	GOA	50	HAA SIB	200	SONG ROI
4	SEE	10	SIB	60	HOK SIB	300	SAAM TOI
5	HAA	11	SIB ET	70	JET SIB	1000	NEUNG PAN

Once you have mastered from one to ten, the rest is easy.

Number's Unit - 10: Sib, 100: Roi, 1,000 Pan, 10,000: Muen, 100,000: Saen, 1,000,000: Laan

Example- 21: Yee sib et, 22: Yee sib song, 23: Yee sib saam, 31: Sam sib et, 32: Saam sib song, 45: See Sib haa, 57: Haa sib jet, 63: Hok sib saam, 71: Jet sib et, 89: Pad sib gao, 98:Gao sib pad, 1200: Nueng pan song roi, 1,312: Nueng pan sam roi sib song

Days of the Week

Monday: Wan Jan
Tuesday: Wan Anghan
Wednesday: Wan Phuut
Thursday: Wan Paruuhat Sabodee

38

Friday: Wan Suk
Saturday: Wan Sow
Sunday: Wan Aatit

Months

January- mók-gà-raa kom
February- gum-paa pan
March- mee-naa kom
April- may-săa-yon
May- préut-sà-paa kom
June- mí-tù-naa-yon
July- gà-rá-gà-daa-kom
August- sĭng hăa kom
September- gan-yaa-yon
October-dtù-laa kom
November- préut-sà-jì-gaa-yon
December- tan-waa kom

Telling the time

This is difficult and most Thais will point to their watch when they want to indicate a specific time, but if you are feeling adventurous and want to learn – here you go

The twenty-four hours of Thailand's day are split into five nominal groups covering a variety of numbers of hours. That means five different ways of saying "o'clock" (and of course two extras for midday and midnight).

The five periods are:

The morning: cháo
The afternoon: bàai
The evening: yen

39

The part of the night before midnight: tûm
The part of the night after midnight: dtee
Midday is tîang wan, and Midnight is tiang keun

To tell the time you'll also need mohng (which roughly translates as o'clock, but is only used for some of the time periods) and the numbers 1 to 59

This is how they are used:

Cháo begins at 6:00am and runs through to 11:00 am.
The construction is number-mohng-cháo.
So, hòk mohng cháo = 6 a.m., jet mohng cháo = 7 a.m. and so on until sìb et mohng cháo = 11 a.m.
Bàai : After midday, we flip to bàai, which runs from 1:00 p.m. to 4:00 p.m.
1:00 p.m. is called bàai mohng, then after that the construction is bàai-number-mohng.
So, bàai song mohng = 2:00 p.m. etc.
Yen: For 5:00 p.m. and 6:00 p.m. we use yen.
They are hâa mohng yen and hok mohng yen respectively.
Tûm: From 7:00 p.m. until 11:00 p.m. we use tûm.

You have to be careful here because the numbers reset to 1. That is to say 7:00 p.m. becomes "one at night". This is said tûm neung

After tûm neung, the construction becomes number-tûm

So, sŏng tûm = 8:00 p.m., saam tûm = 9:00 p.m. and so on until haa tûm = 11:00 p.m.

Dtee Finally, after midnight, we reach the wee small hours and the term dtee is used. This runs from 1:00 a.m. until 5:00 a.m. The construction is dtee-number

So, dtee neung = 1:00 a.m., dtee song = 2:00 a.m. and so on until dtee haa = 5:00 a.m. after which it all starts again at hòk mohng cháo.

To indicate divisions within the hour you just add a number from 1 to 59 after the constructions as outlined above. For example bàai song mohng yee sìp = 2:20 p.m., dtee haa saam sìp jet 5:37 a.m. and so on.

A handy A-Z of commonly used words

English	Thai
A	
about, approximately	bpramaan
address (noun)	tee yoo
to be afraid (of), scared	Glua
after	lang-jaak
afternoon	dtorn bai
again	eek (laew), eek khrang
age	aa-yoo
How old are you?	(khun) aa-yoo taorai
... ago, before	... tee laew, korn, tee paan maa
to agree	hen duai
air-conditioned	mee air
aircon room	ho:ng air
airport	sanaam bin

English	Thai
(to drink) alcohol	(gin) lao
a little (bit)	nid noi
alone	khon diao
already	Laew
alright, okay	riab roi
always, all the time	samoe:, dtalort wee-laa (speak "waylaa")
and	lae, gab
angry	gro:ht, mo:h ho:h (long round "o" sound)
animal	sat (as in "Saturday")
to answer	Dtorb
ant	Mod
arm	khaen
to arrive	(maa) tueng
ash trey	tee khia boori (speak "bully")
to ask	Taam
aunt	bpaa, naa

B

English	Thai
back	Lang
back pain	bpuat lang
bad, evil	leo (speak "layo"), mai dee, (jai) rai, jai dam, yae
bag, baggage, luggage; handbag	gra-bpao, gra-bpau tue:h
banana	Gluai
bank (financial)	tana-khaan
bank account	banchee ("bunchee")
bathroom, toilet	ho:ng naam, sookhaa
to be	bpen, e.g. *I am a man = pom bpen poo chai*
to be (stay)	yoo, e.g. *I am (stay) at home = pom yoo baan*
beach	haad (sai)
beautiful, pretty	suai, suai ngaam
because, as, for	pro-waa
bed	dtiang (no:n)
bedroom	ho:ng no:n
beer	Bia

43

English	Thai
to belive (s.o., s.th.)	chuea
best	dee tee soot
better	dee kwaa
between	rawaang
(to ride) bicycle	(khee) jakkra-yaan
big, large	yai
bird	nok
black	(see) dam
blood	luead
(light) blue	see faa
(dark) blue	see naam ngoen
boat, ship	ruea
body	dtua, raang gai
book (noun)	nang sue:
to be bored (of)	buea
boring	naa buea
bosom, breast, tits	nom
bottle	khuat

English	Thai
bottom, ass(hole)	gon, dtoot
bracelet	gamlai khor mue:
bread	khanom bpang
breakfast	aahaan chao
bridge	sapaan
bright, light	sawaang
broken, out of order	sia (laew)
brother (older)	pee chai
brother (younger)	no:ng chai
brown	(see) naam dtaan
building	aa-khaan
bus, coach	rot but, rot me: ("may"), rot bpra-jam taang
bus station	sataanee rot khon song
(to do) business	(tam) toorakit
businessman	nak toorakit
busy	yoong, mee too-ra, mai waang
but, however	dtae
butter	noey

English	Thai
to buy	sue:

C

to call s.o.	riak
to call (phone) s.o.	to:h haa
to call (phone) back	to:h glab
camera	klo:ng tai roop
can, to be able to, capable of	bpen. e.g.
can, to be able to	dai, saamaat
cannot, impossible	mai dai
cancer	maraeng ("malaeng")
capital	mueang luang
car	rot (yon)
car park	tee jo:t rot
careful, attention!	rawang
cat	maew
chair	gao-ee
to change	bplian

English	Thai
to (ex)change money	lae:k ngoen
cheap, inexpensive	too:k, mai paeng
cheaper	too:k gwaa
cheat, untruthful	khee go:hng
chicken	gai
children, baby	look, dek (plural "dek dek")
chopsticks	dta-kiab
cigarette(s)	boori (speak "bully")
cinema, movie theatre	ro:hng nang
city, town	mueang
clean	sa-aat
climate, weather	aa-gaat
clock, watch	naaligaa
to close, closed	bpid
clothes	suea paa
cloud	me:k
cockroach	malaeng saab
coconut	(loo:k) ma-prao

English	Thai
cold, cool	yen
(to feel) cold	nao
colour	see
(to be) cool, calm; keep cool!	jai yen; jai yen yen
to come	maa
to come back	glab maa
to come from	maa jaak
to come home	glab baan
company (business)	borisat
confused	sab-son
to cook	tam gab khao
cook (noun)	mae/por khrua (female/male)
correct, right	too:k
crocodile	jo-ra-ke:
country	bprate:t
cousin	loo:k pee loo:k no:ng
to cry	ro:ng hai
cup	tuai

English	Thai
D	
to dance	den
dangerous	antarai
daughter	loo:k sao
day	wan (speak "one")
daily, per day	wan la, dtor wan
every day	took wan
day off, holiday	wan yoot
death	kwaam dtai:
(to have) debts	bpen nee
to decide	dtat sin jai
democracy	bprachaa-tipa-dtai
dentist	mor fan (speak "fun")
to explain	a-ti-bai
eye	dtaa
F	
face	naa
factory	ro:hng ngaan

English	Thai
to fall (down)	dtok
family	khro:b khrua
famous	mee chue: siang
fan	pat lom
fast, quick	reo, reo reo (adv.)
(to be) fat	uan
father	por
to feel	roo-suek
(a) few	noi
fewer than, less than ...	noi gwaa
fewest ...	noi tee soot
to fight	soo:
finger	niu mue:
fire	fai (mai)
fish	bplaa
fishing	jab bplaa
fly (insect)	malaeng wan
to fly	bin, nang khrueang bin ("sit airplane")

English	Thai
flood, flooded	naam tuam
flower	dork mai
food	aahaan
foot, feet	tao
football, soccer	foot-born
for	hai, puea
foreigner, Westerner/Caucasian	chao dtaang chaat, farang (speak "fallang")
for free, free of charge	fee
to forget	lue:m
fork	sorm
fridge, refrigerator	dtoo yen
friend	puean
boyfriend/girlfriend	fae:n
fruit	ponlamai
to fuck, have sex	yet, uep, tap, au gan (coll., vulgar)
full	dtem
full (with food, not hungry)	im (laew)

English	Thai
fun, amusement, enjoyable	sanook
funny	dta-lok

G

garlic	gra-tiam
to get	dai, dai rab
to give	hai
glass	kaew
glasses, eyeglasses	wae:n dtaa
to go (to)	bpai (no preposition required)
to go home	glap baan
to go out, go on a trip	bpai tiao
gold	to:ng
good	dee
good (at something), skilled, clever	gaeng
good heart, kind, kind-hearted	jai dee
government	rattabaan
green	(see) khiao
guilty	pid

English	Thai
to feel guilty, to be guilty	roo-suek pid, mee kwaam pid

H

hair	pom
(to get a) haircut	dtat pom
half	khrueng
hand	mue:
handsome	lor
to happen	gerd khuen
happy	dee jai, mee kwaam sook
hard, difficult	yaak, lambaak
hard (not soft)	khaeng
hat, crash helmet	muak
to hate	gliat
to have	mee
head	hua, see-sa
headache	bpuat hua
health	sookapaap
healthy	sookapaap dee

English	Thai
to hear	dai yin
heart	hua jai
heavy (weight)	nak
to help	chuai, chuai luea
Help (me)!	chuai duai
here	tee nee, dtrong nee
his, her	khong khao
to hope	wang
hope (noun)	kwaam wang
(to be) horny	mee aarom, ngian, bpliak ("wet")
hospital	ro:ng payabaan
hot, warm	ro:n
hot-tempered, quick-tempered	jai ro:n ("hot heart")
hotel	ro:hng raem
hour	chua mo:hng
house, home	baan
how	yaang rai, bae:b nai
how long? (time)	naan taorai

English	Thai
how many ...?	gee, maak taorai
how much?	(raa-khaa) taorai, maak taorai
to hug, embrace	gord
hungry	hiu (khao)
husband	saamee, pua

I

ice, ice cubes	naam khaeng
if, in case	taa
important	samkan ("some cun")
impossible	bpen bpai mai dai
in (e.g. one year)	eek (nueng bpee)
in, inside	nai, khaang nai
in, at	tee
intelligent, clever	chalaat
(to be) interested (in)	son jai (nai)
interesting	naa son jai
island	gko (very short "o" sound)

J

English	Thai
jealous	hueng
jeans	gaang gaeng yeen
joke	rueang dta-lok, jo:hk
K	
key	goon jae:
room key, house key	goon jae: ho:ng, goon jae: baan
to kill, to murder	khaa
king	gasat
to kiss	joob
knife	meed
to know, to know (s.o.)	roo, roo jak ...
L	
ladyboy, transvestite, she-male	katoey
language (English, Thai)	paa-saa (ang-krit, tai)
last (as in "last month")	... tee laew, ... gawn
late	sai, duek ("late at nighT")
to laugh	hua ro (short "o" sound)
laundry shop	raan sak reed

English	Thai
law	got-mai
lawyer	nak got-mai
lazy	khee giat
to learn	rian
left	sai
left-hand side	daan sai: mue:
Turn left!	liao sai:
leg(s)	khaa
to lend (money)	hai yue:m (ngoen)
letter	jot mai
to lick	lia
to (speak a) lie	go hok
life	cheewit
to live, to be alive	mee chewit (yoo)
light	fai
light (not heavy)	bao
lighter	fai check
to like	chorb

English	Thai
liquor	lao
to listen (to)	fang
to listen to music	fang ple:ng
little, small	lek, noi
to live in, to stay at	(pak) yoo (tee)
to lock (a door)	lok (bpra-dtoo)
lonely	ngao
long (material)	yao
long (time)	naan
to look	(mo:ng) hen, mo:ng, doo
to look for, search, seek (s.o., s.th.)	haa
to lose (s.th.)	tam hai
to lose (e.g. a game)	pae:
loud, noisy	(siang) dang
to love	rak
love (noun)	kwaam rak
I love you	pom/chan rak khun (male/female)

English	Thai
Do you love me?	khun rak pom/chan mai

M

man	poo chai
manager	poo jat gaan
mango	mamuang
manicure/pedicure	dtat lep
many, much	maak, yoe, lai:
market	dtalaat
to marry	dtaeng ngaan
already married	dtaeng ngaan laew
(Thai, foot) massage	nuad (tai, tao)
traditional massage	nuad paen boran
to masturbate, wank	chuck-wao (coll.)
maybe, perhaps	baang tee, aat-ja
to meet (s.o.)	pob, joer
menstruation, to menstruate	bpra-jam duean, bpen men
(to send a) text message	(faak) khor kwaam
midnight	tiang khue:n

English	Thai
military, soldier	tahaan
milk	nom
minute	natee
mirror, glass (material)	gra-jok
to miss (s.o.)	kid tueng
I miss you	pom/chan kid tueng khun
mistake, fault	kwaam pid
to make a mistake, do wrong	tam pid
to misunderstand	khao jai pid
mobile phone, cell phone	mue: tue:h, mobai:
money	ngoen
to borrow money	yue:m ngoen
to have no money	mai mee ngoen
to owe money, have debts	bpen nee
to send/transfer money	song/faak ngoen
month	duean
monthly	took duean, duean la
more ... than	... maak gwaa

English	Thai
most ...	... suan yai
morning	dtorn chao
Good morning	sawat-dee dtorn chao
mosquito	yoong
mother	mae:
motorcycle	mo-dter-sai
mountain, hill	poo khao
mouth	bpaak
(to watch a) movie	(doo) nang
music	don-dtree
must, have to	dto:ng
my, mine	kho:ng pom/chan (male/female)

N

name	chue:
What's your name?	khun chue: arai
surname/family name	naam sakoon
necessary	jam bpen
neck, throat	khor

English	Thai
necklace	soi: khor
neighbour	puean baan
neighbourhood	taew baan
never	mai koey (loey), e.g. *I never drink beer = pom mai koey gin bia*
new	mai
newspaper	nang-sue pim
next (as in "next month")	... naa
night	khue:n
in the night	dtorn glaang khue:n
tonight	khue:n nee
nipple(s)	hua nom
no	mai, mai chai, bplao
north	nuea
nose	jamook
not at all	mai ... loey
nothing	mai mee arai
not yet	yang (mai)

English	Thai
now, at the moment	dtorn nee, diao nee, khana nee

O

of	kho:ng
often	boi, boi boi
not often	mai boi
old (material)	gao
old (person)	gae:
on	bon
once, twice	nueng khrang (khrang diao), so:ng khrang
only	taonan, kae, yaang diao
to open, open	bpoe:d
opposite	dtrong gan khaam
or	rue:
orange	som
orange juice	naam som
ordinary, normal, usual	tamma-daa
other	... ue:n

P

English	Thai
papaya	malagor
papaya salad	som-dtam
parents	por mae:
passport	nang-sue: dtoe:n taang
to pay	jai
peace	santipaap
to pee, piss	chee, yiao (vulgar)
penis, cock, dick	khuai, ham (speak "hum") [coll., vulgar]
testicles, balls	(khai) ham
perfume	naam horm
petrol, gasoline	naam man (rot)
to fill petrol, gasoline	dtoe:m naam man (rot)
petrol station	bam naam man ("bum naam mun")
photograph, picture	roop paap, roop tai:
to photograph, take a picture	tai: roop
to pick (s.o.) up	rab
pineapple	sapparot

English	Thai
pineapple juice	naam sapparot
plane	khrueang bin
plate	jaan
to play	len
play cards	len pai
please	garoona, bpro:hd
police, policeman	dtam-ruat
police station	sataa-nee dtam-ruat
polite, impolite	soo-paap, mai soo-paap
politics, politician(s)	gaan mueang, nak gaan mueang
poor	jon
popular	tee niyom
possible	bpen bpai dai
powder	bpae:ng
to prefer	chorb ... maak gwaa
pretty	suai
price	raakhaa, khaa
prime minister	nayok rattamon-dtree

English	Thai
problem(s), trouble	bpan-haa
to have a problem	mee bpan-haa
"No problem!"	mai mee bpan-haa, mai bpen rai
profession, occupation	aa-cheep
to promise, promise	san-yaa
to keep a promise	rak-saa san-yaa
proud	poom jai
province	jang-wat ("chang-wat")
to pull	dueng
to push	plak
Q	
quiet	ngiab
quick, fast	reo
quickly	reo reo
R	
radio	witta-yoo
railway station	sataa-nee rot fai
rain	fon

English	Thai
It is raining	fon dtok
to read	aan
really, sure	jing, jing jing (adv.)
to receive	dai rab
red	(see) daeng
to remember	jam (daI)
to rent	chao
rent (noun)	khaa chao
to rest, relax	pak porn
restaurant	raan aahaan, ho:ng aahaan
to return, to come back	glab (maa)
rich	ruai
right, right-hand side	kwaa, daan kwaa mue:
Turn right!	liao kwaa
ring	wae:n
river	mae: naam
road	tanon
room	ho:ng

English	Thai
to run	wing

S

sad	sao jai
salary, monthly income	ngoen duean
salt	gluea
same	muean gan, diao gan
same as ...	muean gab ...
to save money	geb ngoen
to say	bork
(to be) scared	dtok jai
school	ro:hng rian
sea, ocean	talay
by the sea	rim talay
season (cold, hot, rainy)	rue-doo (nao, ro:n, fon)
seat	tee nang
to see	(mo:hng) hen, doo
self (myself, himself etc.)	e:ng
to sell	khai, jam-nai

English	Thai
to send	song
separately	yae:k gan
to pay separately	yae:k gan jai
to have sex, fuck	yet, tap, uep, ao gan
shirt, blouse	suea (chert)
shoe(s)	ro:ng tao
shop, store	raan
short	san, dtia
to show (s.th.)	hai doo
to shower, take a shower	aab naam
Shut up!	hoob bpaak, ngiab, sao wao (Lao dialect)
shy	(khee) ai
sick, ill	bpuai, mai sabai
silk	paa mai
similar	glai gan
single (not married)	so:hd, yang mai mee fae:n
sister (older)	pee sao

English	Thai
sister (younger)	no:ng sao
to sit	nang
skin	piu
skirt, dress	gra-bpro:hng
to sleep	no:n (lab)
sleeping room	ho:ng no:n
slim	porm
slow	chaa
slowly!	chaa chaa
small	lek, noi
to smell (good)	horm
to smell (bad), to stink	men
to smile	yim
to smoke (cigarettes)	soop (boori)
snake	ngoo
snow	heemaa
soap	saboo
socks	toong tao

English	Thai
soldier, military	tahaan
some ...	baang ...
sometimes	baang khrang
son	loo:k chai
(to sing a) song	ro:ng ple:ng
sorry, pardon, excuse me	khor to:ht khrab/kha
sour	bpriao
south	dtai
to speak (about)	pood (tueng)
special, extraordinary	pi-se:t
spider	mae:ng moom
spoon	chorn
sports	geelaa
to stand	yue:n
to start, to begin	roe:m (dton)
stomach	to:ng
stomach ache	bpuad to:ng, jeb to:ng
stone	hin

English	Thai
to stop, to have a break	yoot
strange, weird	bplae:k
street, road	tanon, sai
side-street	soi
strong (physically)	(khae:ng) rae:ng
sound, voice, noise	siang
to suck (s.th.)	doo:t, orm
suit, costume	chut ("choot")
suitcase, bag, baggage, luggage	gra-bpao, gra-bpao dtoe:n taang
sun	pra aatit
sunshine	dae:t
to suppose, to assume	som-moot
(to be) sure	nae jai, nae no:n
surprise, to be surprised	bpralaat jai
sweet	waan
to swim	wai naam, len naam
swimming pool	sa wai naam

T

English	Thai
to take (s.th.)	yip, ao
to take time, to last	chai weelaa ("waylaa")
to talk, to talk about, to chat	khui (gan), pood tueng, sontanaa
tall	soong
tax(es)	paasee
taxi, cab	(rot) teksee
to teach	sorn
teacher	khroo, aajaan
telephone	to:h-rasap
telephone card	bat to:h-rasap
telephone number	boer to:h-rasap
television	(doo) to:h-ratat, tee-wee
to tell	bork
temple	wat
Thailand	mueang tai, bpra-te:t tai
that	nan (speak "none")
there	tee nan
to think (that)	kid (waa), nuek (waa)

English	Thai
thirsty	hiu naam
this	nee
ticket	dtua
air ticket	dtua khrueang bin
bus ticket	dtua rot me:
rail ticket	dtua rot fai
to tickle, ticklish	jakkajee
tiger	suea
tight, stingy, "cheap Charlie"	khee niao
time	weelaa ("waylaa")
at what time ...?	... gee mo:hng
What time is it (now)?	(dtorn nee) gee mo:hng
on time, punctually	dtrong weelaa ("waylaa")
time(s) (one time, two times etc.)	khrang (nueng khrang, so:ng khrang etc.)
every time, each time	took khrang
tired, sleepy	nueay, nguang no:n
to be tired of ...	buea ...
today	wan nee

English	Thai
together	duai gan, ruam gan
tomato	makuea-te:t
tomorrow	proong nee
tongue	lin
too ... (big, small)	... gern bpai
tooth, teeth	fan ("fun")
toothbrush	bpraeng see fan
toothpaste	yaa see fan
to touch (s.th., s.o.)	dtae, jab
tourist	nak to:ng tiao
towel	paa chet dtua
traffic jam	rot dtit
train, railway	rot fai
to translate	bplae
transvestite, ladyboy	katoey
to travel, to go out	dtoe:n taang, bpai tiao
to try	pa-ya-yaam, lo:ng
trousers	gaang gae:ng

English	Thai
to turn (right/left)	liao (kwaa, sai)

U

ugly	naa gliat
umbrella	rom (speak "lom")
uncle	loong
under, below	dtai
to understand	khao jai
I don't understand	pom/chan mai khao jai (male/female)
underpants, panties, knickers	gaang gae:ng nai
to undress, to take off	tord suea (paa), tord ...
unhappy	sia jai, sao jai, mai mee kwaam sook
until, till, to	tueng, jon, jon gratang, jon gwaa, gratang

V

vagina, pussy	yoh-nee (formal), hoy, jim, hee (coll., vulgar)
vegetables	pak
very, many/much	maak, maak maak (adv.)

English	Thai
village	moo baan
visa	wee-saa (from English "visa")
to visit (s.o.)	bpai haa, (bpai) yiam

W

to wait	ror
to wake up	dtue:n no:n
to walk, go for a walk	dtoe:n, dtoe:n len
wallet	gra-bpao ngoen, gra-bpao dtang
to wank, to masturbate	chuck-wao (coll.)
to want (to)	yaak, dto:ng gaan
war	song-khraam
to wash (clothes)	sak (paa)
to watch	doo
to watch TV	doo to:h-ratat, doo tee-wee
(wrist) watch	naaligaa khor mue:
water	naam
drinking water	naam due:m, naam bplao
cold water	naam yen

English	Thai
watermelon	dtaeng mo:h
way	taang
which way?	taang nai
to wear (s.th.)	sai
weather, climate	aa-gaat
week	aatit
weekly	aatit la, took aatit
wet	bpliak
what	arai
what?	arai na
What is this?	nee arai
What's the time?	gee mo:hng
when?	mua-arai
when (temporal conjunction)	weelaa ("waylaa"), dtorn tee, (muea) dtorn
where?	tee nai
Where do you go?	(khun) bpai nai
where (are you/do you come) from?	(khun maa) jaak nai

English	Thai
Where is ...?	... yoo (tee) nai
which, that, who (relative pronoun)	tee
which (person)	khon nai
which (material)	an nai
white	(see) khao
who?	khrai, khon nai
whose ...?	kho:ng khrai
why	tammai, pro arai
wife	panrayaa, mia, fae:n
second wife, mistress	mia noi
(to be) willing	dtem jai
to win	chana
window	naa dtaang
(red/white) wine	wai: (daeng, khao)
with	gab, duai
woman	poo ying
wood(en)	mai
to work	tam ngaan

English	Thai
to work hard	tam ngaan nak
world, earth	lo:hk
to write	khian
wrong, mistaken, false, faulty	pid
to do wrong	tam pid

Y

English	Thai
year	bpee
yearly, every year	bpee la, dtor bpee, took bpee
yellow	(see) lueang
yes	chai, khrab/kha
yesterday	muea-waan (nee)
young (man, woman); not old, still young	noom, sao; yang mai gae:, dek yoo

Popular Thai Recipe

Travelling around Thailand you will enjoy many succulent Thai dishes. Here are the recipes of five that you will come across frequently. Try them out when you return home and again enjoy the authentic taste of Thailand.

PAD THAI NOODLES   KHOA PAT (Fried rice)   THAI GREEN CURRY   THAI RED CURRY   TOM YAM SOUP

PAD THAI NOODLES (Flavoursome Thai noodles)

INGREDIENTS

SERVES 4

1. 8 ounces Thai rice noodles, 1/8
2. 4 tablespoons Thai fish sauce - Naam Plaa
3. 6 tablespoons white vinegar
4. 1 tablespoon tomato paste
5. 6 tablespoons sugar
6. 4 green onions
7. 1 cup dry-roasted unsalted peanuts, Coarsely Ground
8. 1/2 cup vegetable oil
9. 2 garlic cloves, minced
10. 1/2 lb skinless chicken breasts, cut in small pieces (or 1/2 lb of a combination of 2 or all 3) or 1/2 lb pork, cut in chunks (or 1/2 lb of a combination of 2 or all 3) or 1/2 lb raw shrimp (or 1/2 lb of a combination of 2 or all 3)
11. egg

12. bean sprouts
13. 2 tablespoons crushed red pepper flakes
14. 2 limes, cut into wedges

DIRECTIONS

Soak rice noodles in warm water for 20 - 25 minutes - they should be soft but not mushy; they will soften when they are cooked in the liquid.

(Prepare accordingly depending on your choice)Peel and deveign the shrimp, leave the tails intact - cut the chicken and/or pork into 1/8 inch x 1 inch pieces.

Mix together fish sauce, sugar, vinegar, and tomato puree until sugar is dissolved, and set aside.

Slice the scallions on the diagonal 1/4 inch thick, set aside.

Heat a wok and add the oil, then stir-fry the meat and garlic - when meat is cooked (no longer pink) add the drained noodles and quickly stir to coat with oil - quickly add the sauce and stir carefully to avoid breaking the noodles.

Move the noodles to the side and add eggs - let them set a bit then break them up and continue to stir-fry - add additional oil if necessary to keep noodles from sticking- continue to toss until eggs are nicely distributed.

Add 3/4 Cup peanuts, bean sprouts and scallions - toss.

Remove to serving platter, garnish with 1/4 Cup ground peanuts, sprinkle with the chilli flakes, and serve with lime wedges to squeeze over the top.

KHOA PAT (Fried rice) - Khai (chicken) Moo (pork) Gung (shrimp) Neu-a wua (Beef)

INGREDIENTS

SERVES 4-6

1. 4 cups cooked cold jasmine rice (cold rice is essential so the grains will not stick together when stir frying)
2. 3 tablespoons peanut oil
3. 4 cloves freshly minced garlic
4. 1 1/2 cups boneless skinless chicken breasts (its easiest to get thin slices if the meat is still partially frozen) or 1 1/2 cups lean pork (its easiest to get thin slices if the meat is still partially frozen) or 1 1/2 cups beef, thinly sliced (its easiest to get thin slices if the meat is still partially frozen) or Shrimp 1 kilo.
5. 2 eggs
6. 4 green onions, sliced thin
7. 2 teaspoons palm sugar (table sugar is fine if you can't find palm sugar)
8. 3 tablespoons Thai fish sauce (Naam Plaa - no substitutes)
9. 1 tablespoon oyster sauce
10. 3/4 cup frozen peas (not traditional but I like to add them anyway)
11. 1 cucumber, sliced
12. 2 limes, cut into wedges

DIRECTIONS

Heat peanut oil in a wok or large skillet over medium high heat.

While pan is warming, toss the cold rice with your hands, making sure to separate the grains from any clumps.

Add the garlic to the heated wok, and toss until fragrant and golden.

83

Add chicken, beef, pork, or shrimp and stir-fry for about 1 minute.

Push the meat and garlic up the sides making a well in the middle and add eggs.

Scramble eggs for 1 minute in middle of pan then, add green onions and peas and incorporate all ingredients together, stir frying for another minute.

Add rice, turning over rice with pan ingredients several times to coat and stir-frying for 2-3 minutes. You want the rice to begin to have a toasted smell, making sure that all the ingredients are constantly moved around the pan for even cooking.

If your pan seems to have cooled down to the point where the ingredients are no longer sizzling, you may need to turn the heat up slightly.

Sprinkle in the sugar and add the fish sauce and oyster sauce.

Stir-fry all ingredients together for one minute more or until sauces are absorbed and mixture is combined. Transfer to serving platter.

Garnish plate edge with sliced cucumber, lime wedges, and additional whole green onions if desired.

Serve with a small dish of fish sauce and cut red Chile to add zing as required.

THAI GREEN CURRY – Chicken (Khai)

INGREDIENTS

SERVES 4

1. 1 tablespoon vegetable oil
2. 2 shallots, minced
3. 1 inch piece gingerroot, minced
4. 1 -2 tablespoon Thai green curry paste
5. 1 (14 1/2 ounce) can chicken broth
6. 2 cups sliced cooked chicken or 2 cups cooked beef or 2 cups cooked pork
7. 1 (16 ounce) can coconut milk
8. 1 (8-ounce) can. sliced bamboo shoots, drained
9. 1/4 teaspoon salt
10. 1 cup shredded basil leaves
11. lime wedge

DIRECTIONS

Heat oil in a large skillet or wok over high heat; add shallots and ginger. Stir-fry until fragrant, about 1 minute. Reduce heat to medium; stir in curry paste. Stir in chicken broth; cook until the broth is reduced by half, about 10 minutes.

Stir in chicken, coconut milk, bamboo shoots and salt; heat to a boil. Reduce heat; simmer 5 minutes. Stir in basil.

Serve in bowls over steamed rice or noodles with lime wedges on the side for squeezing over.

SPICY THAI RED CURRY – Shrimp (Gung)

INGREDIENTS

SERVES 4

1. 2 tablespoons peanut oil
2. 1/2 cup chopped shallot
3. 1 large red bell pepper, cut into strips

4. 2 medium carrots, trimmed and shredded
5. 2 teaspoons minced garlic
6. 1 1⁄2 tablespoons Thai red curry paste (or to taste)
7. 2 tablespoons fish sauce
8. 2 teaspoons light brown sugar
9. 1 (14 ounce) can coconut milk
10. 1 lb medium shrimp, peeled and deveined
11. 3 tablespoons chopped Thai basil
12. 3 tablespoons chopped fresh coriander / cilantro leaves
13. cooked jasmine rice, accompaniment
14. 1 sprig fresh coriander/ cilantro, garnish

DIRECTIONS

In a large wok or sauté pan, heat the oil over medium-high heat.

Add the shallots, bell peppers, carrots, and garlic, and stir-fry until soft, 2 to 3 minutes.

Add the red curry paste and cook, stirring, until fragrant, 30 seconds to 1 minute.

Stirring, add the fish sauce and sugar, then the coconut milk and bring to a boil.

Simmer until thickened slightly, about 2 minutes.

Add the shrimp and cook, stirring, until pink and just cooked through, about 2 minutes.

Remove from the heat and stir in the basil and coriander/ cilantro.

Serve over jasmine rice, garnished with coriander / cilantro sprigs.

TOM YAM SOUP - Spicy seafood Soup

INGREDIENTS

SERVES 4-6

1. 4-6 cups Chicken Stock
2. 1/2 cup fresh Shiitake Mushrooms, finely chopped
3. 12 raw Shrimp, shells removed (other shellfish optional)
4. 1 stalk Lemon grass , minced
5. 3 Kaffir Lime leaves
6. 3 cloves Garlic, minced
7. 2 Red Chillies, finely chopped
8. 3 tbsp Fish sauce
9. 1/2 can Coconut milk
10. 1 tbsp lime juice, freshly squeezed
11. 1/3 cup fresh coriander/cilantro, chopped
12. 1 tbsp sugar (optional)
13. Extra vegetables of your choice

DIRECTIONS

Boil the chicken stock in a deep cooking pot.

Add lemon grass and boil for 2 more minutes. Include the stalk too if you are using fresh lemon-grass.

Stir in garlic, lime leaves, chilli and mushrooms into the pot and heat it in medium heat, simmer for 2 minutes.

Add Shrimp and extra vegetables (if any) into the pot and simmer until the shrimp is pink and plump.

Reduce to low heat, add fish sauce, limejuice, and coconut milk in it, stir and simmer until hot.

Check for the taste, if salt is not enough add more fish sauce, and if too sour add sugar. Add coconut milk if you taste it too spicy.

Your Thai Tom Yum Soup is now ready to be served hot with fresh coriander / cilantro leaves.

You can add more spice by using Red Thai Curry Paste.

Hilarious Jokes – (Adult)

THAI JOKES

Thai jokes are numerous with ladyboy's usually being the brunt. Here are some that I think you will enjoy.

"How's your new Thai girlfriend, Dave?"
"How do you know her name?"

-

I'm going to Thailand this year and to make sure I don't get any "surprises" I'm asking prostitutes to show me their crotch before I take them to my room.-
Last time I nearly ended up sleeping with a woman!

-

An Irish Catholic boy and a Thai Buddhist boy were talking and the Catholic boy said, "My priest knows more than your Buddha." The Buddhist boy said, "Of course he does, you tell him everything."

-

I just got back from holiday in Bangkok where I came very close to sleeping with a ladyboy. She looked like a woman, she walked like a woman, she talked like a woman and she even kissed like a woman! It was only when she drove me back to her place and reversed parked her car on the first attempt I thought "hang on…"

Nothing says, "I'm a fat ugly bastard with no personality." quite like having a Thai wife.

-

I farted in the bath earlier and started laughing to myself.
"What's so funny?" the wife asked.
"Oh nothing, it's just funny when you fart in the bath and the bubbles tickle your bollocks" I explained.
"Oh yeah, that is funny actually" she replied.
And that's when I knew it was time to send it back to Thailand.

-

My wife was reading the paper and said, "Tut tut, that's terrible. Another woman in India has been gang-raped and hung."
I replied, "Actually it's 'hanged'. In India, women are hanged. In Thailand, women are hung."

-

My Thai wife left me the day after I bought her a new necklace.
I was fuming, fifty fucking quid that thing cost me.
The necklace wasn't cheap, either.

-

I dumped my Thai wife when she told me her balls had dropped.
How was I to know she had just won the lottery?

-

90

I keep making stereotypical jokes about my old man and his new Thai bride. He really doesn't find it amusing… and neither does my Dad.

-

"Dad, what's a ladyboy?"
"Ask your step mother, he knows."

-

I was sitting on the train this morning opposite a really sexy Thai bird. I thought to myself, "Please don't get an erection. Please don't get an erection."
But she did.

-

I'll tell you what I really hate about my new Thai bride.
She keeps leaving the toilet seat up!

-

Went to the new Thai restaurant in town, and it's really weird - there's condom machines in both toilets.

-

"Did you have a good holiday Dave?"
"Amazing. Check out these photos of us at the nudist beach."
"I love your Thai girlfriend, she looks tiny next to you."
"Thanks, but to be fair, she had just been swimming."

-

I met my Thai girlfriend for sex at her place.
She said, "You have condom?"
"Yes," I replied, "But this time, can I wear it?"

91

General Funnies

An old bloke hires a hit-man to kill his wife of 40 years.
The Hitman says. : I'll shoot her just below her left tit"
The husband replies. "I want her dead not fucking kneecapped."

-

I treated the wife to one of those fish pedicures the other day and I must say I was really impressed with the result. Those piranhas don't fuck about.

-

I went to the doctors suffering from premature ejaculation. He said "it must be stressful for your wife. I said "To be perfectly honest doctor, it's getting on her tits."

-

In1872 the Welsh invented the condom by using a sheep's intestine. In 1873 the English refined the idea by taking the intestine out of the sheep out first.

-

The teacher asked Jimmy, "Why is your cat at school today Jimmy?" Jimmy replied crying, "Because I heard my daddy tell my mommy, 'I am going to eat that p*ssy once Jimmy leaves for school today!'"

-

A Chinese fellow walks into a bar with a huge colourful parrot on his shoulder. "Wow", says the bartender, "where did you get that from?" "From China", answered the parrot, "they've got tons of them there!"

-

Teacher: "Kids, what does the chicken give you?"
Student: "Meat!"
Teacher: "Very good! Now what does the pig give you?"
Student: "Bacon!"
Teacher: "Great! And what does the fat cow give you?"
Student: "Homework!"

-

My neighbour just banged on my door shouted
Can I use your phone? there's been an accident along the road and a
Man U fan has been knocked down. He is bleeding to death.
I asked him " Why ...what's wrong with your phone?"
He replied "the camera's shit on mine"

-

Tommy came home from school looking confused, he sat down next
to his father and asked.
"Dad, what's a Pussy?"
His dad went to the bedroom, bought back a playboy, opened the
pages to the centre fold. He then took a marker pen and drew around
her minge region.
"There son, that's a pussy".
The following day Tommy came home again looking confused and
asked.
"Dad, what's a Cunt"
His father leant forward and said
"Remember yesterday when you came home and asked about a pussy
and I drew a circle on that picture."
"Yes dad" replied Tommy
"Well everything outside that circle is a cunt."

-

A rather attractive woman goes up to the bar in a quiet rural pub. She gestures alluringly to the barman who comes over immediately. When he arrives, she seductively signals that he should bring his face close to hers. When he does so, she begins to gently caress his beard which is full and bushy. "Are you the manager?" she asks, softly stroking his face with both hands. "Actually, no" he replies. "Can you get him for me - I need to speak to him?" she asks, running her hands up beyond his beard and into his hair. "I'm afraid I can't" breathes the barman - clearly aroused. "Is there anything I can do?" "Yes there is. I need you to give him a message" she continues huskily, popping a couple of fingers into his mouth and allowing him to suck them gently. "Tell him that there is no toilet paper in the ladies room."

-

Andrew the drover from a huge cattle station in the Australian outback appeared before St. Peter at the Pearly Gates.
"Have you ever done anything of particular merit?" St. Peter asked.
"Well, I can think of one thing," the drover offered.
"Once, on a trip to the back blocks of Broken Hill out in New South Wales I came across a gang of bikers who were threatening a young sheila. I told them to leave her alone, but they wouldn't listen.
So I approached the largest and most heavily tattooed biker and smacked him in the face, kicked his bike over, ripped out his nose ring, and threw it on the ground.
I yelled, "Now, back off!! Or I'll kick the sh*t out of the lot of ya!"
St. Peter was impressed, "When did this happen?"
"A couple of minutes ago."

-

A young man was wandering, lost, in a forest when he came upon a small house. Knocking on the door he was greeted by an ancient Chinese man with a long, gray beard. "I'm lost," said the man. "Can you put me up for the night?" "Certainly," the Chinese man said, "but on one condition. If you so much as lay a finger on my daughter I will inflict upon you the three worst Chinese tortures known to man."

94

"OK," said the man, thinking that the daughter must be pretty old as well, and entered the house. Before dinner the daughter came down the stairs. She was young, beautiful and had a fantastic figure. She was obviously attracted to the young man as she couldn't keep her eyes off him during the meal. Remembering the old man's warning he ignored her and went up to bed alone. But during the night he could bear it no longer and snuck into her room for a night of passion. He was careful to keep everything quiet so the old man wouldn't hear and, near dawn, he crept back to his room, exhausted but happy. He woke to feel a pressure on his chest. Opening his eyes he saw a large rock on his chest with a note on it that read, "Chinese Torture 1: Large rock on chest." "Well, that's pretty crappy," he thought. "If that's the best the old man can do then I don't have much to worry about." He picked the boulder up, walked over to the window and threw the boulder out. As he did so he noticed another note on it that read "Chinese Torture 2: Rock tied to left testicle." In a panic he glanced down and saw the line that was already getting close to taut. Figuring that a few broken bones was better than castration, he jumped out of the window after the boulder. As he plummeted downward he saw a large sign on the ground that read, "Chinese Torture 3: Right testicle tied to bedpost."

-

A blind guy on a bar stool shouts to the bartender, "Wanna hear a blonde joke?" In a hushed voice, the guy next to him says, "Before you tell that joke, you should know something. Our bartender is blonde, the bouncer is blonde. I'm a six foot tall, 200 lb black belt. The guy sitting next to me is six foot two, weighs 225, and he's a rugby player. The fella to your right is six foot five, pushing 300, and he's a wrestler. Each one of us is blonde. Think about it, Mister. Do you still wanna tell that joke?" The blind guy says, "Nah, not if I'm gonna have to explain it five times."

-

A teacher is teaching a class and she sees that Johnny isn't paying attention, so she asks him, "If there are three ducks sitting on a fence, and you shoot one, how many are left?" Johnny says, "None." The teacher asks, "Why?" Johnny says, "Because the shot scared them all off." The teacher says, "No, two, but I like how you're thinking." Johnny then tells the teacher, " Under the desk I am holding on to something hard with a red end, The teacher exclaims! " Johnny, you dirty little boy " Johnny says, "No, its a match, but I like how you're thinking!"

A woman goes to the doctor and complains that her husband is losing interest in sex. The doctor gives her a pill, but warns her that it's still experimental. He tells her to slip it into his mashed potatoes at dinner, so that night, she does just that. About a week later, she's back at the doctor, where she says, "Doc, the pill worked great! I put it in the potatoes like you said! It wasn't five minutes later that he jumped up, raked all the food and dishes onto the floor, grabbed me, ripped all my clothes off, and ravaged me right there on the table!" The doctor says, "I'm sorry, we didn't realize the pill was that strong! The foundation will be glad to pay for any damages." "Nah," she says, "that's okay. We're never going back to that restaurant anyway."

-

A boy is selling fish on a corner. To get his customers' attention, he is yelling, "Dam fish for sale! Get your dam fish here!" A pastor hears this and asks, "Why are you calling them 'dam fish.'" The boy responds, "Because I caught these fish at the local dam." The pastor buys a couple fish, takes them home to his wife, and asks her to cook the dam fish. The wife responds surprised, "I didn't know it was acceptable for a preacher to speak that way." He explains to her why they are dam fish. Later at the dinner table, he asks his son to pass the dam fish. He responds, "That's the spirit, Dad! Now pass the f*cking potatoes!"

-

96

Two factory workers are talking. The woman says, "I can make the boss give me the day off." The man replies, "And how would you do that?" The woman says, "Just wait and see." She then hangs upside down from the ceiling. The boss comes in and says, "What are you doing?" The woman replies, "I'm a light bulb." The boss then says, "You've been working so much that you've gone crazy. I think you need to take the day off." The man starts to follow her and the boss says, "Where are you going?" The man says, "I'm going home, too. I can't work in the dark."

-

Last year I replaced all the windows in my house with that expensive casement type with shutters. Today, I got a call from the contractor who installed them. He was complaining that the work had been completed a whole year ago and I still hadn't paid for them.

Hellloo............ Just because I have fair hair doesn't mean that I am automatically stupid. So, I told him just what his fast talking sales guy had told me last year, that in ONE YEAR these windows would pay for themselves!

Hellloo? It's been a year! I told him. There was only silence at the other end of the line, so I finally just hung up.

He never called back.

I bet he felt like an idiot.

-

Stanley decided to lookup his friend Alf, who was a tight-fisted Yorkshireman. He found Alf at his bungalow in Huddersfield stripping the wallpaper from the dining room. Rather obviously, he remarked, "You're decorating, I see." To which Alf replied, "Nay Stanley lad, I'm moving 'ouse to Bradford."

97

-

At an antiques auction in Leeds, England a wealthy American announced that he had lost his wallet containing £5,000, and he would give a reward of £50 to the person who found it. From the back of the hall a Yorkshire voice shouted, "I'll give £100!"

-

Dwayne is recovering from surgery having had a local anaesthetic when a nurse asks him how he's feeling.' I'm O.K. but I didn't like the four-letter-word the doctor used in surgery'.
'What did he say?' asks the nurse.
'OOPS!'

-

A man goes to the doctor and says: 'Doctor, there's a piece of lettuce sticking out of my bottom.' The doctor asks him to drop his trousers and examines him.
The man asks: 'Is it serious, doctor?' and the doctor replies: 'I'm sorry to tell you, but this is just the tip of the iceberg.'

-

A man left for work one Friday afternoon. Instead of going home, he stayed out the entire weekend hunting with the boys and spending all his wages.
When he finally got home on Sunday night, he was confronted by his very angry wife.
After two hours, she stopped nagging and said: 'How would you like it if you didn't see me for two or three days?' He replied: 'That would be fine with me.' Monday went by and he didn't see his wife. Tuesday and Wednesday came and went with the same results.
Thursday, the swelling went down just enough for him to see her a little out of the corner of his left eye.

-

A magician was working on a cruise ship in the Caribbean. The audience was different each week so he did same tricks over and over. The problem was, the captain's parrot saw all the shows and began to understand how the magician did every trick.

He started shouting in the middle of the show: 'Look, it's not the same hat. Look, he's hiding the flowers under the table. Hey, why are all the cards the ace of spades?' The magician was furious but, as it was the captain's parrot, he could do nothing. Then one day the ship sank and the magician found himself floating on a piece of wood with the parrot.

They glared at each other but said nothing. Finally, after a week, the parrot said: 'OK, I give up. Where's the fucking boat?'

-

A duck walks into a post office and asks the man behind the counter: 'Do you have any corn?' The man answers politely: 'No, we don't have any corn here.' The next day, the duck enters again and asks: 'Do you have any corn?' Annoyed, the man answers: 'No! We don't have any corn.' This goes on for a couple of days until finally, when the duck asks 'Do you have any corn?', the man gets so upset he yells: 'NO! For the last time we don't have any corn, and if you ask again I'll nail your beak to the counter!' The next day, the duck returns and asks: 'Do you have any nails?' The man answers: 'No.' Then the duck asks: ' So do you have any corn?'

-

When NASA started sending up astronauts, they quickly discovered that ballpoint pens would not work at zero gravity.

To combat the problem, NASA scientists spent a decade and $12 billion developing a pen that wrote at zero gravity, upside down, underwater, on almost any surface including glass and at temperatures ranging from below freezing to 300C.

The Russians used a pencil.

-

I stopped at a friend's house the other day and found him stalking around with a fly-swatter. When I asked if he was getting any flies, he answered: 'Yeah, three males and two females.' Curious, I asked how he could tell the difference. He said: 'Three were on a beer can and two were on the phone.'

-

A man goes to the vet about his dog's fleas. The vet says: 'I'm sorry, I'll have to put this dog down.' The man is incredulous and asks why. The vet says: 'Because he's far too heavy.'

Fun quizzes, Brain-teasers, Intelligence test

Thai Knowledge

1. How would a man say," hello " in Thai?
2. How does a woman say, " hello" in Thai?
3. How would a man ask where the toilet is?
4. How would a woman tell a Thai driver that she wants to go to the airport?
5. Who is the current Kind of Thailand?
6. What is Krung Thep Maha Nakhon, better known as?
7. What is one meaning of Mai Pen Ra?
8. What was Thailand known as until 1939?
9. What date did the last major tsunami hit the southern coast of Thailand?
10. What is the currency of Thailand?
11. How would a man tell a Thai that he doesn't understand?
12. How would a woman ask for two bottles of beer in Thai?
13. What is 21 in Thai?
14. What is Monday in Thai?
15. What is the main international airport in Bangkok?
16. Answer in Thai "Sabaii dee Mai?"
17. Answer in English "Khun Chu Arai ?"
18. What sea surrounds Phuket?
19. How do you ask the price in Thai?
20. What is 200 in Thai?
21. What precedes islands names?
22. What is the sea that surrounds Koh Chang?
23. What does 'Chang' mean?
24. What is 155 in Thai?
25. What is the fare for a Baht Bus in Pattaya?
26. What is the national contact sport of Thailand?
27. What two precious gemstones is Thailand famous for?

28. What country borders Thailand to the southeast?
29. What is 1000 in Thai
30. What is the capital city of Thailand?

General Knowledge

1. What organisation did Robert Baden-Powell found in 1908?
2. What code name was given to Nazi Germany's plan to invade Britain during the Second World War?
3. Who said: 'If you want something said, ask a man; if you want something done, ask a woman'?
4. The Intu Metrocentre is a shopping centre in which town?
5. What occupational task is carried out by a sawyer?
6. Who owned the Daily Mirror newspaper between 1984 and 199
7. In the popular children's nursery rhyme what is Wednesday's child full of?
8. Which country only switched to the modern Gregorian Calendar on January 1, 1927?
9. What is the SI unit of luminous intensity?
10. Genuphobia is the fear of what part of the body?
11. What name is given to a cross fruit of tangerines and grapefruits?
12. What do the dots on a pair of dice add up to?
13. How high is a baketball hoop?
14. In photography what does S.L.R stand for?
15. What is the motto of the SAS?
16. Which two countries signed up to the common market in 1973 alongside the U.K?
17. How many years did Nelson Mandela spend in prison?
18. Which star is the nearest to Earth?
19. What is the nearest galaxy to the Solar System?
20. What is the largest bone in the human body?
21. Which nerve forms the link between the eye and the brain?
22. Which country is reputed to have the world's oldest flag design?
23. In which year was the first FA Cup final held at Wembley?

24. What is Agoraphobia the fear of?
25. How many kilograms make up a metric tonne?
26. On what date is U.S Independence day?
27. Who said "I think therefore I am"?
28. In which country was cricketer Ted Dexter born?
29. What was the name of the policeman in Enid Blyton's 'Noddy'?
30. The clavicle is more commonly known as which bone?
31. Which flag is raised when a ship is about to leave port?
32. Who painted the Laughing Cavalier?
33. Who was the father of Ham, Shem and Japheth in the bible?
34. Which country has the longest coastline?
35. Which African country has the shilling as it's currency?
36. Which planet is nearest the sun?
37. What is contained in a dish described as Lyonnaise?
38. What term describes a male swan?
39. Who might make use of a maulstick?
40. What name is given to the Jewish candlestick with special religious meaning?

Brain - teasers

1. A man and women get married and have a baby boy. A year later they have another baby boy, but the two boys are not brothers. WHY?
2. Tommy's mother had three children. The first child was named April. The second child was named May. What was the third child's name?
3. Before Mt. Everest was discovered, what was the highest mountain in the world?
4. How much dirt is there in a hole that measures two feet by three feet by four feet?
5. What word in the English language is always spelled incorrectly?

103

6. In British Columbia you cannot take a picture of a man with a wooden leg. Why not?
7. If you were running a race and you passed the person in 2nd place, what place would you be in now?
8. A farmer has five haystacks in one field and four haystacks in another. How many haystacks would he have if he combined them all in one field?
9. What is greater than God, more evil than the devil, the poor have it, the rich need it, and if you eat it, you'll die?
10. Who makes it, has no need of it. Who buys it, has no use for it. Who uses it can neither see nor feel it. What is it?
11. What can travel around the world while staying in a corner?
12. There was a green house. Inside the green house there was a white house. Inside the white house there was a red house. Inside the red house there were lots of babies. What is it?
13. What call for help, when written in capital letters, is the same forwards, backwards and upside down?
14. One family wants to get through a tunnel. Dad can make it in 1 minute, mom in 2 minutes, son in 4 and daughter in 5 minutes. No more than 2 persons can go through the tunnel at one time, moving at the speed of the slower one. Can they all make it to the other side if they have a torch that lasts only 12 minutes and they are afraid of the dark?
15. How many of each species did Moses take on the ark with him?

Intelligence Test (IQ) These are tough

1. 19, 20, 21, ?, ?, 26, 28, 32, 33, 40 Which two numbers should replace the question marks?
2. Which number is the odd one out? 84129, 32418, 47632, 36119, 67626, 72927
3. Identify two words (one from each set of brackets) that form a connection (analogy), thereby relating to the words in capitals

in the same way.CAT (lash, parade, feline, whiskers) SLEEP (somnambulate, night, bed, Morpheus)

4. A Z B Y D W G T ? Which two letters come next?

5. How many cases do you need if you have to pack 112 pairs of shoes into cases that each hold 28 shoes?

6. Which two words are most opposite in meaning? acquired, derivative, archetypal, elaborate, enigmatic, spasmodic

7. Select two words that are synonyms, plus an antonym of these two synonyms, from the list of words below. excuse, regulate, bestow, condone, concede, condemn, incarcerate.

8. If 4 apples and 6 bananas cost £1.56 and 9 apples and 7 bananas cost £2.60, what is the cost of one apple and one banana?

9. Starting from North, list the following compass points in the correct order working anti-clockwise. ENE WSW SE SSW WNW NNE SSE ESE

10. What number is, logically, missing from this sequence : 348269, 284315, *****, 8438, 4811, 842, 86

11. ABCDEFGH What letter comes two to the right of the letter which is immediately to the left of the letter that comes three to the right of the letter that comes midway between the letter two to the left of the letter C and the letter immediately to the right of the letter F?

12. Identify two words (one from each set of brackets) that form a connection (analogy), thereby relating to the words in capitals in the same way. - QUIRKY (bizarre, irrational, whimsical, erratic) UNCANNY (singular, eerie, esoteric, amazing)

13. Select two words that are synonyms, plus an antonym of these two synonyms, from the list of words - torment, contain, consider, console, assuage, scheme, fraternize

14. In the two numerical sequences, one number that appears in the top sequence should appear in the bottom sequence and vice versa. Which two numbers should be changed round?   3, 6, 9.5, 14.5, 18, 23   -   5, 10, 13.5, 18.5, 22

15. Which word in brackets is closest in meaning to the word in capitals? CHAGRIN (reprehension, revolution, irritation, bedlam, assault)

Answers at the back section, plus check your score and rating

SHORT STORIES

THAI Folklore

The Legend of Princess Manorah

A story told and passed on through generations since the Ayutthaya period and which inspired a poem by King Rama V of Thailand.

Kinnaree Manorah was a princess of Thai legend and was the youngest of the seven Kinnaree daughters of King Prathum and Queen Jantakinnaree. She lived in the mythical Mount Grairat kingdom. The Seven Kinnaree appeared as half woman half swan. They could fly or shed their wings to assume human form as they pleased.

Within the Krairat (Grairat) kingdom was the great Himmapan Forest in which lived strange creatures, unknown to human realms. In the middle of the forest was a beautiful lake which the seven Kinnaree loved to visit regularly on the auspicious day of Panarasi (Full moon day). Nearby, the lake, an old hermit practiced his meditations.

One day, a young man named Prahnbun, was strolling in the Himmapan forest, saw the seven princesses at play at the great pond. Prahnbun, stunned by the beauty of Manorah, thought, "If I can catch her and present her to Prince Suton, son of King Artityawong and Queen Jantaivee of Udon Panjah the Prince would surely fall in love with her. But how will I be able to catch her?"

He knew of the old hermit who meditated nearby in the forest and he decided to seek advice from the wise old man about his plans. The hermit told the young man that to catch the Kinnaree would be very difficult, as they would fly away if anyone frightened them, but that

107

there was a great dragon living deep in the forest that might be able to help him. Prahbun thanked him for his advice and raced off to see the dragon.

The great dragon was not happy to hear Prahnbun's plan but was, eventually persuaded by Prahnbun to give him a magical rope with which he would be able to catch Manorah. Prahnbun thanked the dragon, hurried away to the pond with the magical dragon rope, and crept up to the pond's edge where the Kinnaree were playing. While the Kinnaree were all happily distracted with their play at the water's edge, he struck; throwing the magic rope around the neck of Manorah and caught her so tight, she could not escape. Her sisters fearful of being caught themselves; all took flight and flew away to safety.

Prahnbun then secured Manorah's wings to stop her from flying away and lead her away through the forest heading back to Udon Panjah to present her to the Prince Suton. The Prince happened to be riding through the forest when he came across Prahnbun with his prize. The beauty of Manorah instantly charmed the Prince and when Prahnbun told him that he had captured Manorah for him, the Prince was delighted with Prahnbun's good intentions and rewarded him handsomely.

The Prince returned to his Summer Palace in the forest with Manorah where their love for each other blossomed. When the Prince told his mother and father the whole story, they were very happy and immediately arranged the wedding between the Prince and Princess Manorah who returned to the Udon Panjah palace where they were married and lived happy ever after.

Mai Nak

As stated by tradition, the events occurred during the reign of King Mongkut. The story is about a beautiful young woman named Nak, who lived in the banks of the Phra Khanong canal, and her undying love for her husband, Mak.

With Nak pregnant, Mak is conscripted and sent to war (in some versions of the story the war is against the Shan tribe, while others are not specific), where he is seriously wounded. While he is being nursed back to health in central Bangkok, Nak and their child both die during a difficult childbirth. When Mak returns home, however, he finds his loving wife and child waiting for him. Neighbours who try to warn him that he is living with a ghost are all killed.

One day, as Nak is preparing nam phrik, she drops a lime off the porch. In her haste, she stretches her arm to pick it up from the ground below. Mak sees it and at last realizes his wife is a ghost. Terrified, he tries to find a way to flee without alarming her.

That night, Mak says he has to go downstairs to urinate. He then runs away into the night.

Discovering her husband has fled, Nak pursues him. Mak sees her and conceals himself behind a Blumea balsamifera bush. According to folklore, ghosts are afraid of the sticky Blumea leaves. Mak then runs to Wat Mahabut temple, which a ghost cannot enter, as it is holy ground.

In her grief, Nak terrorizes the people of Phra Khanong, furious at them for causing Mak to leave her. However, Nak's ghost is captured by a powerful exorcist. Confining her in an earthen jar, he throws it into the canal.

There are differing versions of the rest of the story. In one, an old couple new to Phra Khanong finds the jar while fishing; in another two fishermen dredge up the jar. Nak is freed when they opened it.

Nak is conquered again by the venerable monk Somdet Phra Phutthachan. The learned monk confines her spirit in the bone of her forehead and binds it in his waistband. Legend says the waistband is currently in the possession of the royal family.

Admiral Aphakonkiattiwong, the Prince of Chumphon, also claimed to have had the relic. In alternative version, the monk assured Nak that in a future life she would be reunited with her beloved husband, and thus she voluntarily departed for the afterlife.

Mae Nak's story is still very popular because her undying devotion to her husband inspires people of all ages.

A shrine dedicated to Mae Nak is at Wat Mahabut. In 1997, the shrine relocated to nearby Suan Luang District of modern Bangkok.

Thai Short Stories

It's In Here

By Phichetsak Pho-Phayak

The dew saturated the entire hill and the fog seemed to be hiding the morning from the knowledge of humankind. The sun during the cold season came out later than usual, especially in this, the country's northernmost province, but this was no problem for Wiwatchai: waking up at dawn had become second nature to him.

Once he was past primary school age, by two in the morning he had to be at the morning market with his faithful pushcart to carry everything he was hired for, mostly vegetables and fruit that arrived at the market at that time.

When that was over around four in the morning, he had two hours to rest and sleep in a corner next to Aunt Chia's vegetable stall. He'd wakeup again at six, scramble onto his antediluvian motorcycle, and go to Hia Tee's garage to open shop and clean up the place. No particle of dust escaped his broom in this garage the size of two shop houses. And then he tackled the pending work. At eight, three other mechanics came in. Before the heavy work began, they sat in a circle eating breakfast together.

That was during the first years after primary school. Wiwatchai no longer had to be hired to transport vegetables at the market. The monthly salary from Hia Tee's garage was enough for him and his mother to live on, except that on some days he felt like going to help some female vendors he was close to just for the sake of it.

Wiwatchai was only sixteen but he was well respected by his co-workers of the same age. He inspired trust beyond his age by working hard, harder than anyone else in the garage, and never opened his mouth to complain. The important thing that made everyone accept him was his expertise riding his motorcycle motocross-style.

Hia Tee himself was a former motocross rider who had never reached the stars. As a young man the best he did was third place in the B Grade 125cc national competition one year. After that it was downhill,so he no longer had any ground to stand on in the top national field. Wiwatchai was the substitute of his youth, a young competitor who collected victories in splendid fashion in the urban tracks of the North.

This year he had won five of them, so much so that the Thai branch of the Sowa motor oil company had sounded him out to represent it. About this, Hia Tee, who had begun to train Wiwatchai when he didn't even know how to ride a motorcycle yet, felt prouder than the boy himself – Hia Tee who once had been named world-class rider of his time, except that his career had ended faster than it should.

Wiwatchai kept his hesitation about joining the Thai Sowa team to himself. Every rider in the country dreamed of making it to the Sowa team, because it meant big money every month in your pocket and, if you were good enough, competing at world level wasn't beyond dream, even though for Thai people this was still a Herculean undertaking.

He was the only one to know what he thought. He had never been really happy with motocross riding, but since that was what Hia Tee wanted, how could he refuse – Hia Tee who had supported him since he finished primary six two years after his father died.

Many people said Hia Tee should have gone much farther than he did if only he'd been a little more ambitious given his expertise infine-tuning engines. He had earned several awards at national level, which he hung as decorations on the walls. 'I'm showing them to attract customers, that's all,' he'd say, a first-class mechanic who had to skulk in a small repair shop. 'I'm fine here,' he'd say whenever someone mentioned the days when he was a well-paid top mechanic in repair centres in the capital.

Trader who worshiped Love

By Laweng Panjasunthorn

At the approach of the month of October every year it's always like this. I derive satisfaction from little things that happen in nature, ordinary little things that can be noticed by the beginning of the month. They may require some observation, but not too much, except that most people might overlook them, some even dismiss them. But who is really interested? On days in early October when the sky is bright, the sky is a deep blue and white cloud flakes scatter all over the deep blue sky. If you look away for only a moment, the white clouds have changed shape in a seemingly miraculous way, to say nothing of the cool morning wind blowing intimations of chill as if the cold season had sent forth spies in disguise to observe people's behaviour before the last season of the year takes over in the course of time.

Tiny little things I haven't mentioned invite conversation. Most people consider them nonsensical, think it's a waste of time to sit talking about the first cold wind of the season. Aware of this, I don't mention them to anyone except my young girlfriend. I like the month of October because every time this month comes round I am a year older, life goes by slowly, I feel that time agrees with my way of life. I've always listened closely to the sound of time passing through life, up until October last year. At first sight it was like every other day. That morning, the sky was bright, the first cold wind of the season was blowing. I woke up without her beside me.

My beloved had left...

That afternoon, words from her came up on my cell phone.

'Give me some time and then I'll come back.'

I read those words over and over, the only words she had left me. There was nothing I could think of to explain her departure. I tried to call her back but didn't succeed. After that her phone went dead. It was clear that she still didn't want to contact me. I sat reviewing what had happened in earnest, analysing carefully the factors that might have annoyed her and made her leave me. They were mostly little things that shouldn't have mattered. Finally I gave up on what had happened. If I had known in advance, maybe she wouldn't have left like this. The problem I still had to consider was in the second half of her sentence, 'and then I'll come back'. That meant she didn't mean to be gone for ever, but she had left and maybe she would return. Unable to think any further, I stopped thinking temporarily, showered and changed, left the condo unit where I lived and went to stroll idly around a shopping centre, my eyes sweeping the shelves crammed with goods of the supermarket section. I left without having purchased anything .At dusk I went to my regular pub-restaurant where I like to sit with my close friend, ordered a few dishes and a bottle of cold beer and sat reviewing the thirty years of my life so far, an ordinary life with nothing special, nothing outstanding. My last steady job had lasted five years. At the time, I was on the editorial team of a small magazine. One morning of an easy day I resigned from that steady job and then lived on the income derived from writing columns in two magazines. One column assessed films and songs with relevance to our way of life and ended on sharp precepts that gave plain writing an appearance of depth. The other column was in a women's magazine and featured modern-day women's lives. I wrote about how to think, how to live, fashion, love, the dreams of modern young women, in simple terms and from a man's point of view. This column of mine had quite a following. The fee for it was raised every year. One column four times a month and the other twice a month provided a steady income. Properly handled it was enough for me to live on. The rest of the time I spent writing short stories and poems

I sent to magazines for publication at times. Writing had value enough to sustain the other parts of an ordinary life. Three years ago I began instalment payments on a conveniently located medium sized condo unit to live in. My girlfriend came over and spent the night with me often but she wasn't willing to move in with me for good. She kept saying it wasn't time yet. Three years full of happiness when she was by my side. I didn't wish for anything else in life, until now when hollowness is back in my life once again.

I met my girlfriend in the month of May shortly after I had given up my steady job.

Memory

By Than Yutthachaivodin

Today is Thewan's sixty-fifth birthday but he isn't thinking of taking his woman out to dinner somewhere.

'Look, it's raining hard,' he grumbles when he sees the rain in the halo of the street lamppost near Tha Phae Gate while thinking how impressive this picture always is when visiting Chiang Mai in the rainy season. Sure, this time he's come for a special occasion, but what the occasion is he can't remember. It seems to be on the tip of his tongue. Hard as he tries he can't think of it, as with some implement that can't be found when it is truly needed.

114

'Where the hell are you hiding, you nasty memory?' Thewan mutters sotto voce as he sits looking at what is happening in the street from the hotel window.

After a moment he tells his woman to call room service and have dinner brought up to the room.

'Ann, I hope you don't mind if we eat quietly in this room.'

Quite some time has passed before Thewan says,

'As you wish. I've just ordered Chiang Mai and Vienna sausages as well as roast duck, your favourite snacks. And stout this once.'

'Excellent. How long has it been since I last had stout?' the elderly man mumbles as if talking to himself.

'If the doctor didn't forbid it, you'd be drinking it all the time, I bet, but don't get drunk, please, while we are together, I don't want our dinner to be spent in drunkenness.'

'When the doctor forbids me to leave the house, I won't come to Chiang Mai again.'

'If you keep strong and healthy, who would dare to forbid you?'

Thewan looks at her before nodding his head and then he says with a sad face, 'I'm not a strong man for a young woman like you any longer, as you know very well.'

'That's not important. Actually I'm forty years old, I haven't been a young woman for quite some time,' Ann says without looking at him.

She seems to be dreamingly staring in the direction of the window.

'How can you say that? It's not true at all. But haven't you ever felt sorry being involved with someone old like me? Someone as beautiful as you should be doing much better than this.'

'I like it actually, don't worry.'

'With a man who … who can't remember your birthday, like that?'

Thewan retorts in a low voice and with a blank look.

'It's nothing worth remembering. Just remembering who I am is enough.'

'What will happen if I forget you,' Thewan queries again.

'Well, I'd disappear from your life.' Ann's eyes hold his then she smiles coolly.

Half an hour goes by. There is a knock on the door. Ann gets up from her chair and walks over to open the door. It's room service. The waiter pushing a small trolley brings it to the edge of the round table by the window before lifting the dishes and a bottle of beer and two glasses he puts down on the table. The two remaining bottles of beer he places in the refrigerator (the mini-bar has only other beer brands Thewan doesn't like; so the woman ordered stout for him instead).

Thewan sees Ann thank the young waiter and hand him over a tip by the door and then she goes back and sits down as before.

'Do you remember that today besides being my birthday there's something else to remember?' Suddenly Thewan remembers what makes today so important, so he asks after taking a swig of the stout.

'Who would forget how America got a beating from outside by commercial airliners. Three thousand dead in two fell swoops.' He heaves a sigh. 'How crazy that it should happen on a day when I should have fun celebrating, but that was still more distant from us than when the tsunami struck in southern Thailand on your birthday. That's how I feel.'

'So you do remember my birthday.' Ann smiles, pleased

A Muay Thai Story

By Derby Shaw

It all started with a man named Tea. A Bangkok local who's help I enlisted in finding a local gym. I knew what kind of gym I wanted. A large, clean, *farang* (foreigner) catering gym was not it. No; I wanted that grungy, janky, beaten-down, grimy, dilapidated, foreign-to-foreigners kind of third world gym. And I got more than I bargained for. I followed Tea through a series of alleys, which became passageways, which became tunnels, and suddenly we were there. It crept up on me because no signs discern that this is a boxing gym. And you'd *never* suspect that any talent made it's way out of this place, let alone a former champion at Bangkok's prestigious Rajadamnern stadium. But there was, and his name was Jak, and he was my trainer for the day. And by "for the day", I mean thirty minutes of the most gruelling madness ever. Jak would call out "One! One two!" and then I would throw punch combos and then swing my leg for all it was worth, like it was attached by a flabby piece of skin and my goal was to kick it right off.

At one point a beer-bellied man in a Redbull shirt strolled in and Tea barked at me to *wai* (the Thai version of a bow) the hell out of him. He must be a person of interest, but how in the devil was I supposed to differentiate between him and the locals sipping whiskey and scratching their buttcracks out front? He would come to be known as "the boss", and was the promoter for this particular gym. This was the guy to get in with if I was going to be fighting competitively. Which I already knew I would be, because when I finished my workout that day, I was hooked.

117

The next couple of weeks the intensity was upped significantly. I entered the ring and learned new moves, combos, how to block, shadow box, weight lifting techniques, and more. The most satisfying move was the elbow. If I struck the punching bag, the whole bag, it's chain, and the ceiling even, would rock violently when I made collision. My knee however was total garbage. Jak can rattle the punching bag with knees, but I just awkwardly smidge it a little to the side. I knew what I needed to improve. I was learning so much, so fast, and despite the language barrier, I had little kids translating, and Jak actually apologized to ME for not being able to speak English! Can you believe that? Everyone there was so helpful, and they took it one step further when they gave me my own pair of red Muay Thai trunks emblazoned with my name on the front. I had reached an important milestone in my training, and it would be only a matter of time before I was in that ring fighting for real.

Well, it would have been. Let me take a brief detour in the story to tell you about a little issue I have had ever since I moved to Bangkok. I love this place. My body doesn't. My body despises it! In a little under a year, I have had eye surgery twice, teeth mysteriously break while I was sleeping, blackouts, seizures, piercings get pulled out by people's hugs, fevers... to name a few. But the icing on the cake came three months into my training, just as I was about to declare my candidacy to fight. I woke up one day with a bump on my right elbow. A bump that wasn't there when I went to bed. A bump that was the size of a McDonald's cheeseburger. I looked like a creepy forest troll. This setback meant that I wouldn't be fighting anytime soon. I had to retire from training until this bump went away on it's own, since surgery and home remedies did literally nothing to alleviate it. Nothing would have either, had I not gone directly against the doctor's orders to cancel my trip to Laos. It was there that a drunken upside-down dive into the river ripped my arm bandages off, and the water entering the hole in my arm cleaned it out and caused it to dissipate. I don't know. I'm not sure of the technical explanation behind it. But the bump was gone which meant that once I got back from Laos, I was ready to fight again.

Back at the gym, I was better than ever. I was hungrier, that's for sure. Training became a routine affair, and I'd be at that gym no less than three times a week. I developed a much larger arsenal of techniques, and having attended a Thai language school in Silom meant that I could actually understand what the hell people were saying to me. Likewise, they could understand me when I said, "I'm ready to fight." This was something I found myself repeating constantly, wondering if I ever would truly be granted my request. Then one day, I had a date: February 8th. A little less than three weeks away. Having something tangible changes *everything*. The first major difference is that anything you ever considered "fun" in your life is going to have to be relinquished. Fifteen days before your fight, you need to quit drinking, smoking, and "bap bap bap," the sound that comes from hitting your palms together rapidly. I'll let you guess what that one means. You need to be running everyday. Twice! And you should be doing, at the bare minimum, hmm, three-hundred and fifty sit-ups daily.

I was assigned a new trainer to train me intensively and exhaustively. His name was Parinya, a cool guy with a defined jawbone and impressive English skills. As for his credentials, well, let me just state that he is fighting in a tournament in Russia next month where the grand champion takes home *three million baht*. That's a lot of money, kids. Parinya puts on the protection pads, which I regretfully admit is not enough to protect him from my wild aim and occasional kick to the "banana" region, and then he coaxes me into throwing crazy combos. Parinya also shows no mercy. Even though he wears pads that are made to be hit, he manages to make them into a specialized boxing glove and smacks me with them when I forget to keep my guard up. One time he smacked me on the side of the face so hard, I literally didn't even see him throw it. I just felt a ringing, burning sensation on my face.

After we finish striking drills, I hop into the ring with a guy who calls himself Yay, or "big" in Thai. We engage in *plam*, an activity where we lock up arms, exchange knees to the ribs or the abs, and try to throw the other guy right on his ass. Despite Yay being a foot and a half shorter than me, he throws me to the ground twenty two times for every one time I take him down. I've been counting. And the really embarrassing thing is when I train with one of the younger guys who live literally under the ring, and they dodge ninety-nine percent of my punches. That is somewhat of an anti-confidence booster.

As the days wound down, and February 8th loomed, I found myself more and more unsure of myself. My left kick, which should be my dominant kick from my normal fighting stance (I'm a southpaw) just didn't feel right. My foot was constantly in pain and a daily foot massage couldn't fix that. Luckily my right one was like a rocket, but still. When the playbill came out and my Thai opponent was listed, I asked about how much experience the guy had and everyone just responded with laughter. "Don't worry," they said. "Just have a *jai-su* and you'll be okay." Well, my strong heart means nothing if I'm fighting a guy who's been in fifty fights already. Getting tossed around by Yay constantly taught me that my distinct height advantage over everyone was no longer an advantage. It didn't matter how tall I was. The bigger they come, the harder they fall. I was getting pushed to my physical limits, as well as my sanity. Typically me and Parinya would spar for five minutes, then take a one minute break before going another five minutes. But now I wasn't even being allowed that one minute. My stamina was better, but I was still breathing so hard I'd nearly vomit.

Two days before my fight, when I expected the hardest workout of all, I was turned around at the gym. I needed to rest up, they told me. Take it easy. But, how would I? I was so hyped for this fight. I spent those next couple of days trying to study the pre-fight dance ritual, called the *ram muay*. It turns out I wouldn't even have to do the dance. The dance would be necessary if either of the fighters were Thai. But neither were. In a last minute twist, when I arrived at Thepasit staduim in Pattaya hours before my fight, I looked at my opponent's name: Ivan the Russian Twin Tiger. Hmm. You know, I could be wrong but, this guy doesn't sound Thai. Whatever. And then I saw him. And for the first time since I began training, I felt *scared*. This guy was the biggest human being I had ever seen in my life. Whereas I was worried that I would be disallowed to fight being eighty-one kilos in the eighty kilo weight class, there was NO way that man was within fifteen kilos of eighty. He looked like the Incredible Hulk. My promoter, a.k.a. "the boss", verbally lashed out at the promoter of the gym for allowing such a mismatch. They scrambled to find me another opponent but failed to. I had already accepted my fate and at this point I just wanted to get into the ring. The pressure was on, and it didn't help that U.S. marines were coming up to me and telling me I needed to win this fight *for our country*. I heard a warning bell ring and it was time to fight.

What happened in that ring was nothing short of sheer brutality. I'd give you the play by play, but the fact of the matter is, the ring is a time machine. You walk in, and suddenly you are transported to the end of the fight. Well, maybe it's not that dramatic, but I can tell you that time flies when someone is trying to punch your head off. As expected, Ivan the Russian Twin Tiger was strong. Each time his gloves made contact with my head (which was rather frequently, mind you), I felt my neck, my head, my whole body jolt backwards, and I could tell it was only a matter of time before blood started spewing out of random orifices on my body. When the blood did finally matriculate, it was after a monstrous hook to the face. I put my guard up, but it was too late. The punch caught me, and once I lowered my fists the crowd saw my face and there was a very audible, "Holy shit!" that came out of the crowd. Ivan tried to finish me, but I thrust a knee into his abdomen that humbled him, hunched him over, and gave me a brief window of time to finish him.

I didn't take that chance. The first round wasn't even over yet, and I was absolutely gassed. I used that time to inhale deeply, to try to gain back some energy. Instead, Ivan got his back and started swinging and kicking wildly for my face. The bell rang right when I needed it to, and that was the end of round one. Back at my corner, my Thai boxing posse watered me down and shouted strategies at me, but none of it--and I mean, none of it registered. As the adrenaline coursed through my veins, all I could think about was, "How am I going to survive another round?" Eventually I stood up, because sitting wasn't helping, and waited for the next round to start. Ding! And then I had a strategy. I need to knock this big lug out.

I ran at him, and we exchanged some punches. Then, some kicks. I realized I couldn't back away from him. I needed to keep the pressure, and not back down. We had a moment of sheer epicness, where I punched, and he punched, and I punched back, and so forth. The crowd was loving it. But eventually his punches started coming quicker than mine, and I had to step out of this situation. I backed up to the ropes and Ivan the Dragon or Bear or whatever he is called blasted me in the face and my mouthguard went flying into the lap of some lucky audience member. I needed this break. I was feeble and trembling. And there was blood everywhere. Hell, I think there was even blood on the ceiling. As my mouth guard was being fetched, the ref called the doctor over to look at my face. He pointed his little magical flashlight in my eyes, took all of five seconds to observe me, then told the ref, "*May dai.*" I knew that phrase, and I knew it well. "Cannot." In this situation, the only thing that could not happen was for me to continue the fight. The ref waved his hands in the air, and that was it. The fight was finito.

My face was a wreck, and I needed stitches both above and below the eye, but to be honest, I wasn't hurting that bad. It was more just the disappointment that ate me up inside. I went back to my corner of people, all laying out on a picnic mat, and was welcomed by a surprisingly warm reception. Parinya was a little pissed that I didn't keep my hands up, but then he told me that he lost his first six fights. And this is coming from the guy who is fighting for a 3 million baht jackpot next month! Then, one by one, all of the other fighters approached me and told me they had lost their first fight as well. This cheered me up and put me in good spirits. Plus, no more training, no more need to abstain from drinking. I was getting drunk tonight boy!

Before the long drive back to Bangkok, we all sat on the beautiful Pattaya beach and sipped whiskey and caught crabs barehanded. Sitting in the back of the pickup truck, mildly drunk, and my throbbing head using another Thai fighter as a pillow, I looked up at the stars and felt so small. What had happened here tonight was one of the biggest events of my life. But from the perspective of the stars, it was just a tiny little fraction of the universe. It was yet another one of the hundreds of fights happening in Thailand at that very moment. For me, this was a revolution. For the guys that live at my gym, sleep under the ring, and train every single day, this was simply one of the hundreds of fights they will accumulate in their lifetime. Hell, they may not even remember this night five years from now. But for me, this was a night I will never forget. A journey I will always take to heart. All thanks to the friendliest and most receptive people I have met, across dozens of countries travelled. Thailand, thank you. Thank you for turning me into a warrior.

Why The Tuk do we use the Tuk-Tuk?

By Neil Ray.

This question has been vexing me for some time, and try as I may, the answer eludes me. What is the great thing about the Tuk-tuk? We know it's synonymous with Thailand, and The Tourist Authority would be at a complete loss without it. But really, what use is a Tuk-tuk other than to pollute the streets of Bangkok, provide tourist photo opportunities and make the driver a happy man.

I very rarely take a Tuk-tuk, mainly based on a number of factors. One is that it's noisy, and open to all the traffic fumes. It's expensive. It's no quicker than a normal taxi once stuck in a jam, and for the average Farang, we end up with knees under chin in the most uncomfortable position. There may be electric Tuk-tuks around but I've never seen one and anyway - isn't that a golf cart? The normal taxi is air conditioned, has a meter, has nice vinyl covered seats and runs on eco friendly gas. How about that for a counter argument?

Its true, old Thai ladies can be seen with a stack of market goodies piled high in striped bags, sat awkwardly amongst their shopping in the back of the Bangkok Tuk-tuk. Maybe I'm getting cynical in my old age, but chances are the driver is her brother, father, son, husband

123

or nephew and she feels obliged to use his farting old machine. After all she could be sat in a nice air conditioned eco friendly taxi, with the goodies in the trunk, but the family might get upset.

There's always the cost to consider and unfortunately again we draw a blank. In a moment of weakness I took a Tuk-tuk from Suan Plu, off Sathorn road to the BTS one evening. The apartment had its own Tuk-tuk but it stops at 6pm, as well as at lunch time – well the driver has to eat. It was the usual rainy Friday evening gig with no available taxis anywhere. I was considering the dangers of a motorbike taxi in the rain, when along came Mr. Tuk-tuk honking his friendly horn. Ok we'll give it a go. It soon dawned on me this was a big mistake. Sat in the Sathorn road traffic at 6.30 in a Tuk-tuk was not a great idea. I could be in a taxi watching the meter tick over. As it was, the fare was undoubtedly rising but I didn't know by how much. Any fee negotiated beforehand was definitely history and our friendly toothless driver was already getting his mental calculator going. Why is it they never have change? It's worth stacking up twenties for the moment, because no Tuk-tuk man I know has ever seen a 20 Baht note. 100 Baht, yes, and lots of them. But a twenty change from a hundred? No change khap.

So, indeed as expected it was 80 Baht for the short trip to Lumphini – I got off before I lost the will to live and walked to the Metro. Make that 100 Baht.

"No change khap."

I then made another mistake. I asked "Why Tuk-tuk so expensive - Can sit in car with air con, pay less. Tuk-tuk noisy, take long time, big traffic, not so nice. Why you cost more?" My toothless Tuk-tuk man smiled his toothless smile and muttered something about his family, the sick buffalo and fuel costs and how long it took and so on.

Does the taxi driver have no family or sick buffalo? Does his car run on fresh air? Never mind.

124

So the question remains unanswered. At night the Tuk-tuk turns into a mobile light show which after a boat load of Leo does no one any good. It's noisy, smelly and doesn't get you there any faster. But the tourists love it and not surprisingly, so do the Tuk-tuk drivers. Oh well, what the tuk tuk.

A Funny Story

By David Umfahrer

I had a funny thing happen to me while cycling from Malaysia to Vietnam. I was cycling towards the Cambodian border in Thailand. Couldn't find a guest house for ages and had to ride into the evening. Absolutely exhausted from cycling over 100km that day, I finally come to a place that looked like a hotel although I couldn't really tell because it was dark, I was exhausted, .and the signs were all written in Thai. A ladyboy stood at the front, which is a common sight in Thailand, so didn't think anything of it. I asked him/her if this was the hotel, "yes" she replied. I asked her if she knew how much it was per night. She said something like "500bhat," which I thought was a bit expensive but being exhausted, I didn't really care. I parked my bicycle, walked inside, went up the reception counter, and asked for the room. The reception asked for 300bhat, which was cheaper than the ladyboy said. I thought that it was a bit strange, why would the ladyboy say 500? The ladyboy then walks in, stands beside me and grabs my ass. I'm thinking 'what the fuk is going on here.' I turn back to the receptionist and she takes a box of condoms from under the counter and puts them in front of me on the counter. Then I realised what was happening, the ladyboy was asking 500 to have sex with him/ her, not the room...and I'd agreed to it!

I shook my head and saying "No, no!" my face must have been bright red I'm sure the receptionist and the ladyboy thought that I am saying no to the condoms and that I want to take the ladyboy without a condom or something, making the situation even more awkward.

125

Panicking and embarrassed, I grabbed my room key, ran to my room and locked the door, leaving very early the following day.

Ladyboys of Bangkok

By Anthony Shambrook

It was the end of our first night out in the big City and it felt hot and sticky walking along Sakhumvit road at 2am. It had been a great night out as my mate and I had experienced the wonder of the bar scene in the frantic yet friendly City of Bangkok. Tone the Drone and myself had arrived from UK earlier in the day and although knackered we went straight out. It had been a long day and night but our adrenaline was pumping to explore this wonderland. It lived up to its reputation and we went from one bar area to another soaking in the ambience. We soon found are bearings and our hotel was in a Soi (street) just off the main Sakhumvit road. It is difficult to describe the feeling of Bangkok, The heat is bearable and the aromatic smells from the food-stalls waft around, which is different in each area, all we could smell was a cacophony of delicious aromas with no noxious petrol fumes which we expected. from being on a main road. Anyhow , I digress, sorry.

We were walking to the hotel, which was a feat in itself considering the amount of Singha beer we had consumed.. Considering the late hour, the Bangkok Road was alive and buzzing with life. A cackle of lady-boys approached, Six in all. I call them a cackle because that's all they did....cackle. Tone and me looked at each other and, keeping our heads down tried to walk past them without being noticed. We had only seen lady boys for the first time a few hours earlier while exploring the bar scene at Nana plaza. We found them amusing and entertaining while in the bars, but walking along the streets we didn't know. They surrounded us and asked the same questions that we had been asked all night. We are you from? How long you staying? Do you want a lady.? Although we had only been there for a few hours it becomes easy to tell the todger possessed ladies from the real ones. Not wanting to offend, we laughed and joked with them. They came

126

closer and stated rubbing themselves against us, which became a little disconcerting. We had heard the tales about how some of the lady boys were pick pockets, so. I put my hand in my pocket to protect my wallet, however, there was no need, there was already one in there, and by the look of horror on Tone the Drone's face he also had a pocket visitor, either that or he was getting his todger rubbed. Either way we soon sobered up. I slapped my pocket, removed the hand of an irate but still cackling lady boy and then me and Tone legged it, with the laughing lady boys shouting and cackling behind us. That was our first night in Thailand, but we had many more adventures during the fortnight we stayed.

What's in a name

Whilst sitting in a newly opened bar, the owner came over, sat down and started talking to our small group. A Thai friend of his came in with another Thai man. Being a good host, Paul the owner, stood up, shook his friends hand and introduced himself to the other Thai.

"Hi, I'm Paul."

"Piss room" said the Thai extending his hand.

"Oh," said Paul, taken aback."It's over there," he said pointing to the toilet.

Phisrum then spoke to his Thai friend, giving Paul a strange look before going to sit at the bar,

Paul leant over to us and said, "He didn't even go, and I still don't know his name."

Although it is a strange name to us, Phisrum is commonplace in Thailand as is Bum and Poo. Unfortunately, these are girls names, and I have several friends with Bum's for wives.

Don't Poop on Your Girlfreind

127

One night after a good drinking sesh, and while on my way home, I decided to buy some shell fish at a local vendors. These tiny crustaceans resemble the good old British cockle. However, unlike the good old cockle, they live in fresh water and instead of being boiled they are dried in the sun. This method is fine for the Thais as they have cast iron stomachs.

I ate a dollop before I went to bed. I awoke a few hours later feeling a little gaseous in the bottomly department. My girlfriend of a few months had her back turned and was fast asleep. Too bone idle to get out of bed, I decided to vent a little wind and gave a little nudge to my sphincter. I suddenly realised that it wasn't just wind, it was Montezuma's revenge, and projectile poop drenched the back of my girlfriend.

Embarrassed I lay there planning my next course of action. how could I explain my way out of this. There was no need. My girlfriend calmly got out of bed, took a shower, returned with a fresh sheet, and told me to take a shower while she cleaned the bed. I returned to a clean bed and my girlfriend was outside soaking poopy-sheet in a bowl of soapy water.

For the next few days I kept apologising, but my lovely lass just smiled and told me it was no problem. Thai ladies don't turn a dram into a crisis. That's why we luv em.

We have been happily married for four years, although I don't eat the shellfish any more.

Two good old classics that are now public domain and copyright unlisted.

The Bride Comes to Yellow Sky

by Stephen Crane

The great Pullman was whirling onward with such dignity of motion that a glance from the window seemed simply to prove that the plains of Texas were pouring eastward. Vast flats of green grass, dull-hued spaces of mesquite and cactus, little groups of frame houses, woods of light and tender trees, all were sweeping into the east, sweeping over the horizon, a precipice.

A newly married pair had boarded this coach at San Antonio. The man's face was reddened from many days in the wind and sun, and a direct result of his new black clothes was that his brick-colored hands were constantly performing in a most conscious fashion. From time to time he looked down respectfully at his attire. He sat with a hand on each knee, like a man waiting in a barber's shop. The glances he devoted to other passengers were furtive and shy.

The bride was not pretty, nor was she very young. She wore a dress of blue cashmere, with small reservations of velvet here and there and with steel buttons abounding. She continually twisted her head to regard her puff sleeves, very stiff, straight, and high. They embarrassed her. It was quite apparent that she had cooked, and that she expected to cook, dutifully. The blushes caused by the careless scrutiny of some passengers as she had entered the car were strange to see upon this plain, under-class countenance, which was drawn in placid, almost emotionless lines.

They were evidently very happy. "Ever been in a parlor-car before?" he asked, smiling with delight.

"No," she answered, "I never was. It's fine, ain't it?"

"Great! And then after a while we'll go forward to the diner and get a big layout. Finest meal in the world. Charge a dollar."

"Oh, do they?" cried the bride. "Charge a dollar? Why, that's too much -- for us -- ain't it, Jack?"

"Not this trip, anyhow," he answered bravely. "We're going to go the whole thing."

Later, he explained to her about the trains. "You see, it's a thousand miles from one end of Texas to the other, and this train runs right across it and never stops but four times." He had the pride of an owner. He pointed out to her the dazzling fittings of the coach, and in truth her eyes opened wider as she contemplated the sea-green figured velvet, the shining brass, silver, and glass, the wood that gleamed as darkly brilliant as the surface of a pool of oil. At one end a bronze figure sturdily held a support for a separated chamber, and at convenient places on the ceiling were frescoes in olive and silver.

To the minds of the pair, their surroundings reflected the glory of their marriage that morning in San Antonio. This was the environment of their new estate, and the man's face in particular beamed with an elation that made him appear ridiculous to the negro porter. This individual at times surveyed them from afar with an amused and superior grin. On other occasions he bullied them with skill in ways that did not make it exactly plain to them that they were being bullied. He subtly used all the manners of the most unconquerable kind of snobbery. He oppressed them, but of this oppression they had small knowledge, and they speedily forgot that infrequently a number of travelers covered them with stares of derisive enjoyment. Historically there was supposed to be something infinitely humorous in their situation.

"We are due in Yellow Sky at 3:42," he said, looking tenderly into her eyes.

"Oh, are we?" she said, as if she had not been aware of it. To evince surprise at her husband's statement was part of her wifely amiability. She took from a pocket a little silver watch, and as she held it before her and stared at it with a frown of attention, the new husband's face shone.

"I bought it in San Anton' from a friend of mine," he told her gleefully.

"It's seventeen minutes past twelve," she said, looking up at him with a kind of shy and clumsy coquetry. A passenger, noting this play, grew excessively sardonic, and winked at himself in one of the numerous mirrors.

At last they went to the dining-car. Two rows of negro waiters, in glowing white suits, surveyed their entrance with the interest and also the equanimity of men who had been forewarned. The pair fell to the lot of a waiter who happened to feel pleasure in steering them through their meal. He viewed them with the manner of a fatherly pilot, his countenance radiant with benevolence. The patronage, entwined with the ordinary deference, was not plain to them. And yet, as they returned to their coach, they showed in their faces a sense of escape.

To the left, miles down a long purple slope, was a little ribbon of mist where moved the keening Rio Grande. The train was approaching it at an angle, and the apex was Yellow Sky. Presently it was apparent that, as the distance from Yellow Sky grew shorter, the husband became commensurately restless. His brick-red hands were more insistent in their prominence. Occasionally he was even rather absent-minded and far-away when the bride leaned forward and addressed him.

As a matter of truth, Jack Potter was beginning to find the shadow of a deed weigh upon him like a leaden slab. He, the town marshal of Yellow Sky, a man known, liked, and feared in his corner, a prominent person, had gone to San Antonio to meet a girl he believed he loved, and there, after the usual prayers, had actually induced her to marry him, without consulting Yellow Sky for any part of the transaction. He was now bringing his bride before an innocent and unsuspecting community.

Of course, people in Yellow Sky married as it pleased them, in accordance with a general custom; but such was Potter's thought of his duty to his friends, or of their idea of his duty, or of an unspoken form which does not control men in these matters, that he felt he was heinous. He had committed an extraordinary crime. Face to face with this girl in San Antonio, and spurred by his sharp impulse, he had gone headlong over all the social hedges. At San Antonio he was like a man hidden in the dark. A knife to sever any friendly duty, any form, was easy to his hand in that remote city. But the hour of Yellow Sky, the hour of daylight, was approaching.

He knew full well that his marriage was an important thing to his town. It could only be exceeded by the burning of the new hotel. His friends could not forgive him. Frequently he had reflected on the advisability of telling them by telegraph, but a new cowardice had been upon him. He feared to do it. And now the train was hurrying him toward a scene of amazement, glee, and reproach. He glanced out of the window at the line of haze swinging slowly in towards the train.

Yellow Sky had a kind of brass band, which played painfully, to the delight of the populace. He laughed without heart as he thought of it. If the citizens could dream of his prospective arrival with his bride, they would parade the band at the station and escort them, amid cheers and laughing congratulations, to his adobe home.

He resolved that he would use all the devices of speed and plains-craft in making the journey from the station to his house. Once within that safe citadel he could issue some sort of a vocal bulletin, and then not go among the citizens until they had time to wear off a little of their enthusiasm.

The bride looked anxiously at him. "What's worrying you, Jack?"

132

He laughed again. "I'm not worrying, girl. I'm only thinking of Yellow Sky."

She flushed in comprehension.

A sense of mutual guilt invaded their minds and developed a finer tenderness. They looked at each other with eyes softly aglow. But Potter often laughed the same nervous laugh. The flush upon the bride's face seemed quite permanent.

The traitor to the feelings of Yellow Sky narrowly watched the speeding landscape. "We're nearly there," he said.

Presently the porter came and announced the proximity of Potter's home. He held a brush in his hand and, with all his airy superiority gone, he brushed Potter's new clothes as the latter slowly turned this way and that way. Potter fumbled out a coin and gave it to the porter, as he had seen others do. It was a heavy and muscle-bound business, as that of a man shoeing his first horse.

The porter took their bag, and as the train began to slow they moved forward to the hooded platform of the car. Presently the two engines and their long string of coaches rushed into the station of Yellow Sky.

"They have to take water here," said Potter, from a constricted throat and in mournful cadence, as one announcing death. Before the train stopped, his eye had swept the length of the platform, and he was glad and astonished to see there was none upon it but the station-agent, who, with a slightly hurried and anxious air, was walking toward the water-tanks. When the train had halted, the porter alighted first and placed in position a little temporary step.

"Come on, girl," said Potter hoarsely. As he helped her down they each laughed on a false note. He took the bag from the negro, and bade his wife cling to his arm. As they slunk rapidly away, his hang-dog glance perceived that they were unloading the two trunks, and also that the station-agent far ahead near the baggage-car had turned

133

and was running toward him, making gestures. He laughed, and groaned as he laughed, when he noted the first effect of his marital bliss upon Yellow Sky. He gripped his wife's arm firmly to his side, and they fled. Behind them the porter stood chuckling fatuously.

THE California Express on the Southern Railway was due at Yellow Sky in twenty-one minutes. There were six men at the bar of the "Weary Gentleman" saloon. One was a drummer who talked a great deal and rapidly; three were Texans who did not care to talk at that time; and two were Mexican sheep-herders who did not talk as a general practice in the "Weary Gentleman" saloon. The barkeeper's dog lay on the board walk that crossed in front of the door. His head was on his paws, and he glanced drowsily here and there with the constant vigilance of a dog that is kicked on occasion. Across the sandy street were some vivid green grass plots, so wonderful in appearance amid the sands that burned near them in a blazing sun that they caused a doubt in the mind. They exactly resembled the grass mats used to represent lawns on the stage. At the cooler end of the railway station a man without a coat sat in a tilted chair and smoked his pipe. The fresh-cut bank of the Rio Grande circled near the town, and there could be seen beyond it a great, plum-colored plain of mesquite.

Save for the busy drummer and his companions in the saloon, Yellow Sky was dozing. The new-comer leaned gracefully upon the bar, and recited many tales with the confidence of a bard who has come upon a new field.

" -- and at the moment that the old man fell down stairs with the bureau in his arms, the old woman was coming up with two scuttles of coal, and, of course -- "

The drummer's tale was interrupted by a young man who suddenly appeared in the open door. He cried: "Scratchy Wilson's drunk, and has turned loose with both hands." The two Mexicans at once set down their glasses and faded out of the rear entrance of the saloon.

134

The drummer, innocent and jocular, answered: "All right, old man. S'pose he has. Come in and have a drink, anyhow."

But the information had made such an obvious cleft in every skull in the room that the drummer was obliged to see its importance. All had become instantly solemn. "Say," said he, mystified, "what is this?" His three companions made the introductory gesture of eloquent speech, but the young man at the door forestalled them.

"It means, my friend," he answered, as he came into the saloon, "that for the next two hours this town won't be a health resort."

The barkeeper went to the door and locked and barred it. Reaching out of the window, he pulled in heavy wooden shutters and barred them. Immediately a solemn, chapel-like gloom was upon the place. The drummer was looking from one to another.

"But, say," he cried, "what is this, anyhow? You don't mean there is going to be a gun-fight?"

"Don't know whether there'll be a fight or not," answered one man grimly. "But there'll be some shootin' -- some good shootin'."

The young man who had warned them waved his hand. "Oh, there'll be a fight fast enough if anyone wants it. Anybody can get a fight out there in the street. There's a fight just waiting."

The drummer seemed to be swayed between the interest of a foreigner and a perception of personal danger.

"What did you say his name was?" he asked.

"Scratchy Wilson," they answered in chorus.

"And will he kill anybody? What are you going to do? Does this happen often? Does he rampage around like this once a week or so? Can he break in that door?"

"No, he can't break down that door," replied the barkeeper. "He's tried it three times. But when he comes you'd better lay down on the floor, stranger. He's dead sure to shoot at it, and a bullet may come through."

Thereafter the drummer kept a strict eye upon the door. The time had not yet been called for him to hug the floor, but, as a minor precaution, he sidled near to the wall. "Will he kill anybody?" he said again.

The men laughed low and scornfully at the question.

"He's out to shoot, and he's out for trouble. Don't see any good in experimentin' with him."

"But what do you do in a case like this? What do you do?"

A man responded: "Why, he and Jack Potter -- "

"But," in chorus, the other men interrupted, "Jack Potter's in San Anton'."

"Well, who is he? What's he got to do with it?"

"Oh, he's the town marshal. He goes out and fights Scratchy when he gets on one of these tears."

"Wow," said the drummer, mopping his brow. "Nice job he's got."

The voices had toned away to mere whisperings. The drummer wished to ask further questions which were born of an increasing anxiety and bewilderment; but when he attempted them, the men merely looked at him in irritation and motioned him to remain silent. A tense waiting hush was upon them. In the deep shadows of the room their eyes shone as they listened for sounds from the street. One man made three gestures at the barkeeper, and the latter, moving like a ghost, handed him a glass and a bottle. The man poured a full glass

136

of whisky, and set down the bottle noiselessly. He gulped the whisky in a swallow, and turned again toward the door in immovable silence. The drummer saw that the barkeeper, without a sound, had taken a Winchester from beneath the bar. Later he saw this individual beckoning to him, so he tiptoed across the room.

"You better come with me back of the bar."

"No, thanks," said the drummer, perspiring. "I'd rather be where I can make a break for the back door."

Whereupon the man of bottles made a kindly but peremptory gesture. The drummer obeyed it, and finding himself seated on a box with his head below the level of the bar, balm was laid upon his soul at sight of various zinc and copper fittings that bore a resemblance to armor-plate. The barkeeper took a seat comfortably upon an adjacent box.

"You see," he whispered, "this here Scratchy Wilson is a wonder with a gun -- a perfect wonder -- and when he goes on the war trail, we hunt our holes -- naturally. He's about the last one of the old gang that used to hang out along the river here. He's a terror when he's drunk. When he's sober he's all right -- kind of simple -- wouldn't hurt a fly -- nicest fellow in town. But when he's drunk -- whoo!"

There were periods of stillness. "I wish Jack Potter was back from San Anton'," said the barkeeper. "He shot Wilson up once -- in the leg -- and he would sail in and pull out the kinks in this thing."

Presently they heard from a distance the sound of a shot, followed by three wild yowls. It instantly removed a bond from the men in the darkened saloon. There was a shuffling of feet. They looked at each other. "Here he comes," they said.

A MAN in a maroon-coloured flannel shirt, which had been purchased for purposes of decoration and made, principally, by some Jewish women on the east side of New York, rounded a corner and walked into the middle of the main street of Yellow Sky. In either hand the man held a long, heavy, blue-black revolver. Often he yelled, and these cries rang through a semblance of a deserted village, shrilly flying over the roofs in a volume that seemed to have no relation to the ordinary vocal strength of a man. It was as if the surrounding stillness formed the arch of a tomb over him. These cries of ferocious challenge rang against walls of silence. And his boots had red tops with gilded imprints, of the kind beloved in winter by little sledding boys on the hillsides of New England.

The man's face flamed in a rage begot of whisky. His eyes, rolling and yet keen for ambush, hunted the still doorways and windows. He walked with the creeping movement of the midnight cat. As it occurred to him, he roared menacing information. The long revolvers in his hands were as easy as straws; they were moved with an electric swiftness. The little fingers of each hand played sometimes in a musician's way. Plain from the low collar of the shirt, the cords of his neck straightened and sank, straightened and sank, as passion moved him. The only sounds were his terrible invitations. The calm adobes preserved their demeanor at the passing of this small thing in the middle of the street.

There was no offer of fight; no offer of fight. The man called to the sky. There were no attractions. He bellowed and fumed and swayed his revolvers here and everywhere.

The dog of the barkeeper of the "Weary Gentleman" saloon had not appreciated the advance of events. He yet lay dozing in front of his master's door. At sight of the dog, the man paused and raised his revolver humorously. At sight of the man, the dog sprang up and walked diagonally away, with a sullen head, and growling. The man yelled, and the dog broke into a gallop. As it was about to enter an alley, there was a loud noise, a whistling, and something spat the ground directly before it. The dog screamed, and, wheeling in terror, galloped headlong in a new direction. Again there was a noise, a whistling, and sand was kicked viciously before it. Fear-stricken, the dog turned and flurried like an animal in a pen. The man stood laughing, his weapons at his hips.

138

Ultimately the man was attracted by the closed door of the "Weary Gentleman" saloon. He went to it, and hammering with a revolver, demanded drink.

The door remaining imperturbable, he picked a bit of paper from the walk and nailed it to the framework with a knife. He then turned his back contemptuously upon this popular resort, and walking to the opposite side of the street, and spinning there on his heel quickly and lithely, fired at the bit of paper. He missed it by a half inch. He swore at himself, and went away. Later, he comfortably fusilladed the windows of his most intimate friend. The man was playing with this town. It was a toy for him.

But still there was no offer of fight. The name of Jack Potter, his ancient antagonist, entered his mind, and he concluded that it would be a glad thing if he should go to Potter's house and by bombardment induce him to come out and fight. He moved in the direction of his desire, chanting Apache scalp-music.

When he arrived at it, Potter's house presented the same still front as had the other adobes. Taking up a strategic position, the man howled a challenge. But this house regarded him as might a great stone god. It gave no sign. After a decent wait, the man howled further challenges, mingling with them wonderful epithets.

Presently there came the spectacle of a man churning himself into deepest rage over the immobility of a house. He fumed at it as the winter wind attacks a prairie cabin in the North. To the distance there should have gone the sound of a tumult like the fighting of 200 Mexicans. As necessity bade him, he paused for breath or to reload his revolvers.

POTTER and his bride walked sheepishly and with speed. Sometimes they laughed together shamefacedly and low.

"Next corner, dear," he said finally.

139

They put forth the efforts of a pair walking bowed against a strong wind. Potter was about to raise a finger to point the first appearance of the new home when, as they circled the corner, they came face to face with a man in a maroon-colored shirt who was feverishly pushing cartridges into a large revolver. Upon the instant the man dropped his revolver to the ground, and, like lightning, whipped another from its holster. The second weapon was aimed at the bridegroom's chest.

There was silence. Potter's mouth seemed to be merely a grave for his tongue. He exhibited an instinct to at once loosen his arm from the woman's grip, and he dropped the bag to the sand. As for the bride, her face had gone as yellow as old cloth. She was a slave to hideous rites gazing at the apparitional snake.

The two men faced each other at a distance of three paces. He of the revolver smiled with a new and quiet ferocity.

"Tried to sneak up on me," he said. "Tried to sneak up on me!" His eyes grew more baleful. As Potter made a slight movement, the man thrust his revolver venomously forward. "No, don't you do it, Jack Potter. Don't you move a finger toward a gun just yet. Don't you move an eyelash. The time has come for me to settle with you, and I'm goin' to do it my own way and loaf along with no interferin'. So if you don't want a gun bent on you, just mind what I tell you."

Potter looked at his enemy. "I ain't got a gun on me, Scratchy," he said. "Honest, I ain't." He was stiffening and steadying, but yet somewhere at the back of his mind a vision of the Pullman floated, the sea-green figured velvet, the shining brass, silver, and glass, the wood that gleamed as darkly brilliant as the surface of a pool of oil -- all the glory of the marriage, the environment of the new estate. "You know I fight when it comes to fighting, Scratchy Wilson, but I ain't got a gun on me. You'll have to do all the shootin' yourself."

His enemy's face went livid. He stepped forward and lashed his weapon to and fro before Potter's chest. "Don't you tell me you ain't got no gun on you, you whelp. Don't tell me no lie like that. There ain't a man in Texas ever seen you without no gun. Don't take me for no kid." His eyes blazed with light, and his throat worked like a pump.

"I ain't takin' you for no kid," answered Potter. His heels had not moved an inch backward. "I'm takin' you for a -- -- -- fool. I tell you I ain't got a gun, and I ain't. If you're goin' to shoot me up, you better begin now. You'll never get a chance like this again."

So much enforced reasoning had told on Wilson's rage. He was calmer. "If you ain't got a gun, why ain't you got a gun?" he sneered. "Been to Sunday-school?"

"I ain't got a gun because I've just come from San Anton' with my wife. I'm married," said Potter. "And if I'd thought there was going to be any galoots like you prowling around when I brought my wife home, I'd had a gun, and don't you forget it."

"Married!" said Scratchy, not at all comprehending.

"Yes, married. I'm married," said Potter distinctly.

"Married?" said Scratchy. Seemingly for the first time he saw the drooping, drowning woman at the other man's side. "No!" he said. He was like a creature allowed a glimpse of another world. He moved a pace backward, and his arm with the revolver dropped to his side. "Is this the lady?" he asked.

"Yes, this is the lady," answered Potter.

There was another period of silence.

"Well," said Wilson at last, slowly, "I s'pose it's all off now."

"It's all off if you say so, Scratchy. You know I didn't make the trouble." Potter lifted his valise.

"Well, I 'low it's off, Jack," said Wilson. He was looking at the ground. "Married!" He was not a student of chivalry; it was merely that in the presence of this foreign condition he was a simple child of the earlier plains. He picked up his starboard revolver, and placing both weapons in their holsters, he went away. His feet made funnel-shaped tracks in the heavy sand.

The Idiots

by Joseph Conrad

We were driving along the road from Treguier to Kervanda. We passed at a smart trot between the hedges topping an earth wall on each side of the road; then at the foot of the steep ascent before Ploumar the horse dropped into a walk, and the driver jumped down heavily from the box. He flicked his whip and climbed the incline, stepping clumsily uphill by the side of the carriage, one hand on the footboard, his eyes on the ground. After a while he lifted his head, pointed up the road with the end of the whip, and said--

"The idiot!"

The sun was shining violently upon the undulating surface of the land. The rises were topped by clumps of meagre trees, with their branches showing high on the sky as if they had been perched upon stilts. The small fields, cut up by hedges and stone walls that zig-zagged over the slopes, lay in rectangular patches of vivid greens and yellows, resembling the unskilful daubs of a naive picture. And the landscape was divided in two by the white streak of a road stretching in long loops far away, like a river of dust crawling out of the hills on its way to the sea.

"Here he is," said the driver, again.

In the long grass bordering the road a face glided past the carriage at the level of the wheels as we drove slowly by. The imbecile face was red, and the bullet head with close-cropped hair seemed to lie alone, its chin in the dust. The body was lost in the bushes growing thick along the bottom of the deep ditch.

It was a boy's face. He might have been sixteen, judging from the size--perhaps less, perhaps more. Such creatures are forgotten by time, and live untouched by years till death gathers them up into its compassionate bosom; the faithful death that never forgets in the press of work the most insignificant of its children.

"Ah! there's another," said the man, with a certain satisfaction in his tone, as if he had caught sight of something expected.

There was another. That one stood nearly in the middle of the road in the blaze of sunshine at the end of his own short shadow. And he stood with hands pushed into the opposite sleeves of his long coat, his head sunk between the shoulders, all hunched up in the flood of heat. From a distance he had the aspect of one suffering from intense cold.

"Those are twins," explained the driver.

The idiot shuffled two paces out of the way and looked at us over his shoulder when we brushed past him. The glance was unseeing and staring, a fascinated glance; but he did not turn to look after us. Probably the image passed before the eyes without leaving any trace on the misshapen brain of the creature. When we had topped the ascent I looked over the hood. He stood in the road just where we had left him.

The driver clambered into his seat, clicked his tongue, and we went downhill. The brake squeaked horribly from time to time. At the foot he eased off the noisy mechanism and said, turning half round on his box--

"We shall see some more of them by-and-by."

"More idiots? How many of them are there, then?" I asked.

"There's four of them--children of a farmer near Ploumar here. . . . The parents are dead now," he added, after a while. "The grandmother lives on the farm. In the daytime they knock about on this road, and they come home at dusk along with the cattle. . . . It's a good farm."

We saw the other two: a boy and a girl, as the driver said. They were dressed exactly alike, in shapeless garments with petticoat-like skirts. The imperfect thing that lived within them moved those beings to howl at us from the top of the bank, where they sprawled amongst the tough stalks of furze. Their cropped black heads stuck out from the bright yellow wall of countless small blossoms. The faces were purple with the strain of yelling; the voices sounded blank and cracked like a mechanical imitation of old people's voices; and suddenly ceased when we turned into a lane.

I saw them many times in my wandering about the country. They lived on that road, drifting along its length here and there, according to the inexplicable impulses of their monstrous darkness. They were an offence to the sunshine, a reproach to empty heaven, a blight on the concentrated and purposeful vigour of the wild landscape. In time the story of their parents shaped itself before me out of the listless answers to my questions, out of the indifferent words heard in wayside inns or on the very road those idiots haunted. Some of it was told by an emaciated and sceptical old fellow with a tremendous whip, while we trudged together over the sands by the side of a two-wheeled cart loaded with dripping seaweed. Then at other times other people confirmed and completed the story: till it stood at last before me, a tale formidable and simple, as they always are, those disclosures of obscure trials endured by ignorant hearts.

When he returned from his military service Jean-Pierre Bacadou found the old people very much aged. He remarked with pain that the work of the farm was not satisfactorily done. The father had not the energy of old days. The hands did not feel over them the eye of the master. Jean-Pierre noted with sorrow that the heap of manure in the

144

courtyard before the only entrance to the house was not so large as it should have been. The fences were out of repair, and the cattle suffered from neglect. At home the mother was practically bedridden, and the girls chattered loudly in the big kitchen, unrebuked, from morning to night. He said to himself: "We must change all this." He talked the matter over with his father one evening when the rays of the setting sun entering the yard between the outhouses ruled the heavy shadows with luminous streaks. Over the manure heap floated a mist, opal-tinted and odorous, and the marauding hens would stop in their scratching to examine with a sudden glance of their round eye the two men, both lean and tall, talking in hoarse tones. The old man, all twisted with rheumatism and bowed with years of work, the younger bony and straight, spoke without gestures in the indifferent manner of peasants, grave and slow. But before the sun had set the father had submitted to the sensible arguments of the son. "It is not for me that I am speaking," insisted Jean-Pierre. "It is for the land. It's a pity to see it badly used. I am not impatient for myself." The old fellow nodded over his stick. "I dare say; I dare say," he muttered. "You may be right. Do what you like. It's the mother that will be pleased."

The mother was pleased with her daughter-in-law. Jean-Pierre brought the two-wheeled spring-cart with a rush into the yard. The gray horse galloped clumsily, and the bride and bridegroom, sitting side by side, were jerked backwards and forwards by the up and down motion of the shafts, in a manner regular and brusque. On the road the distanced wedding guests straggled in pairs and groups. The men advanced with heavy steps, swinging their idle arms. They were clad in town clothes; jackets cut with clumsy smartness, hard black hats, immense boots, polished highly. Their women all in simple black, with white caps and shawls of faded tints folded triangularly on the back, strolled lightly by their side. In front the violin sang a strident tune, and the biniou snored and hummed, while the player capered solemnly, lifting high his heavy clogs. The sombre procession drifted in and out of the narrow lanes, through sunshine and through shade, between fields and hedgerows, scaring the little birds that darted away in troops right and left. In the yard of Bacadou's farm the dark ribbon wound itself up into a mass of men and women pushing at the door with cries and

145

greetings. The wedding dinner was remembered for months. It was a splendid feast in the orchard. Farmers of considerable means and excellent repute were to be found sleeping in ditches, all along the road to Treguier, even as late as the afternoon of the next day. All the countryside participated in the happiness of Jean-Pierre. He remained sober, and, together with his quiet wife, kept out of the way, letting father and mother reap their due of honour and thanks. But the next day he took hold strongly, and the old folks felt a shadow--precursor of the grave--fall upon them finally. The world is to the young.

When the twins were born there was plenty of room in the house, for the mother of Jean-Pierre had gone away to dwell under a heavy stone in the cemetery of Ploumar. On that day, for the first time since his son's marriage, the elder Bacadou, neglected by the cackling lot of strange women who thronged the kitchen, left in the morning his seat under the mantel of the fireplace, and went into the empty cow-house, shaking his white locks dismally. Grandsons were all very well, but he wanted his soup at midday. When shown the babies, he stared at them with a fixed gaze, and muttered something like: "It's too much." Whether he meant too much happiness, or simply commented upon the number of his descendants, it is impossible to say. He looked offended --as far as his old wooden face could express anything; and for days afterwards could be seen, almost any time of the day, sitting at the gate, with his nose over his knees, a pipe between his gums, and gathered up into a kind of raging concentrated sulkiness. Once he spoke to his son, alluding to the newcomers with a groan: "They will quarrel over the land." "Don't bother about that, father," answered Jean-Pierre, stolidly, and passed, bent double, towing a recalcitrant cow over his shoulder.

He was happy, and so was Susan, his wife. It was not an ethereal joy welcoming new souls to struggle, perchance to victory. In fourteen years both boys would be a help; and, later on, Jean-Pierre pictured two big sons striding over the land from patch to patch, wringing tribute from the earth beloved and fruitful. Susan was happy too, for she did not want to be spoken of as the unfortunate woman, and now she had children no one could call her that. Both herself and her

146

husband had seen something of the larger world--he during the time of his service; while she had spent a year or so in Paris with a Breton family; but had been too home-sick to remain longer away from the hilly and green country, set in a barren circle of rocks and sands, where she had been born. She thought that one of the boys ought perhaps to be a priest, but said nothing to her husband, who was a republican, and hated the "crows," as he called the ministers of religion. The christening was a splendid affair. All the commune came to it, for the Bacadous were rich and influential, and, now and then, did not mind the expense. The grandfather had a new coat.

Some months afterwards, one evening when the kitchen had been swept, and the door locked, Jean-Pierre, looking at the cot, asked his wife: "What's the matter with those children?" And, as if these words, spoken calmly, had been the portent of misfortune, she answered with a loud wail that must have been heard across the yard in the pig-sty; for the pigs (the Bacadous had the finest pigs in the country) stirred and grunted complainingly in the night. The husband went on grinding his bread and butter slowly, gazing at the wall, the soup-plate smoking under his chin. He had returned late from the market, where he had overheard (not for the first time) whispers behind his back. He revolved the words in his mind as he drove back. "Simple! Both of them. . . . Never any use! . . . Well! May be, may be. One must see. Would ask his wife." This was her answer. He felt like a blow on his chest, but said only: "Go, draw me some cider. I am thirsty!"

She went out moaning, an empty jug in her hand. Then he arose, took up the light, and moved slowly towards the cradle. They slept. He looked at them sideways, finished his mouthful there, went back heavily, and sat down before his plate. When his wife returned he never looked up, but swallowed a couple of spoonfuls noisily, and remarked, in a dull manner--

"When they sleep they are like other people's children."

She sat down suddenly on a stool near by, and shook with a silent tempest of sobs, unable to speak. He finished his meal, and remained idly thrown back in his chair, his eyes lost amongst the black rafters of the ceiling. Before him the tallow candle flared red and straight, sending up a slender thread of smoke. The light lay on the rough, sunburnt skin of his throat; the sunk cheeks were like patches of darkness, and his aspect was mournfully stolid, as if he had ruminated with difficulty endless ideas. Then he said, deliberately--

"We must see . . . consult people. Don't cry. . . . They won't all be like that . . . surely! We must sleep now."

After the third child, also a boy, was born, Jean-Pierre went about his work with tense hopefulness. His lips seemed more narrow, more tightly compressed than before; as if for fear of letting the earth he tilled hear the voice of hope that murmured within his breast. He watched the child, stepping up to the cot with a heavy clang of sabots on the stone floor, and glanced in, along his shoulder, with that indifference which is like a deformity of peasant humanity. Like the earth they master and serve, those men, slow of eye and speech, do not show the inner fire; so that, at last, it becomes a question with them as with the earth, what there is in the core: heat, violence, a force mysterious and terrible--or nothing but a clod, a mass fertile and inert, cold and unfeeling, ready to bear a crop of plants that sustain life or give death.

The mother watched with other eyes; listened with otherwise expectant ears. Under the high hanging shelves supporting great sides of bacon overhead, her body was busy by the great fireplace, attentive to the pot swinging on iron gallows, scrubbing the long table where the field hands would sit down directly to their evening meal. Her mind remained by the cradle, night and day on the watch, to hope and suffer. That child, like the other two, never smiled, never stretched its hands to her, never spoke; never had a glance of recognition for her in its big black eyes, which could only stare fixedly at any glitter, but failed hopelessly to follow the brilliance of a sun-ray slipping slowly along the floor. When the men were at work she spent long days between her three idiot children and the childish grandfather, who sat grim, angular, and immovable, with his feet near the warm ashes of

148

the fire. The feeble old fellow seemed to suspect that there was something wrong with his grandsons. Only once, moved either by affection or by the sense of proprieties, he attempted to nurse the youngest. He took the boy up from the floor, clicked his tongue at him, and essayed a shaky gallop of his bony knees. Then he looked closely with his misty eyes at the child's face and deposited him down gently on the floor again. And he sat, his lean shanks crossed, nodding at the steam escaping from the cooking-pot with a gaze senile and worried.

Then mute affliction dwelt in Bacadou's farmhouse, sharing the breath and the bread of its inhabitants; and the priest of the Ploumar parish had great cause for congratulation. He called upon the rich landowner, the Marquis de Chavanes, on purpose to deliver himself with joyful unction of solemn platitudes about the inscrutable ways of Providence. In the vast dimness of the curtained drawing-room, the little man, resembling a black bolster, leaned towards a couch, his hat on his knees, and gesticulated with a fat hand at the elongated, gracefully-flowing lines of the clear Parisian toilette from which the half-amused, half-bored marquise listened with gracious languor. He was exulting and humble, proud and awed. The impossible had come to pass. Jean-Pierre Bacadou, the enraged republican farmer, had been to mass last Sunday--had proposed to entertain the visiting priests at the next festival of Ploumar! It was a triumph for the Church and for the good cause. "I thought I would come at once to tell Monsieur le Marquis. I know how anxious he is for the welfare of our country," declared the priest, wiping his face. He was asked to stay to dinner.

The Chavanes returning that evening, after seeing their guest to the main gate of the park, discussed the matter while they strolled in the moonlight, trailing their long shadows up the straight avenue of chestnuts. The marquise, a royalist of course, had been mayor of the commune which includes Ploumar, the scattered hamlets of the coast, and the stony islands that fringe the yellow flatness of the sands. He had felt his position insecure, for there was a strong republican element in that part of the country; but now the conversion of Jean-Pierre made him safe. He was very pleased. "You have no idea how influential those people are," he explained to his wife. "Now, I am sure, the next communal election will go all right. I shall be re-elected." "Your ambition is perfectly insatiable, Charles," exclaimed the marquise, gaily. "But, ma chere amie," argued the husband, seriously, "it's most important that the right man should be mayor this year, because of the elections to the Chamber. If you think it amuses me . . ."

Jean-Pierre had surrendered to his wife's mother. Madame Levaille was a woman of business, known and respected within a radius of at least fifteen miles. Thick-set and stout, she was seen about the country, on foot or in an acquaintance's cart, perpetually moving, in spite of her fifty-eight years, in steady pursuit of business. She had houses in all the hamlets, she worked quarries of granite, she freighted coasters with stone--even traded with the Channel Islands. She was broad-cheeked, wide-eyed, persuasive in speech: carrying her point with the placid and invincible obstinacy of an old woman who knows her own mind. She very seldom slept for two nights together in the same house; and the wayside inns were the best places to inquire in as to her whereabouts. She had either passed, or was expected to pass there at six; or somebody, coming in, had seen her in the morning, or expected to meet her that evening. After the inns that command the roads, the churches were the buildings she frequented most. Men of liberal opinions would induce small children to run into sacred edifices to see whether Madame Levaille was there, and to tell her that so-and-so was in the road waiting to speak to her about potatoes, or flour, or stones, or houses; and she would curtail her devotions, come out blinking and crossing herself into the sunshine; ready to discuss business matters in a calm, sensible way across a table in the kitchen of the inn opposite. Latterly she had stayed for a few days several times with her son-in-law, arguing against sorrow and misfortune with composed face and gentle tones. Jean-Pierre felt the convictions imbibed in the regiment torn out of his breast--not by arguments but by facts. Striding over his fields he thought it over. There were three of them. Three! All alike! Why? Such things did not happen to everybody--to nobody he ever heard of. One--might pass. But three! All three. Forever useless, to be fed while he lived and . . . What

150

would become of the land when he died? This must be seen to. He would sacrifice his convictions. One day he told his wife--

"See what your God will do for us. Pay for some masses."

Susan embraced her man. He stood unbending, then turned on his heels and went out. But afterwards, when a black soutane darkened his doorway, he did not object; even offered some cider himself to the priest. He listened to the talk meekly; went to mass between the two women; accomplished what the priest called "his religious duties" at Easter. That morning he felt like a man who had sold his soul. In the afternoon he fought ferociously with an old friend and neighbour who had remarked that the priests had the best of it and were now going to eat the priest-eater. He came home dishevelled and bleeding, and happening to catch sight of his children (they were kept generally out of the way), cursed and swore incoherently, banging the table. Susan wept. Madame Levaille sat serenely unmoved. She assured her daughter that "It will pass;" and taking up her thick umbrella, departed in haste to see after a schooner she was going to load with granite from her quarry.

A year or so afterwards the girl was born. A girl. Jean-Pierre heard of it in the fields, and was so upset by the news that he sat down on the boundary wall and remained there till the evening, instead of going home as he was urged to do. A girl! He felt half cheated. However, when he got home he was partly reconciled to his fate. One could marry her to a good fellow--not to a good for nothing, but to a fellow with some understanding and a good pair of arms. Besides, the next may be a boy, he thought. Of course they would be all right. His new credulity knew of no doubt. The ill luck was broken. He spoke cheerily to his wife. She was also hopeful. Three priests came to that christening, and Madame Levaille was godmother. The child turned out an idiot too.

Then on market days Jean-Pierre was seen bargaining bitterly, quarrelsome and greedy; then getting drunk with taciturn earnestness; then driving home in the dusk at a rate fit for a wedding, but with a

151

face gloomy enough for a funeral. Sometimes he would insist on his wife coming with him; and they would drive in the early morning, shaking side by side on the narrow seat above the helpless pig, that, with tied legs, grunted a melancholy sigh at every rut. The morning drives were silent; but in the evening, coming home, Jean-Pierre, tipsy, was viciously muttering, and growled at the confounded woman who could not rear children that were like anybody else's. Susan, holding on against the erratic swayings of the cart, pretended not to hear. Once, as they were driving through Ploumar, some obscure and drunken impulse caused him to pull up sharply opposite the church. The moon swam amongst light white clouds. The tombstones gleamed pale under the fretted shadows of the trees in the churchyard. Even the village dogs slept. Only the nightingales, awake, spun out the thrill of their song above the silence of graves. Jean-Pierre said thickly to his wife--

"What do you think is there?"

He pointed his whip at the tower--in which the big dial of the clock appeared high in the moonlight like a pallid face without eyes--and getting out carefully, fell down at once by the wheel. He picked himself up and climbed one by one the few steps to the iron gate of the churchyard. He put his face to the bars and called out indistinctly--

"Hey there! Come out!"

"Jean! Return! Return!" entreated his wife in low tones.

He took no notice, and seemed to wait there. The song of nightingales beat on all sides against the high walls of the church, and flowed back between stone crosses and flat gray slabs, engraved with words of hope and sorrow.

"Hey! Come out!" shouted Jean-Pierre, loudly.

The nightingales ceased to sing.

"Nobody?" went on Jean-Pierre. "Nobody there. A swindle of the crows. That's what this is. Nobody anywhere. I despise it. Allez! Houp!"

He shook the gate with all his strength, and the iron bars rattled with a frightful clanging, like a chain dragged over stone steps. A dog near by barked hurriedly. Jean-Pierre staggered back, and after three successive dashes got into his cart. Susan sat very quiet and still. He said to her with drunken severity--

"See? Nobody. I've been made a fool! Malheur! Somebody will pay for it. The next one I see near the house I will lay my whip on . . . on the black spine . . . I will. I don't want him in there . . . he only helps the carrion crows to rob poor folk. I am a man. . . . We will see if I can't have children like anybody else . . . now you mind. . . . They won't be all . . . all . . . we see. . . ."

She burst out through the fingers that hid her face--

"Don't say that, Jean; don't say that, my man!"

He struck her a swinging blow on the head with the back of his hand and knocked her into the bottom of the cart, where she crouched, thrown about lamentably by every jolt. He drove furiously, standing up, brandishing his whip, shaking the reins over the gray horse that galloped ponderously, making the heavy harness leap upon his broad quarters. The country rang clamorous in the night with the irritated barking of farm dogs, that followed the rattle of wheels all along the road. A couple of belated wayfarers had only just time to step into the ditch. At his own gate he caught the post and was shot out of the cart head first. The horse went on slowly to the door. At Susan's piercing cries the farm hands rushed out. She thought him dead, but he was only sleeping where he fell, and cursed his men, who hastened to him, for disturbing his slumbers.

Autumn came. The clouded sky descended low upon the black contours of the hills; and the dead leaves danced in spiral whirls under

153

naked trees, till the wind, sighing profoundly, laid them to rest in the hollows of bare valleys. And from morning till night one could see all over the land black denuded boughs, the boughs gnarled and twisted, as if contorted with pain, swaying sadly between the wet clouds and the soaked earth. The clear and gentle streams of summer days rushed discoloured and raging at the stones that barred the way to the sea, with the fury of madness bent upon suicide. From horizon to horizon the great road to the sands lay between the hills in a dull glitter of empty curves, resembling an unnavigable river of mud.

Jean-Pierre went from field to field, moving blurred and tall in the drizzle, or striding on the crests of rises, lonely and high upon the gray curtain of drifting clouds, as if he had been pacing along the very edge of the universe. He looked at the black earth, at the earth mute and promising, at the mysterious earth doing its work of life in death-like stillness under the veiled sorrow of the sky. And it seemed to him that to a man worse than childless there was no promise in the fertility of fields, that from him the earth escaped, defied him, frowned at him like the clouds, sombre and hurried above his head. Having to face alone his own fields, he felt the inferiority of man who passes away before the clod that remains. Must he give up the hope of having by his side a son who would look at the turned-up sods with a master's eye? A man that would think as he thought, that would feel as he felt; a man who would be part of himself, and yet remain to trample masterfully on that earth when he was gone? He thought of some distant relations, and felt savage enough to curse them aloud. They! Never! He turned homewards, going straight at the roof of his dwelling, visible between the enlaced skeletons of trees. As he swung his legs over the stile a cawing flock of birds settled slowly on the field; dropped down behind his back, noiseless and fluttering, like flakes of soot.

That day Madame Levaille had gone early in the afternoon to the house she had near Kervanion. She had to pay some of the men who worked in her granite quarry there, and she went in good time because her little house contained a shop where the workmen could spend their wages without the trouble of going to town. The house stood alone

154

amongst rocks. A lane of mud and stones ended at the door. The sea-winds coming ashore on Stonecutter's point, fresh from the fierce turmoil of the waves, howled violently at the unmoved heaps of black boulders holding up steadily short-armed, high crosses against the tremendous rush of the invisible. In the sweep of gales the sheltered dwelling stood in a calm resonant and disquieting, like the calm in the centre of a hurricane. On stormy nights, when the tide was out, the bay of Fougere, fifty feet below the house, resembled an immense black pit, from which ascended mutterings and sighs as if the sands down there had been alive and complaining. At high tide the returning water assaulted the ledges of rock in short rushes, ending in bursts of livid light and columns of spray, that flew inland, stinging to death the grass of pastures.

The darkness came from the hills, flowed over the coast, put out the red fires of sunset, and went on to seaward pursuing the retiring tide. The wind dropped with the sun, leaving a maddened sea and a devastated sky. The heavens above the house seemed to be draped in black rags, held up here and there by pins of fire. Madame Levaille, for this evening the servant of her own workmen, tried to induce them to depart. "An old woman like me ought to be in bed at this late hour," she good-humouredly repeated. The quarrymen drank, asked for more. They shouted over the table as if they had been talking across a field. At one end four of them played cards, banging the wood with their hard knuckles, and swearing at every lead. One sat with a lost gaze, humming a bar of some song, which he repeated endlessly. Two others, in a corner, were quarrelling confidentially and fiercely over some woman, looking close into one another's eyes as if they had wanted to tear them out, but speaking in whispers that promised violence and murder discreetly, in a venomous sibillation of subdued words. The atmosphere in there was thick enough to slice with a knife. Three candles burning about the long room glowed red and dull like sparks expiring in ashes.

The slight click of the iron latch was at that late hour as unexpected and startling as a thunder-clap. Madame Levaille put down a bottle she held above a liqueur glass; the players turned their heads; the whispered quarrel ceased; only the singer, after darting a glance at the door, went on humming with a stolid face. Susan appeared in the doorway, stepped in, flung the door to, and put her back against it, saying, half aloud--

"Mother!"

Madame Levaille, taking up the bottle again, said calmly: "Here you are, my girl. What a state you are in!" The neck of the bottle rang on the rim of the glass, for the old woman was startled, and the idea that the farm had caught fire had entered her head. She could think of no other cause for her daughter's appearance.

Susan, soaked and muddy, stared the whole length of the room towards the men at the far end. Her mother asked--

"What has happened? God guard us from misfortune!"

Susan moved her lips. No sound came. Madame Levaille stepped up to her daughter, took her by the arm, looked into her face.

"In God's name," she said, shakily, "what's the matter? You have been rolling in mud. . . . Why did you come? . . . Where's Jean?"

The men had all got up and approached slowly, staring with dull surprise. Madame Levaille jerked her daughter away from the door, swung her round upon a seat close to the wall. Then she turned fiercely to the men--

"Enough of this! Out you go--you others! I close."

One of them observed, looking down at Susan collapsed on the seat: "She is--one may say--half dead."

Madame Levaille flung the door open.

"Get out! March!" she cried, shaking nervously.

156

They dropped out into the night, laughing stupidly. Outside, the two Lotharios broke out into loud shouts. The others tried to soothe them, all talking at once. The noise went away up the lane with the men, who staggered together in a tight knot, remonstrating with one another foolishly.

"Speak, Susan. What is it? Speak!" entreated Madame Levaille, as soon as the door was shut.

Susan pronounced some incomprehensible words, glaring at the table. The old woman clapped her hands above her head, let them drop, and stood looking at her daughter with disconsolate eyes. Her husband had been "deranged in his head" for a few years before he died, and now she began to suspect her daughter was going mad. She asked, pressingly--

"Does Jean know where you are? Where is Jean?"

"He knows . . . he is dead."

"What!" cried the old woman. She came up near, and peering at her daughter, repeated three times: "What do you say? What do you say? What do you say?"

Susan sat dry-eyed and stony before Madame Levaille, who contemplated her, feeling a strange sense of inexplicable horror creep into the silence of the house. She had hardly realised the news, further than to understand that she had been brought in one short moment face to face with something unexpected and final. It did not even occur to her to ask for any explanation. She thought: accident--terrible accident--blood to the head--fell down a trap door in the loft. . . . She remained there, distracted and mute, blinking her old eyes.

Suddenly, Susan said--

"I have killed him."

157

For a moment the mother stood still, almost unbreathing, but with composed face. The next second she burst out into a shout--

"You miserable madwoman . . . they will cut your neck. . . ."

She fancied the gendarmes entering the house, saying to her: "We want your daughter; give her up:" the gendarmes with the severe, hard faces of men on duty. She knew the brigadier well--an old friend, familiar and respectful, saying heartily, "To your good health, Madame!" before lifting to his lips the small glass of cognac--out of the special bottle she kept for friends. And now! . . . She was losing her head. She rushed here and there, as if looking for something urgently needed--gave that up, stood stock still in the middle of the room, and screamed at her daughter--

"Why? Say! Say! Why?"

The other seemed to leap out of her strange apathy.

"Do you think I am made of stone?" she shouted back, striding towards her mother.

"No! It's impossible. . . ." said Madame Levaille, in a convinced tone.

"You go and see, mother," retorted Susan, looking at her with blazing eyes. "There's no money in heaven--no justice. No! . . . I did not know. . . . Do you think I have no heart? Do you think I have never heard people jeering at me, pitying me, wondering at me? Do you know how some of them were calling me? The mother of idiots--that was my nickname! And my children never would know me, never speak to me. They would know nothing; neither men--nor God. Haven't I prayed! But the Mother of God herself would not hear me. A mother! . . . Who is accursed--I, or the man who is dead? Eh? Tell me. I took care of myself. Do you think I would defy the anger of God and have my house full of those things--that are worse than animals who know the hand that feeds them? Who blasphemed in the night at the very church door? Was it I? . . . I only wept and prayed for mercy .

158

. . and I feel the curse at every moment of the day--I see it round me from morning to night . . . I've got to keep them alive--to take care of my misfortune and shame. And he would come. I begged him and Heaven for mercy. . . . No! . . . Then we shall see. . . . He came this evening. I thought to myself: 'Ah! again!' . . . I had my long scissors. I heard him shouting . . . I saw him near. . . . I must--must I? . . . Then take! . . . And I struck him in the throat above the breastbone. . . . I never heard him even sigh. . . . I left him standing. . . . It was a minute ago. How did I come here?"

Madame Levaille shivered. A wave of cold ran down her back, down her fat arms under her tight sleeves, made her stamp gently where she stood. Quivers ran over the broad cheeks, across the thin lips, ran amongst the wrinkles at the corners of her steady old eyes. She stammered--

"You wicked woman--you disgrace me. But there! You always resembled your father. What do you think will become of you . . . in the other world? In this . . . Oh misery!"

She was very hot now. She felt burning inside. She wrung her perspiring hands--and suddenly, starting in great haste, began to look for her big shawl and umbrella, feverishly, never once glancing at her daughter, who stood in the middle of the room following her with a gaze distracted and cold.

"Nothing worse than in this," said Susan.

Her mother, umbrella in hand and trailing the shawl over the floor, groaned profoundly.

"I must go to the priest," she burst out passionately. "I do not know whether you even speak the truth! You are a horrible woman. They will find you anywhere. You may stay here--or go. There is no room for you in this world."

Ready now to depart, she yet wandered aimlessly about the room, putting the bottles on the shelf, trying to fit with trembling hands the covers on cardboard boxes. Whenever the real sense of what she had heard emerged for a second from the haze of her thoughts she would fancy that something had exploded in her brain without, unfortunately, bursting her head to pieces--which would have been a relief. She blew the candles out one by one without knowing it, and was horribly startled by the darkness. She fell on a bench and began to whimper. After a while she ceased, and sat listening to the breathing of her daughter, whom she could hardly see, still and upright, giving no other sign of life. She was becoming old rapidly at last, during those minutes. She spoke in tones unsteady, cut about by the rattle of teeth, like one shaken by a deadly cold fit of ague.

"I wish you had died little. I will never dare to show my old head in the sunshine again. There are worse misfortunes than idiot children. I wish you had been born to me simple--like your own. . . ."

She saw the figure of her daughter pass before the faint and livid clearness of a window. Then it appeared in the doorway for a second, and the door swung to with a clang. Madame Levaille, as if awakened by the noise from a long nightmare, rushed out.

"Susan!" she shouted from the doorstep.

She heard a stone roll a long time down the declivity of the rocky beach above the sands. She stepped forward cautiously, one hand on the wall of the house, and peered down into the smooth darkness of the empty bay. Once again she cried--

"Susan! You will kill yourself there."

The stone had taken its last leap in the dark, and she heard nothing now. A sudden thought seemed to strangle her, and she called no more. She turned her back upon the black silence of the pit and went up the lane towards Ploumar, stumbling along with sombre determination, as if she had started on a desperate journey that would last, perhaps, to the end of her life. A sullen and periodic clamour of waves rolling over reefs followed her far inland between the high hedges sheltering the gloomy solitude of the fields.

Susan had run out, swerving sharp to the left at the door, and on the edge of the slope crouched down behind a boulder. A dislodged stone went on downwards, rattling as it leaped. When Madame Levaille called out, Susan could have, by stretching her hand, touched her mother's skirt, had she had the courage to move a limb. She saw the old woman go away, and she remained still, closing her eyes and pressing her side to the hard and rugged surface of the rock. After a while a familiar face with fixed eyes and an open mouth became visible in the intense obscurity amongst the boulders. She uttered a low cry and stood up. The face vanished, leaving her to gasp and shiver alone in the wilderness of stone heaps. But as soon as she had crouched down again to rest, with her head against the rock, the face returned, came very near, appeared eager to finish the speech that had been cut short by death, only a moment ago. She scrambled quickly to her feet and said: "Go away, or I will do it again." The thing wavered, swung to the right, to the left. She moved this way and that, stepped back, fancied herself screaming at it, and was appalled by the unbroken stillness of the night. She tottered on the brink, felt the steep declivity under her feet, and rushed down blindly to save herself from a headlong fall. The shingle seemed to wake up; the pebbles began to roll before her, pursued her from above, raced down with her on both sides, rolling past with an increasing clatter. In the peace of the night the noise grew, deepening to a rumour, continuous and violent, as if the whole semicircle of the stony beach had started to tumble down into the bay. Susan's feet hardly touched the slope that seemed to run down with her. At the bottom she stumbled, shot forward, throwing her arms out, and fell heavily. She jumped up at once and turned swiftly to look back, her clenched hands full of sand she had clutched in her fall. The face was there, keeping its distance, visible in its own sheen that made a pale stain in the night. She shouted, "Go away!"-- she shouted at it with pain, with fear, with all the rage of that useless stab that could not keep him quiet, keep him out of her sight. What did he want now? He was dead. Dead men have no children. Would

161

he never leave her alone? She shrieked at it--waved her outstretched hands. She seemed to feel the breath of parted lips, and, with a long cry of discouragement, fled across the level bottom of the bay.

She ran lightly, unaware of any effort of her body. High sharp rocks that, when the bay is full, show above the glittering plain of blue water like pointed towers of submerged churches, glided past her, rushing to the land at a tremendous pace. To the left, in the distance, she could see something shining: a broad disc of light in which narrow shadows pivoted round the centre like the spokes of a wheel. She heard a voice calling, "Hey! There!" and answered with a wild scream. So, he could call yet! He was calling after her to stop. Never! . . . She tore through the night, past the startled group of seaweed-gatherers who stood round their lantern paralysed with fear at the unearthly screech coming from that fleeing shadow. The men leaned on their pitchforks staring fearfully. A woman fell on her knees, and, crossing herself, began to pray aloud. A little girl with her ragged skirt full of slimy seaweed began to sob despairingly, lugging her soaked burden close to the man who carried the light. Somebody said: "The thing ran out towards the sea." Another voice exclaimed: "And the sea is coming back! Look at the spreading puddles. Do you hear--you woman--there! Get up!" Several voices cried together. "Yes, let us be off! Let the accursed thing go to the sea!" They moved on, keeping close round the light. Suddenly a man swore loudly. He would go and see what was the matter. It had been a woman's voice. He would go. There were shrill protests from women--but his high form detached itself from the group and went off running. They sent an unanimous call of scared voices after him. A word, insulting and mocking, came back, thrown at them through the darkness. A woman moaned. An old man said gravely: "Such things ought to be left alone." They went on slower, shuffling in the yielding sand and whispering to one another that Millot feared nothing, having no religion, but that it would end badly some day.

Susan met the incoming tide by the Raven islet and stopped, panting, with her feet in the water. She heard the murmur and felt the cold caress of the sea, and, calmer now, could see the sombre and confused

162

mass of the Raven on one side and on the other the long white streak of Molene sands that are left high above the dry bottom of Fougere Bay at every ebb. She turned round and saw far away, along the starred background of the sky, the ragged outline of the coast. Above it, nearly facing her, appeared the tower of Ploumar Church; a slender and tall pyramid shooting up dark and pointed into the clustered glitter of the stars. She felt strangely calm. She knew where she was, and began to remember how she came there--and why. She peered into the smooth obscurity near her. She was alone. There was nothing there; nothing near her, either living or dead.

The tide was creeping in quietly, putting out long impatient arms of strange rivulets that ran towards the land between ridges of sand. Under the night the pools grew bigger with mysterious rapidity, while the great sea, yet far off, thundered in a regular rhythm along the indistinct line of the horizon. Susan splashed her way back for a few yards without being able to get clear of the water that murmured tenderly all around and, suddenly, with a spiteful gurgle, nearly took her off her feet. Her heart thumped with fear. This place was too big and too empty to die in. To-morrow they would do with her what they liked. But before she died she must tell them--tell the gentlemen in black clothes that there are things no woman can bear. She must explain how it happened. . . . She splashed through a pool, getting wet to the waist, too preoccupied to care. . . . She must explain. "He came in the same way as ever and said, just so: 'Do you think I am going to leave the land to those people from Morbihan that I do not know? Do you? We shall see! Come along, you creature of mischance!' And he put his arms out. Then, Messieurs, I said: 'Before God--never!' And he said, striding at me with open palms: 'There is no God to hold me! Do you understand, you useless carcase. I will do what I like.' And he took me by the shoulders. Then I, Messieurs, called to God for help, and next minute, while he was shaking me, I felt my long scissors in my hand. His shirt was unbuttoned, and, by the candle- light, I saw the hollow of his throat. I cried: 'Let go!' He was crushing my shoulders. He was strong, my man was! Then I thought: No! . . . Must I? . . . Then take!--and I struck in the hollow place. I never saw him fall. . . .

163

The old father never turned his head. He is deaf and childish, gentlemen. . . . Nobody saw him fall. I ran out . . . Nobody saw. . . ."

She had been scrambling amongst the boulders of the Raven and now found herself, all out of breath, standing amongst the heavy shadows of the rocky islet. The Raven is connected with the main land by a natural pier of immense and slippery stones. She intended to return home that way. Was he still standing there? At home. Home! Four idiots and a corpse. She must go back and explain. Anybody would understand. . . .

Below her the night or the sea seemed to pronounce distinctly--

"Aha! I see you at last!"

She started, slipped, fell; and without attempting to rise, listened, terrified. She heard heavy breathing, a clatter of wooden clogs. It stopped.

"Where the devil did you pass?" said an invisible man, hoarsely.

She held her breath. She recognized the voice. She had not seen him fall. Was he pursuing her there dead, or perhaps . . . alive?

She lost her head. She cried from the crevice where she lay huddled, "Never, never!"

"Ah! You are still there. You led me a fine dance. Wait, my beauty, I must see how you look after all this. You wait. . . ."

Millot was stumbling, laughing, swearing meaninglessly out of pure satisfaction, pleased with himself for having run down that fly-by-night. "As if there were such things as ghosts! Bah! It took an old African soldier to show those clodhoppers. . . . But it was curious. Who the devil was she?"

Susan listened, crouching. He was coming for her, this dead man. There was no escape. What a noise he made amongst the stones. . . . She saw his head rise up, then the shoulders. He was tall--her own man! His long arms waved about, and it was his own voice sounding a little strange . . . because of the scissors. She scrambled out quickly, rushed to the edge of the causeway, and turned round. The man stood still on a high stone, detaching himself in dead black on the glitter of the sky.

"Where are you going to?" he called, roughly.

She answered, "Home!" and watched him intensely. He made a striding, clumsy leap on to another boulder, and stopped again, balancing himself, then said--

"Ha! ha! Well, I am going with you. It's the least I can do. Ha! ha! ha!"

She stared at him till her eyes seemed to become glowing coals that burned deep into her brain, and yet she was in mortal fear of making out the well-known features. Below her the sea lapped softly against the rock with a splash continuous and gentle.

The man said, advancing another step--

"I am coming for you. What do you think?"

She trembled. Coming for her! There was no escape, no peace, no hope. She looked round despairingly. Suddenly the whole shadowy coast, the blurred islets, the heaven itself, swayed about twice, then came to a rest. She closed her eyes and shouted--

"Can't you wait till I am dead!"

She was shaken by a furious hate for that shade that pursued her in this world, unappeased even by death in its longing for an heir that would be like other people's children.

165

"Hey! What?" said Millot, keeping his distance prudently. He was saying to himself: "Look out! Some lunatic. An accident happens soon."

She went on, wildly--

"I want to live. To live alone--for a week--for a day. I must explain to them. . . . I would tear you to pieces, I would kill you twenty times over rather than let you touch me while I live. How many times must I kill you--you blasphemer! Satan sends you here. I am damned too!"

"Come," said Millot, alarmed and conciliating. "I am perfectly alive! . . . Oh, my God!"

She had screamed, "Alive!" and at once vanished before his eyes, as if the islet itself had swerved aside from under her feet. Millot rushed forward, and fell flat with his chin over the edge. Far below he saw the water whitened by her struggles, and heard one shrill cry for help that seemed to dart upwards along the perpendicular face of the rock, and soar past, straight into the high and impassive heaven.

Madame Levaille sat, dry-eyed, on the short grass of the hill side, with her thick legs stretched out, and her old feet turned up in their black cloth shoes. Her clogs stood near by, and further off the umbrella lay on the withered sward like a weapon dropped from the grasp of a vanquished warrior. The Marquis of Chavanes, on horseback, one gloved hand on thigh, looked down at her as she got up laboriously, with groans. On the narrow track of the seaweed-carts four men were carrying inland Susan's body on a hand-barrow, while several others straggled listlessly behind. Madame Levaille looked after the procession. "Yes, Monsieur le Marquis," she said dispassionately, in her usual calm tone of a reasonable old woman. "There are unfortunate people on this earth. I had only one child. Only one! And they won't bury her in consecrated ground!"

166

Her eyes filled suddenly, and a short shower of tears rolled down the broad cheeks. She pulled the shawl close about her. The Marquis leaned slightly over in his saddle, and said--

"It is very sad. You have all my sympathy. I shall speak to the Cure. She was unquestionably insane, and the fall was accidental. Millot says so distinctly. Good-day, Madame."

And he trotted off, thinking to himself: "I must get this old woman appointed guardian of those idiots, and administrator of the farm. It would be much better than having here one of those other Bacadous, probably a red republican, corrupting my commune."

I hope you enjoyed the shorties. Please enjoy the full Novel - Siam Storm – A Thailand Adventure.

Siam Storm

A Thailand Adventure

Robert A Webster

Copyright © 2012 Robert A Webster

— Prologue —

Somchay noticed a change in the aroma within the temple. The fragrant jasmine was replaced by something that he'd come across before. It smelt similar to the sweet nutty scent given off by cakes at the village bakery; almonds. However, he knew this wasn't cake, but something more modern and far more sinister.

The wispy curls of vapour emanating from essence sticks, suddenly erupted into large plumes of smoke. Somchay cried out, clasping the holy box to his chest. The other monks now got to their feet, rushing toward their Prime Master. Confusion reigned as one by one, the coughing, spluttering monks fell to the floor.

Somchay fell against the golden statue of the Buddha. Unable to see through the haze in the now smoke filled temple, he could hear his brother monks coughing and convulsing, fighting desperately for their lives. He clutched onto the holy box as darkness enveloped him. A hooded monk then came over to his lifeless body, prising the small golden box from his hand.

* **In Appendix**

169

— Chapter One —

The ancient stage was set. The delicate scent of jasmine and lotus blossom, drifted soothingly through the warm candlelit main hall of the Wat. Inside, warrior monks of the Tinju order knelt with their foreheads touching the marble floor, arms extended in front of them. Above them, Prince Siddhartha Gautama journeyed around the mural walls on his way to enlightenment. The monks remained deep in meditation and awaited the moment, like crouching lions awaiting the scent of their prey.

Located in dense jungle and surrounded by mountains, the Wat was around 2000 years old and had been built by villagers and monks in Salaburi, a remote village near the south-eastern Thai/Cambodian border town of Pong-Nam-Rom. The Wat, although small in comparison to other Thai temples, had gleaming domes and arches covered in gold leaf, with intricate carved statues depicting Buddha's journey through life, both as a prince and a pauper.

The Wat, built against a mountain to the rear of the village was meticulously maintained. There was a large door at the front, a small door at the rear and a door at the side, leading to a meditation room. The outside walls were adorned with mosaic-tiled murals, depicting a nobleman on a horse, smiling down upon a poor, decrepit individual. It was believed this was the moment when Prince Siddhartha Gautama decided to give up his earthly possessions and begin his journey to enlightenment, eventually becoming known as Buddha and entering Nirvana whilst still alive.

Inside the meditation room was an embalmed corpse on a stone slab, a foetus in a glass jar, preserved in a clear liquid made from the bark of a local tree, and a skeleton. The monks entered this room for intense meditation on the journey through life, reflecting on birth, death, and the afterlife. Further away, a small tunnel led to a large cave, barred by a heavy golden gate. On either side of the gate monks stood, armed with bows and arrows. With their swords glinting at their sides, they guarded the treasure within the cave: a jewel-encrusted gold box, housing four teeth of the Lord Buddha.

The monks, reincarnations of those who had died before them, had dedicated their lives in the Wat to this purpose from the time they were one day old.

The inhospitable terrain, humidity, many biting insects and lack of trails ensured the centuries-old isolation of the Wat and village. Because of the bountiful jungle resources, they were self-sufficient in food and rich in plant life for medicines, with no need for the trappings of the outside world.

****

The holy relics were brought from China by a trader and presented to King Bumnalonkorn two thousand years ago. The King had a golden box, encrusted with locally mined rubies and sapphires, made to house the relics. He chose a site in the heart of the jungle, which he named Salaburi. He brought in the best artisans from the Siamese Kingdom to construct the Wat, which took 12 years. Once completed, the bejewelled box was placed into the gated cave, hidden inside a small gold statue of Buddha.

To protect the relics, the kingdom's best Chang warriors were chosen. Dedicating their lives to Buddha and the current ruler, they honed their fighting skills. These warrior monks became the Tinju and their fearsome reputation in all forms of combat became legendary. The early kings of Siam used Tinju monks as bodyguards and assassins throughout the centuries.

The people involved with the building of Wat developed into a small community, making up the population of Salaburi village. A new civilisation was created, cut off from the outside world, and developed its own culture.

****

Once a year, on the current King's birthday, the relics were taken to the *Temple of the Emerald Buddha at the Imperial Palace in Bangkok, where the current King would worship them for continued wisdom in his rule.

Apart from the current King, his Chief of the Palace Guards, and the Tinju, nobody else was aware of the existence of the holy relic. The Chief of the Palace Guards responsibility was to transport the Tinju to and from the palace. Large army transports would arrive at Pong-Nam-Rom, where the monks would be waiting. They would get into the vehicles, and proceed to the Imperial Palace in Bangkok. The monks would enter the Temple of the Emerald Buddha, forming rows on either side of the aisle.

The Prime Master would walk over to the Emerald Buddha, remove the golden box from his robe, and place it at the foot of the statue. He would then pray alone for several moments before joining the other monks to await the King's arrival.

****

The day before the journey, the box was taken from the cave, brought to the Wat, and placed in the open hands of a large Buddha statue. The Tinju performed their ceremony, praying for Buddha's protection on the great journey

The Prime Master stood in front of the large golden statue of a smiling Buddha. The statue, approximately 20 feet tall, was of the Buddha sitting in the lotus position, with the matchbox sized golden box in its open hands.

Somchay had been Prime Master of the Tinju for four years, and although 58 years old, had the strength of a lion and the speed of a striking snake. His mentor, the former Prime Master Vitchae, after losing his sight had handed over the honour to him, as he was unable to perform his duties.

Somchay, with his head bowed and hands together in the 'Wai' position, chanted mantras for enlightenment, wisdom, and courage, which continued for several minutes. He then fell silent.

Two hooded monks stood either side of the statue and lit more of the scented essence sticks positioned around the statue in small sand traps. This took several minutes, and as small wisps of smoke started emanating from the sticks, the air started to fill with a fragrant aroma. After all 30 sticks were lit; Somchay took the small box from the statue's hands and turned to face the prone monks. He held the box high above his head. He uttered a command in an ancient Siamese dialect and the monks shouted their praise to Lord Buddha.

Somchay then continued chanting Mantras, until the horrific event unfolded.

****

The assailant put the holy relic in his tunic pocket. He squinted through the smoke at the blurred orange-clad figures of the monks, now either dead or convulsing on the marble floor. One monk in particular caught his gaze. He stared for several moments, until the monk's body ceased all movement. He made his way to the back door of the temple. Once outside, he removed his S-16 respirator and took a gulp of fresh air. He took off his robe, revealing a camouflage under-garment. He bundled up his robe, along with his remaining cyanide flares. Tying the parcel to his back, he took a deep breath and ran off toward the jungle.

With the back door of the temple left ajar, there was a dull thud as the other hooded monk came stumbling outside. He had used his robe to

174

filter the gas and held his breath as the deadly cyanide gas billowed out around him. Somehow, he had found the strength to run out of the gas stream into the fresh air. Letting out his breath in a loud throaty roar, he inhaled, deeply filling his lungs with air. Still wheezing, the monk bent over and vomited. Turning his head, he saw the figure disappear into the jungle, and then collapsed, unconscious.

— Chapter Two —

The silence was broken by a high-pitched screech, followed by several beeps, and a hand emerged from underneath a bundle of blankets, slapping the top of an alarm clock; Stu was awake. He mumbled, farted, scratched his gonads, and rolled out of bed. He made his way over to the light switch. 'Bloody freezing,' he thought. 'But never mind. This time tomorrow I will be basking in sunshine.' He looked over to an armchair, where a bundle of fur lay staring at Stu as he switched on the light.

"Come on lazy dog; get your useless carcass up," said Stu. "You're going on holiday."

Stu moved back to Cleethorpes four years ago. He now lived in a flat above a hair salon, with his old boxer dog, Chunky. Although born and raised in the seaside town, he had moved away at the age of seventeen to join the Royal Navy. After serving fourteen years, he left the navy and spent several years moving around the country before deciding to return to Cleethorpes. He would set up a furniture business and purchase a cheap dilapidated shop house there, which he fixed up and rented out to a hairdresser. The downstairs flat behind the shop, he leased to his friend, Spock.

Although he'd had several women in his life they never stayed with him long, possibly due to the fact they didn't really like how he spent most of his time on the piss with Spock, so he remained alone with his faithful canine companion. Chunky, purchased several years ago as an eighteen-month-old unwanted pet, when brought from the animal rescue shelter to meet her new owner, thought she would have an easy life. Poor misguided animal.

The neighbours knew Chunky for her affection and stupidity, with the local fire department having been called out on many occasions to free her head from the many railings and other obstacles that she had managed to become stuck in.

Now into December, England was cold, with icy chills that cut to the bone. Keeping extremities warm became a full time task. The long periods of darkness caused deep depression among many of its inhabitants.

Because England was not to his liking during the winter months, Stu decided to take a holiday. His staff could take care of his business, while his mum would take care of Chunky.

Stu was short but stocky, with a well-formed beer gut. He would be the perfect weight for his height if he was six-feet-five, but he fell short of that by over a foot. His mousy brown hair always appeared uncombed, mainly because it was and although he thought he looked handsome, in reality he had looks that only a mother could love. Not a rich man, but never short of money, he worked hard for what he earned, having the reputation of being thrifty, or 'as tight as a duck's arse in water,' as most people said of him.

His friend Spock lived in the downstairs flat. The pair had been mates since childhood and had kept in contact throughout the years. They shared many drunken adventures whenever Stu was in town. Including getting the neighbourhood closed off by armed police, who were looking for a crazy man in a checked shirt waving a shotgun around. This was a shitfaced Stu, who had borrowed Spock's air rifle to look for a comet with its telescopic sights, supposed to be easily viewed in the northeast night sky. Because Stu didn't know which direction was northeast, he went outside and searched the sky using the rifle's sights, but to no avail, so he gave up, went inside, and drank more beer. Within ten minutes, the street swarmed with armed police, searching for the crazy man with a gun.

Spock recently finished a relationship with his long-time girlfriend, who decided after ten years together that she didn't really like him. She did, however, like her boss at the fish-processing factory where she worked. She even liked his new black eye and crooked nose, courtesy of Spock.

Stu found a flight on the internet to Pattaya via Bangkok. After finding out this was in Thailand, advertised as the 'Land of Smiles', and because they thought that it looked tropical enough and it was cheap, they booked a return flight from Manchester. They had spoken to several local lads who had been to Pattaya, who told them it was the dogs bollix.

Stu took a hot shower, pulled on his jeans and a thick shirt, and made himself a cup of tea. He opened a tin of dog food, which he scooped into a bowl. Leaving Chunky with her snout buried in the food, he went into living room. He sat in his armchair and went through everything in his mind. Bags packed, check. Tickets, passport, traveller's cheques, check. Condoms, check. Dog food, 16 days supply, check. Train tickets, check. He knew that he had forgotten something, but couldn't think what. Then he realised. "Shit!" He got out of his armchair and raced off downstairs.

"Spock, are you awake!" He bellowed through the door of the downstairs flat.

"Yes matey...I'll be up in ten minutes."

Spock, his real name Peter Harris, was around Stu's age. With his large build and shaven head, he resembled a large primate. He had been given his nickname at school because of his uncanny resemblance to Star Trek's resident Vulcan. He loved his newly single life, loved the parties, and loved his work as a hygiene engineer, a dustbin man.

Spock was the life and soul of any party with his unusual party tricks. He would sit down, lift his legs to his neck, break wind, and ignite the lethal gas, producing a blue flame as methane met spark. He wore a top denture, because he lost all his top teeth in a run-in with a wooden club wielded by an unhappy customer during his stint as a bouncer

179

several years ago. Therefore, his other favourite trick was to drop his denture into someone's pint of beer, then, with a big cheerful grin, apologise, and offer to finish off their drink. This practice had all but ceased because one night at their favourite Indian restaurant, 'The Tiger of Bengal,' a spannered Spock decided to put his denture into a girl's drink. In went the false teeth, but instead of shrieking hysterically, the girl calmly finished her drink, tipped out the denture and promptly threw it across the restaurant. Everyone found this amusing, except for Spock. The false gnashers were passed along, with Spock running around trying, unsuccessfully, to find them. The customers were in an uproar. The denture was eventually found buried in a half-eaten bowl of Bombay mix. After being taken to the kitchen and cleaned, it was brought back to Spock on a small silver platter by a very perturbed Indian waiter. The restaurant was now known as 'The Teeth of Bengal.'

After Chunky was taken to her residence for the next 16 days, the lads caught a train to Manchester airport. They had not gone far when Spock opened his small hand luggage and produced a half-full bottle of whisky.

"Still three hours until we get to the airport, so we might as well finish this off," said Spock and continued, "after all, we are on holiday and it would be a shame not to."

They arrived in plenty of time and checked in their luggage. After being allocated aisle seats and told about the free drink service on the flight, they felt even happier.

On the aeroplane, they met Nick, who was in the seat next to Spock and, as luck would have it, was also travelling to Pattaya. Nick was staying three weeks, as he did not want to be in England over Christmas. He chuckled and told them that he would have a better Christmas in Pattaya. Nick lived with his sister in Brighton, a southern English coastal resort. He made the journey many times a year, both for leisure pursuits and business, which, as he explained, was buying copy designer clothes and watches to sell back in the U.K. He gave

Spock and Stu information about what to expect in Pattaya. The two lads listened intently, especially about the girls. The only time they spoke was when Stu asked about brothels, to which Nick replied, chuckling, "There aren't any; wait and see."

That became his standard reply to all their questions.

"Wait and see; just remember lads, whatever you do; fall in love with the place, but don't fall in love with the girls."

Nick was a typical 'Jack the Lad'. Fairly tall and lean, he spoke with a slight cockney accent, which he explained he had picked up after spending many years in London working on construction sites.

'Too puny for a builder, probably a sandwich boy,' thought Stu.

The three got on like a house on fire and decided to stick together in Pattaya.

Stu and Spock had not booked a hotel. A friend advised them that it would be cheaper, and easier, to find a hotel once they arrived. This worried them both, but Nick confirmed it, stating that he always stayed at the same hotel, which always had plenty of available rooms, even during high season, (November to March). This eased both their minds.

After a twelve-hour flight, they landed at Bangkok's Don Muang International Airport at the local time of 16:50. Once off the plane, the first priority involved several cigarettes in one of the smoking rooms within the airport. They collected their luggage and headed into the main airport building. They felt grimy and weary, but Nick assured them that it would soon pass once they arrived in Pattaya. Stu and Spock stopped at a currency exchange kiosk and converted £100's worth of traveller's cheques into Thai Baht. They made their way to the sliding exit doors, and Stu and Spock took in the sights, especially the beautiful olive skinned women walking around the airport. They giggled like two naughty schoolboys. It was the same as when they

181

were ten years old and their classmate, Mary Tate, lifted her skirt and pulled down her knickers behind the school bike shed. She gave the two embarrassed young lads a glimpse of something they would spend their entire adult life pursuing.

Nick walked on, shaking his head. 'These two are in for a big shock,' he thought.

Stopping at the automatic sliding exit doors, Spock and Stu glanced at each other; they then both looked straight ahead and, in unison, said, "Well, Thailand, we're here."

They took another pace forward, the automatic doors slid open, and they stepped out of the cool air-conditioned airport building into the warm night.

Spock and Stu faced each other and together hollered,

"Fuck me it's hot!"

— Chapter Three —

An eerie surreal aura surrounded the village of Salaburi. The villagers wandered around aimlessly, in a state of shock and disbelief. It had been two days since the deadly intrusion on their holy domain.

Pon lay in the monks living quarters, drifting in and out of consciousness. He had been that way since Khun Cenat found his near-lifeless body outside the rear of the temple as he strolled around the grounds. While checking that Pon was alive, Cenat noticed that the rear door of the temple was open. Confused, he approached the door, smelling an unusual aroma; he put his robe over his nose and mouth and entered.

In the main hall, the smoke had almost cleared. Cenat gagged when he saw his comrades and family lying dead on the floor, with their features and bodies contorted. He saw the body of the Prime Master leaning against the statue of Buddha. Feeling dizzy and devoid of rational thought, Cenat left the temple and went back outside to tend the fallen Pon. Then, as if in a hypnotic trance, hoisted the monk over his shoulder and carried him to the living area.

Vitchae is sitting in the classroom, listening to Khun Tangrit as he gave lessons to the young monks on the teachings of Buddha. Vitchae, the former Prime Master, was eighty-six-years-old and the oldest monk. With his sight completely gone, he liked to sit in on the lessons of the youngsters, especially when the ceremony of the 'great journey' was held. He enjoyed talking to the older monks, excluded from the ceremony because he was deemed too old to make the pilgrimage to Bangkok. The door of the classroom burst open. Cenat stumbled in with Pon over his shoulder. He put the unconscious Pon down on a mat and struggled to catch his breath.

"What's happening?" asked the old blind Master.

183

The young students rushed to aid Cenat and Pon.

Slipping in and out of consciousness, Pon felt too weak to tell them much. They put him on a small sleeping mat, where monks tended him, administering medicinal herbs. Several hours passed, and after Cenat regained his faculties, he relayed what he witnessed in the temple. The others first reactions were shock and horror, followed by disbelief, and then rage. Vitchae told them that they needed to get a message to His Majesty, the King. They would send a monk to the meeting point at the pre-arranged time the following day and relay what happened. The wise King would decide what to do.

Cenat, at Seventy-four-years-old, was the youngest of the elder monks, so was chosen to make the arduous trek through the jungle. With no compass or navigational aids, and with tracks or roads to follow, he relied on his memory and knowledge of the terrain.

The trek took many hours and he arrived early morning. Even though his most recent visit to the palace had been four years ago, the meeting point was still familiar. At a nearby food stall, the owner gave him a large bowl of pad Thai noodles, which he gratefully accepted. The owners of the stall had been there for many years and expected the monks. They usually arrived, ate, and blessed the food stall, before being driven away in large army transport trucks. The arrival of a single monk confused them, but the stall owners never asked questions.

Three large UNIMOG army trucks stopped beside the lone monk, who stood on a circular patch of earth alongside the road. The Chief of the Palace Guard, who always came along for this assignment, leapt out from the leading truck and approached Cenat.

Khun Taksin Sawalsdee was a retired army Lieutenant Colonel, who had held the title for eight years. It was an enviable position. He and his family loved living at the palace, and enjoyed the power that came along with the prestigious title.

Taksin listened to Cenat intently and formulated the next course of action. He would have to inform the King, but first needed to secure the area until they could gather all the facts. Who could have committed such a terrible act and why?

He phoned the nearest army garrison in Pong-Nam-Rom. That used to be his old infantry command and the commander was a good friend and excellent soldier, so Taksin requested five of his best infantry soldiers. He strode over to the second troop carrier and spoke to a lieutenant sitting in the passenger seat. The lieutenant got on his radio and gave an order to the other troop carriers. The large vehicles turned around and headed off back along the motorway towards Bangkok.

Taksin stayed with Cenat. He could see that the old monk looked weary, but enraged. Taksin explained that when infantrymen arrived, he would send them along to the village with him and find out what happened. The old monk glared at him and spoke in his ancient Siamese dialect, but realising Taksin did not understand, quickly reverted to Thai language.

"I will take your soldiers, but the Tinju will make any investigations and report directly to the King."

Taksin knew the fearsome reputation of his charges and nodded. 'They can do their investigation and I will do mine,' he thought. He gave Cenat his card with his mobile telephone number. He knew that most of the monks would never have seen a phone, let alone know how to use one, but it was all he could think to do while they waited for the soldiers.

Twenty minutes later, five non-commissioned officers pulled up in two army jeeps. A Master Sergeant leapt out of the lead jeep, snapped to attention, and saluted Taksin. Taksin returned the salute and informed the Sergeant he wanted him and his men to go to the village with Cenat, assess the situation, make the area secure and report to him, and only him. The sergeant returned to the jeep and gave instructions to the men. They then filed into the second jeep, leaving

185

Taksin with one jeep for his own use. They bunched up in the jeep to make room for Cenat. Taksin turned to face Cenat, giving him a long respectful Wai. The old monk returned the Wai and looked at the men waiting in the jeep.

"It's this way, and a long walk, so please keep up," he said as he turned and walked towards the jungle-covered hills. The five soldiers scrambled out of the jeep and ran to catch up to him.

The trek through the jungle proved to be gruelling for the young soldiers. Despite having trained in tropical forests and carrying out many combat simulations in different jungle terrains, nothing could have prepared them for this. It was now dark, with the moon hidden by the dense tree canopy. In the pitch-blackness, they tied themselves together with vine and, even though attached to the monk, could not see what lurked underfoot. Even carrying their .45mm service handguns and a portable GPS monitor with a location tracker, they still felt terrified. The elderly monk never spoke, and although the many biting insects attacked the soldiers relentlessly, the old monk never appeared to be touched. The soldiers, not prepared for this, had not brought along any rations. After ten hours of rapidly stomping through mud, over rocks, and trying to avoid walking into trees, a young corporal collapsed. The other soldiers rallied around him. The old monk came over to the huddled group of soldiers, knelt down and said,

"We will stop for a short while and eat."

Cenat stood up, untied himself and walked off into the darkness. Confused, the soldiers started a fire and huddled around it. Hot, thirsty and exhausted, they chatted about the day's events. Almost an hour later, the monk returned with two, small dead pythons around his neck, a bunch of bananas, several coconuts, and a bag made from banana leaves. The old monk just appeared by the fire, making the soldiers nervous. Cenat prepared and cooked the snakes; they drank the coconut milk and ate its milky flesh. The monk opened the bag, spilling the contents in front of the soldiers. He laid out several

186

unfamiliar fruits, and banana leaf packages. He peeled back the leaves to reveal a foul smelling paste. Cenat told them to rub on their uncovered areas, informing them that it would keep insects away and relieve the stings and bites already received. While the soldiers complied, the monk split open the fruits, which had a sickly sweet aroma. Cenat then took a white poppy pod from his tunic, opened it, crushed the seeds between two stones, and sprinkled the powder over the open fruits. He gave the soldiers half each, saying,

"Eat this. It will give you power and dull any pain."

He then tied himself back to the soldiers and waited until the last one had eaten his fruit.

"Come on, we still have a long way to go."

"How long?" asked one weary soldier.

"Oh, we are well over halfway," replied Cenat as he turned and walked ahead.

****

Pon had now regained consciousness, although his chest felt like it was on fire with every breath. Vitchae stayed at his bedside most of the time and the young monks came in to administer herbal medicines prepared by the elder monks. Pon told Vitchae what he witnessed in the temple and about the other hooded monk next to the statue. He explained how the incense sticks had flared up and given off a strange aroma, and how he'd filtered the gas with his tunic, before running out. Then he fell silent, stared at the ceiling, and whispered,

"I am ashamed, Master. I have to retrieve the holy relic and avenge my brothers."

Vitchae felt confused and thought, 'How was somebody able to get amongst the Tinju unnoticed and wipe out the most diligent warriors

187

in the kingdom? Moreover, why? Who could have possibly known so much about the whereabouts of Salaburi, the layout of the temple, the holy relic's location, and the timing of the ceremony? Only the monks and a few villagers knew this.'

He looked down at Pon and, in his dark world, muttered, "Don't be ashamed for living, young Pon. You are our only warrior left, the only hope for the survival of our creed and culture. You will deal out our vengeance. Of that I am certain."

The old man started chanting a prayer to Buddha for strength for Pon. He knew 'an eye for an eye' was not the Buddhist way, but he felt sure greed played a part in this crime.

Cenat and the soldiers arrived at the village during the early hours of the morning. It had taken them 18 hours to trek through the hostile terrain and they felt tired, hungry, and sore. Cenat took them straight to the monk's quarters, which were not usually open for outsiders, but these were exceptional circumstances and no other places were yet available. He woke two young monks and gave instructions to feed the soldiers. His old bones ached and his body cried out for rest, but nevertheless he went to Pon's sick bed, knowing he would find Vitchae there. Cenat had been trekking for almost two days, but he had a duty and a Tinju never rested until that duty was fulfilled. Vitchae sat beside the sleeping Pon, his eyes open, staring straight ahead. Unsure as to whether he was asleep or awake, Cenat gave a respectful Wai to the old master. Vitchae felt Cenat's presence and returned the Wai. Cenat sat beside Vitchae.

Cenat enquired about Pon, and was relieved to hear that he would be fine once the poison was expelled from his system. Cenat told Vitchae of his meeting with Taksin, the arrival of the soldiers and told him that the King would be informed.

"Good," said the elder monk. "You have done well, my old friend. This duty is concluded, so now go to rest."

188

Cenat headed to where he left the soldiers. They were all huddled in a group, sound asleep, with their food untouched. Cenat sat down and ate.

The Master Sergeant awoke four hours later and looked around at his surroundings. He woke his men, who slowly arose and surveyed the room. Two of the younger monks sat in deep meditation behind the soldiers and, when the soldiers awoke, one of them slipped out of the room. The other monk Wai-ed the group and pointed to the food covered by a fashee, a wicker dome used to keep insects off food.

"Please eat. We shall bring fruit and water."

They returned the Wai, removed the Fashee, and heartily tucked in.

Once they'd eaten, the soldiers left the quarters and went outside into the hot, humid grounds of the Wat. The villagers and the monks were already busy fetching large brittle blue rocks and what appeared to be white charcoal. The monks crushed this to powder and mixed it with other powders and a thick, sticky, amber liquid. The soldiers, not quite sure what to do, wandered aimlessly around the village for several hours, until Cenat retrieved them and put them to work with a carpenter, making what looked like canoes from cut-down trees.

Fifty-nine large bundles lay out in a line along the back of the Wat, each wrapped in a cloth that gave off a pungent odour, making the soldiers gag. The fifty-eight bodies had been recovered from the temple while Cenat was away. Another body was later found unceremoniously dumped behind some rocks, several metres from the cave's mouth. The remaining monks gathered around their fallen brother. They had seen the 5mm puncture-mark that the dead monk had at the back of his neck.

"You know what this means," said Vitchae to the elders, who nodded.

Now knowing the assailant had used a *pitou, Vitchae not only knew how the perpetrator got in, he also thought he knew who it was. He

189

would follow up on this after seeing his fallen brothers safely on their way to Nirvana. The dead monk was swathed and placed with the others.

The monks, villagers, and soldiers worked long into the night on their appointed tasks. On the twilight of the third day, they all gathered at the rear of the Wat, on the large area the monks used for combat training and as general meeting place for the village. Pon joined the remaining monks. Although still weak, he felt that he must see his brothers off on their last journey.

A long marble altar stood about four feet off the ground in the centre of the area. On the altar lay the fifty-nine coffins, each lined with hammered gold obtained from within the mountains. Each contained a body, swathed in a hessian cloth and covered with hardened blue-white clay, coated with a thick, syrupy substance. The remaining monks, dressed in ceremonial robes, stood behind the large altar, facing the kneeling villagers and soldiers, chanting from Holy Scriptures. Cenat warned the soldiers to keep their heads bowed below the altar. They asked Cenat many questions, to which he replied, "It is the way of the Tinju," and when asked about the substance covering the bodies, he just said, "Wharm lorn," sunblaze.

The twilight slowly gave way to darkness, the chanting stopped, and starting from the left, two young monks lit the coffins.

Each ignited immediately, and vivid orange and yellow flames filled the night air. Within a few seconds, the flames turned blue. The monks, villagers, and soldiers assumed a prostrate position lower than the altar. The flames glowed white for a split second, then ¬— whoosh— a column of white light as bright and as hot as the sun shot into the night sky. It was over in an instant and the silence and blackness of the night returned.

They remained silent for several moments. Vitchae got to his feet, and beckoned everyone to rise. The smell of scorched wood filled their nostrils, and all that now remained on the altar was fifty-nine glowing

190

blobs of gold. The following day they would be taken to the sacred burial site, but for now, the monks would meditate and reflect on their own, while the villagers and soldiers would party and celebrate the holy ones' lives.

Pon now felt stronger. After being given medicinal herbs and King Cobra liver, he had regained most of his strength. It had been five days since the terrible event took place. He knew that if he wanted to catch the culprit and avenge his brothers, he would have to leave soon, although he did not yet know whom he was chasing. At Cenat's suggestion, he traded with one of the soldiers a gold nugget with the Buddha's image intricately carved on it for his mobile phone. The young Corporal thought he had made a good trade. 'This must be worth a fortune,' he thought. 'That is if we ever get out of here.' The soldier taught Pon how to use the phone but as there was no signal in this area, he could only pretend. Pon thought he had the gist of his new tool and Cenat gave him Taksin's card. 'This is a start', he thought.

He packed his cloth holdall with dried food, liquids, edible roots, and leaves, along with small round clay containers containing various powders, including sunblaze, the mobile phone, and his ornaments. Laid out beside him was his *glave, his sword, which resembled a Samurai sword, with seven inches of the rear side serrated, used for sawing through animal bone and cutting up carcasses for easy transport. The handle was engraved and hollow, with a tight-fitting flip top, which contained his pitou.

Pon meditated. He had listened to Vitchae telling him of his suspicions, but as the old master told him, he had no firm proof. Pon was confused and unable to understand why anyone would do this, although in the next few minutes he would learn, who.

Vitchae entered and went over to Pon, accompanied by an old woman from the village. Pon felt shocked, because villagers, especially women, were not allowed. 'It must be important,' he thought. Vitchae introduced the woman as Banti Meesilli. Pon recognised her from his

191

morning pilgrimages around the village, when he and the other monks would go to acquire food, a ritual to learn humility. The villagers were always happy to give food in return for a blessing.

The pair sat down in front of Pon. Vitchae encouraged Banti to tell him about her son. She tearfully explained that eight years ago her youngest son, Dam, went into the jungle to hunt, but never returned. She had always feared that wild tigers killed and ate him. She told Pon of her young son's bravery and skill as a hunter and her pride at her eldest son being a Tinju, although Banti was unsure which monk was her son, as only the Prime Master and a few elder monks knew from which family the monks were taken. She went on to explain that Dam became close to a Tinju named Jinn, who, at four years his senior, was the right age to be his brother. She handed Pon a clear resin covered charcoal drawing.

"That was my beloved son, Dam," Banti told him.

Pon looked at the sketch as Banti stood up. She Wai-ed the monks and looking distraught, announced,

"With Jinn being murdered in the temple, it now means that I have lost both my sons. Please find who is responsible. I beg you."

Banti left the room, leaving her drawing with Pon, who had a strange feeling about this woman.

Once Banti left, Pon asked Vitchae,

"Master, I don't understand. What has this woman's dead son to do with this?"

Vitchae explained,

"Her son went into the jungle and never returned; everyone presumed he was killed by a tiger, but these timid animals avoid any contact with us. Dam is the only person in Salaburi unaccounted for during my lifetime. I knew young Dam; he was a strong boy and extremely well taught in the way of the Tinju. I spoke to him two days before his disappearance, but our conversation did not end well. He is who I suspect is responsible for this. Pon thought for a moment. He remembered the lad who always hung around the temple and trained with them. He wondered at the time why a villager was allowed so much freedom around the holy temple.

Pon knew Jinn; they were almost the same age. He knew how much Jinn had grieved for his brother after Dam's disappearance was announced.

Pon folded the drawing of Dam and placed it in his bag.

"Master, now I must leave," he said, feeling a sense of direction.

"Yes, young warrior, and I pray that Buddha will guide and protect you," Vitchae replied.

— Chapter Four —

The lads pulled up in a taxi outside the reception area of a large hotel. The two-hour journey from Bangkok airport allowed Stu and Spock to take in all the sights, with the modern buildings and motorways of the sprawling Bangkok metropolis surprising them. They had expected to see dirt tracks and wooden shacks. Pattaya also had the same effect as the taxi drove along streets lined with modern hotels, restaurants, shops and, to their relief, McDonalds and KFC.

They checked into the Siam Sawasdsee Hotel. Stu and Spock could not believe the price; only 450 Baht a night, which they calculated to be about seven pounds sterling. They made their way to their rooms on the third floor.

The large furnished rooms came with a small fridge stocked with beer, soft drinks, and bottled water. In the en-suite bathroom, alongside the toilet was small hose with a nozzle, which Nick explained was a sort of portable bidet that fired a strong jet of water up your jaxey. 'Aqueous toilet roll,' thought Spock.

A patio door led out onto a small balcony and Nick, having the corner room, had a small opening window behind his door. The instructions from Nick were, "Quick shit, shower, shave, shampoo and then go out."

It was past eight o'clock and, though jetlagged from the long journey, Spock and Stu wanted to see the place known as 'Sin City.'

Nick explained that the streets joined or branched off the main roads and were known as Sois; some were numbered and some named. Nick planned to start in Soi 6, informing them that it was a, 'short time Soi.'

"Great," said Stu, not knowing what he was talking about. They walked out of the hotel and got on a Baht bus, one of the many small covered pick-up trucks that circled the city's one-way traffic system. Stu and Spock noticed them on the way to Soi 6 bars, each with loud music, and many people dancing, waving, and having a whale of a time.

Soi 6 joined Second Road, which led to the beach road and was lined with small and large air-conditioned bars on both sides. Each bar had its windows covered by signs or dark glass, making it difficult to see inside. Young, scantily-clad women sat in groups outside the bars, chatting and fixing their makeup, like a group of muggers waiting for a victim.

The lads paid the 10-baht bus fare and went into the first bar, which was on the corner of the Soi. The women sitting outside leapt up, surrounded them, and dragged them inside, in the nicest possible way.

In the dimly lit bar, the lads were taken over to an L-shaped sofa. They sat down and ordered three bottles of Singha beer, the local Thai brew; it was slightly sweet, with a hint of nut in the flavour, and a lot stronger than most European beers.

The beer got brought over by a young, scantily-clad woman, followed by two equally skimpily dressed women. One woman sat next to Nick, while the other two ladies sat on either side of Stu and Spock, sitting close together like two Catholic nuns at a rugby team party. They had a mortal fear of being stitched up with a katoey, a ladyboy. They'd heard stories from their mates at home who had been to Thailand and were allegedly stitched up with a katoey.

"Make sure you check their feet size, check for an Adam's apple and check between their legs before you go anywhere near any of those girls," they were advised by a friend in England. This played on their minds, even more so now that they were in the situation, even though Nick tried to reassure them the stories were untrue.

196

"What a load of bollocks," he would say.

Still unsure, Stu ignored the two girls and turned to Nick.

"Are we in a brothel, mate?"

It amused Nick to observe these Pattaya virgins in action. He remembered his first time here and knew he had acted the same.

"No mate, not exactly," he mused. He then leaned over and said something to the girl sitting next to Stu. With a look of annoyance and disbelief, she looked at Stu, stood up, and lifted her short skirt to reveal her bare pubic region.

"Me not ladyboy. Me lady...Sure!"

This came as a shock to both Stu and Spock, as flashes of Mary Tate went through both their minds. The woman then spent the next few moments convincing them that she was indeed a woman. Ten minutes later, thoroughly reassured and enjoying their ice-cold beers, Stu turned to face Spock, who had a stupid, dopey contented grin on his face.

"What an amazing little place," he said, looking down between his legs at his naked mid section and approving of the oral dexterity of his temporary, but amenable, new friend.

"Yeah!" replied a chilled out Spock, looking down at his own small sack-emptier doing her thing, very expertly, he thought. All memories of Mary Tate disappeared.

Several beers later, after the girls finished giving relief to the three grateful lads and were given their reward for their services, namely 500 Baht and a few glasses of overpriced wine cooler, the lads decided it was time to move on. They paid their bill and, with Nick mumbling about the price of the ladies' drinks, strolled out into the hot night. Sacks empty, spinning heads and slightly juiced, they made

197

their way down Soi 6. They ran the gauntlet of women jumping off their seats, screaming at them to come into their bars, informing them that they were sexy men and fondling their now empty sacks and todgers. They resisted further temptation and got on a Baht bus at Beach Road.

"Where to next matey?" Spock enquired.

"Soi 8," Nick replied.

"What's there?" asked Stu.

Nick chuckled. "Wait and see."

Soi 8 buzzed with life. Music blared out from the many open-air bars with every bar trying to out-volume the others. Only a musical cacophony was heard, as one bar played the Eagles, with another playing the Scorpions, etc. However, that only contributed to the lively atmosphere of Soi 8. Girls screeched at passing customers to "Come inside please." The occasional bell rang at various bars, much to the delight of the women working there, as that was the signal that they would be getting a free drink. Lights flashed. Street vendors walked around selling everything from chewing gum to fake watches. They went from bar to bar, looking for any drunken, gullible foreigner, egged on by the girls to "Buy me this darling." The customer would be promised undying, everlasting love. At least until his money ran out.

The atmosphere of Soi 8 was indescribable. Young men, old men with big beaming smiles sat at the bars playing bar games, Connect Four, Jenga, Swallow the Sausage. There was the occasional crash of wood heard as a foreigner lost at Jenga, and yet again had to ring the bell. An occasional holiday couple walked past, with the husband's head bent down looking at the floor while his wife glared at him, ensuring that he wasn't peeking at the girls.

The lads positioned themselves at one of Nick's regular bars. He said hello to Wan, the mamasan, bar manager. He introduced Stu and Spock, who could only manage a grunt as they tried to take in the never before experienced sights and sounds. Wan gave instructions to two women, who went to a large freezer and removed two small packages. They went over to Stu and Spock, popped open a 'pah-yen', cold towel, and proceeded to rub the ice-cold towel over Stu and Spock's neck and arms. The two lads cooed with satisfaction, as the heat was intense for them, even at night. They weren't prepared for Thailand's heat, so the pah-yen provided a welcome relief.

Three bottles of ice-cold beer were placed in front of them, along with a small wooden pot containing their bill. They took a long slow mouthful of their amber fluid, followed rapidly by several more. They bought drinks for the two girls who had wiped them down and while Nick spoke with the mamasan, the two lads made small talk with their newly acquired companions. The women asked where they came from, how long they planned to stay, and did they have ladies? They seemed to show more interest when the two lads said they did not have ladies. However, they became disappointed when the woman with Spock asked,

"I go with you, sexy man?"

Spock towered over the woman, but she was undaunted. Spock, not quite fully grasping what she'd meant, replied, "I don't think we are leaving yet, love."

The girl glared at Spock, said something to her friend, got off her stool and went over to talk to another older foreigner sitting the opposite side of the bar, much to the merriment of Nick who had been ear wigging in on the exchange.

After the girls buggered off, Spock decided he would do one of his 'party pieces' but, as his dentures would not fit in a bottle, it was the 'flaming arsehole' that would make its debut. He got off his stool, went to a small wicker armchair, sat down, lifted his legs either side

199

of his neck and held his lighter to his sphincter to await the arrival of its methane fuel. Right on cue, a bright blue flame shot out from his arse, followed a second later by a shorter flame. 'A good result,' he thought, 'double bubble.'

People at the bar were in uproar, clapping excitedly and asking for one more performance. Spock took a bow and walked back to his stool, laughter still echoing around the area. He now attracted several more women around him and, along with Stu, looked liked a couple of cats that got the cream.

Nick, not wanting to be upstaged by these new upstarts at his regular drinking hole, went over to the wicker chair previously occupied by Spock. The bar fell silent as all eyes turned toward Nick. Adopting the same position as Spock, he held a lighter in place, strained his bowels and distorted his facial muscles for extra power, making him appear like a clay gargoyle. He felt the twinges of pressure, so ignited the lighter. A short blue flame rushed out from his sphincter, followed by a yellow fire.

Stu turned to face Spock.

"Maybe not a good trick to try while wearing nylon shorts," he stated. They both fell about laughing, while Nick jumped around like a headless chicken trying to extinguish his flaming shorts.

After a few minutes, the commotion calmed down, apart from the odd sporadic chortles from Stu and Spock. Nick stood next to them at the bar, with a bag of ice held to his arse by a small motherly girl. He occasionally winced as the bag moved position to give the woman's arm a rest.

With several more beers consumed, they approached being spannered. Although the tiredness had worn off, the lads thought that they'd had too much excitement for one night and presumed Nick would want to go back to the hotel. On the contrary; according to Nick, the night had just got started. The girl who he sent to buy him replacement shorts at the market returned a few minutes later. Nick dismissed his Florence Nightingale and announced they were moving on. Nick counted his change and gave the girl a 20 Baht tip, which she gratefully accepted.

"That's not a lot for a tip," said Stu.

"Nick kee-neow," the mamasan said. "A cheap-Charlie."

They paid their bill and Stu and Spock left a 100 Baht tip.

"You'll learn," Nick told them.

They headed off up Soi 8 to join Second Road.

They walked along against the flow of traffic. Buying food at one of the many barbecue stands en-route, they walked along, happily chomping on small bits of sweet pork, onions, peppers, and green chillies on wooden skewers. They ate sweet banana pancakes, cooked at another street stand. With food in their stomach, they steadily sobered up. Getting their second wind and having fun, they walked among the many sporadic outcrops of bars, having girls latch onto them, trying to drag them in.

"Buy one drink, just one, please, sexy man," pleaded the girls, followed by the grabbing of an appendage. It amused Nick and Stu to observe a woman, who weighed approximately eight stones, trying to move a 20 stone Spock.

They arrived at a small bar amongst several others, situated on the ground floor of a row of four-storey buildings. These bars seemed more subdued than the hectic Soi 8. Several girls sat behind the bar, while others sat on stools in front, laughing and joking with customers or playing bar games with their new beaus. The three entered and, although Nick's sphincter was still throbbing, it had eased enough for him to sit on a barstool. They ordered beers and Nick introduced Spock and Stu to the bar owner, a middle-aged Thai man known as Charlie. Although not his real name, he thought it sounded more

201

foreigner friendly. Nick explained they would have a few quiet drinks and then move on to a go-go bar for an hour before the bars officially closed at one o'clock.

"But," added Charlie, with an impish look in his eye, "some bars still stay open after hours."

Charlie's wife came over, who, although well into her forties, still had her youthful looks. They could tell she must have been an absolute stunner in her younger years. 'I'd shag it,' thought Stu, now feeling ready for more action.

"Would you like to take a lady to sleep with you tonight?" she asked the newbies.

"Well," said Spock, "there's nothing like being forward."

"We're okay, thanks," replied Stu.

The conversation ebbed, so Stu started looking around at the girls, some dressed in slacks and blouses, with other in dresses. Compared with Soi's six and eight, Stu thought these girls looked plain. He noticed a girl sitting behind the bar reading a dictionary. Noticing Stu looking, she smiled and held up her English/Thai for Beginners book. Stu smiled back and she returned to her reading. Stu felt a little awkward and tapped Charlie's wife on the shoulder, and stammered,

"What's that girl's name?"

"Dao," replied Charlie's wife, smiling. "She is a good lady, only worked the bar for 3 weeks. Do you want me to have her come over and sit with you?"

"No...only asking," Stu said, blushing.

"Are you sure?" she asked.

"Yes, I'm sure, thanks anyway, but I think we're about to leave."

Stu took note of the sign behind the bar. 'HAPPY WORLD BAR.' The lads left the bar, walked down the Soi, to Beach Road, and jumped onto a Baht bus. Getting off at Walking Street, they walked about a third of the way along until they reached 'Champion a Go-Go.'

Passing a small beer bar, one of the smiling girls, an older but attractive woman, shouted "Hello" to Nick who boasted, "I've done her. Sturdy old tug, but a good shag."

An attractive young woman, dressed in a white thong, small white bra and knee-length black boots held the door to Champion open for them.

"Welcome," she cheerily shrilled. "Would you like some drink?"

The long, raised stage had five chrome poles set at its centre at varying distances apart. As Guns and Roses blasted out 'Sweet Child o' Mine', five girls danced and swayed around the poles, occasionally crouching down with legs opening and closing like a goldfish's mouth. They were all dressed the same as the girl who had opened the door and welcomed them, although some had removed their thongs and had them twirling around in their hands.

After drinking several glasses of draft Singha and watching the acrobatics of the ever-alternating ladies of the pole, they felt renewed vigour in their loins. Nick explained the routine for taking girls back to the hotel. "Pay the bar fine, take the lady to your room, do the business then, in the morning give them 500 Baht. Though they will ask for 1,000 Baht, only give them, 500."

This felt alien to Stu and Spock, but if this was the time-old method, then who were they to argue with tradition, and besides, they were horny again. Spock noticed that Stu did not appear to be his usual cheerful self. Though he looked at the chrome pole molesters, his mind seemed to be elsewhere. However, he just put this down to tiredness and hoped that his old mate would be ok tomorrow. Spannered and rapidly moving toward shitfaced, they just burbled on about nothing. Spock occasionally grabbed a passing dancer and played with her breasts, but he did buy her a drink as a reward. The girls didn't flinch, hoping they might hook him in and get a short time, quick shag, and 1,000 Baht.

They decided that it was time to move on before the bars closed. They walked into a small bar outside, sat down, and ordered more drinks. They seemed to be finishing their drinks a lot quicker and, not being used to the strength of Thai beer, plus the long session, they were wankered. Spock attempted to speak to the woman 'Nick had done' who had now gone from, a sturdy old tug, to a raving beauty in Spock's drunken mind. Nick drooled over another woman, who just smiled. Spock looked up and, when his eyes focused on the spinning room, asked, "Where's Stu?"

Nick turned his head away from his sodden companion. "I don't know. He was here a minute ago."

They remained concerned for all of ten seconds before resuming their drunken mating rituals. Stu and Spock had each taken a name card from the hotel and given instructions to follow, should they become separated.

****

Spock was the first awake and with a belch and a fart, re-joined the living. He checked his watch; 3:30pm.

"That can't be right," he said aloud.

He tried to recall the events from the night before, but his memory was sketchy; he remembered nothing after leaving Soi 8.

With a raging thirst, he went over to the small fridge, took out a bottle of water, and gulped down the cool refreshing liquid. He let out another rasping fart, still trying to search his memory. There came a groan from his bed followed by a quilt being tossed off.

'Oh yeah, I remember now,' thought Spock, vaguely regaining his faculties. He looked at the smiling woman.

"Men!" she exclaimed.

Spock, not understanding that men, meant bad smell, thought it meant good morning in Thai, so he returned the greeting, much to the confusion of Lek. He remembered that this was the sturdy old tug who Nick had done before, but she now looked a lot less attractive. He then remembered about Stu disappearing. Putting on his jeans, he walked out of his room and banged on Stu's door.

"Stu! Are you okay, matey?"

Spock heard mumbling and then Stu said, "Yes mate, but I feel rough."

"Me too," said Spock through the door. "I'm going back to my room. See you later."

Spock returned to his room, where Lek lay naked on the bed. He could not recall having sex the previous night, so decided that it would be a great shame to allow his todger twinge go to waste. He took out condoms from the bedside table and presented them to Lek. She slid over to the standing Spock, rolled the condom over his manhood and placed the wrapped package into her mouth.

Stu was awake, but only just. His head throbbed, and his mouth felt as dry as the bottom of a birdcage. Confused, he looked around, becoming aware that this wasn't his house. Where was his shabby wallpaper? Where was Chunky? He then came to his senses, remembering where he was. He could not remember much from the

205

previous night. He recalled being in Happy World Bar and then going to a go-go bar, but nothing else He checked his watch. 3:45pm. 'That can't be right,' he thought. He then realised there was someone in bed with him. Nervously, he turned to see a figure huddled under the quilt with their back turned. 'Oh no! What did I do?' He gingerly pulled the light quilt off the figure, revealing a naked olive-skinned back. The figure moved, turning to face him.

He looked at her face, then down her body, at the pert breasts, with small pink-brown nipples, like juicy raspberries. Stu had never seen anything so lovely. A small black-haired triangle was delicately nestled between her crossed-over legs. He stared at her as a vague memory came back. He thought about the film, 'The Godfather' and how Michael Corleone felt the 'thunderbolt' after meeting his Italian sweetheart. He'd never experienced this before. Nick's words of wisdom were still ringing in his ears: 'Don't fall in love with the girls.'

He remembered where he'd first seen her, but couldn't recall how she had ended up here. His head throbbed, but he was glad to be in this wonderland and as happy as a 'pig in shit' to be right here, right now. The slumbering figure looked at Stu, smiled and said,

"Good morning, pompui."

Stu, unaware that pompui meant fatty, stared at this lovely lady and replied,

"Good morning, Dao."

— Chapter Five —

Somsak Meesilli, nicknamed Dam, meaning black, and now 25 years old, sat on the back of an open Toyota Hilux pick-up truck. He donned his monk's robes in order to get a ride easier. The truck headed east towards Phnom Penh, the capital city of Cambodia. Dam trekked through jungle and mountains for four days, before he made his way to a minor road. He'd managed to hitch a ride from a passing Cambodian market trader. The man was surprised at seeing a monk in the middle of nowhere, especially a Thai monk. He told Dam to get onto the back, and continued on to Phnom Penh.

Dam wanted to go home. He lived with his benefactor and guardian, an Irishman named Andrew Towhey, for seven years. They lived in Caw Kong, a small town 12 kilometres from Phnom Penh. He lived in a large, luxurious bungalow with Towhey and Miguel, a Spaniard, who came to Cambodia with Towhey many years earlier. Dam's life was good. He had money in his pocket, ate well, drank well, had transport and many women. He was pleased when Andrew gave him this task.

Dam tapped at the small hard package in his robe pocket. He thought about Jinn and watching him die in the smoke filled temple. He felt a twinge of remorse.

"Sorry, my brother," he said aloud. The sadness soon left him as his thoughts drifted back further, to growing up in the village of Salaburi.

Dam was born and raised in Salaburi. His mother, Banti, told him at an early age that his older brother had been taken to be a Tinju. Although sad that he would be raised as an only son, he had two sisters.

Dam was a small child with a darker complexion compared to the other villagers; hence his nickname. He was an inquisitive boy who would often wander around the temple to watch the monk's combat training. He was a loner, preferring to watch the monks, explore, and discover secret little places around the temple. One day when Dam was seven years old, he was exploring the small mountainous hills at the side of the temple. He made his way around some rocks and noticed a cave. At the mouth of the cave stood two hooded monks, with bows slung over their shoulders, standing in front of a large golden gate. The guards, on hearing him, scrambling over the rocks, immediately swung their bows into a firing position and, as quick as lightning, removed arrows from their quivers and pointed the deadly weapons at Dam, who froze in his tracks. The two monks recognised him as a village boy and shouted at him to leave immediately and never return or they would kill him.

Gripped by panic and fear, the young boy turned in his tracks, scrambling and stumbling back up the rocks. The cave became his nemesis.

Dam was determined to become a Tinju Warrior, even though his mother explained that Tinju were specially chosen and unlike his brother, he was not a reincarnation, so could never become a Tinju. Several years later, whilst on one of his jaunts to the temple, he was mimicking the monk's moves with kendo sticks. He became aware of someone behind him. He spun around and faced a smiling monk, who looked around 14 years old. Staring at the monk for a few seconds, he said, "Hello, my name's Dam."

"Hello Dam, my name's Jinn."

Dam instantly knew Jinn to be his brother.

Many years passed, and although it was unusual for monks to associate so closely with villagers, Vitchae, the Prime Master, noticing the friendship develop between Dam and Jinn, wasn't unduly concerned. Dam was a likeable lad, who made the monks laugh with his comical antics. Jinn taught Dam everything that he had learned about hand-to-hand combat and weapons, with Dam allowed on the training ground to mock fight with the other monks. Although he usually got a good beating, he was undeterred. He thought that one day he would become a Tinju like his big brother. He did his schooling with his brother, learning about the wisdom of Buddha. The Tinju forged their own weapons and were taught how to fold steel, mixed with locally mined black iron ore. This, when mixed with other metals, became a strong pliable material easily folded and shaped. It was from this metal that they made their glaves and swords. The weapons were given to the novice monks at ten-years-old, an age at which they were considered capable of undertaking the great journey, and meeting the current King, The Living Buddha. These weapons were the monks' responsibilities and stayed with them for life. They were given unsharpened and undecorated, it being down to the monk to keep them sharpened and maintained, and up to them what decoration was engraved. The monks spent their days with combat, fitness training, meditation, and spiritual learning. Dam enjoyed every painful minute. He and Jinn became inseparable.

Jinn reached his 17th birthday, the age eligible to take the, Trial of the Warrior.

The Trial of the Warrior was the hardest event in the monks' lives, being the time they progressed from Novice to Warrior: the time of becoming a man.

The trial consisted of several stages. First, a Master would trek toward Pong-Nam-Rom. After given a two-hour head start, which for a fit Master would take about 9 hours; the novice would then have to chase after him. When, or if, he caught up, he would then engage the Master in combat with kendo sticks. The novice needed to reach the Master before he reached Pong-Nam-Rom. This meant the novice sprinting through the jungle for at least 20kms. If the Master reached Pong-Nam-Rom before being caught, or the novice proved unworthy in combat, the novice would fail. He would then have to re-take the test the next day, and every day after, until successful.

The novice would return to the village and, armed with his sword, he would have to navigate an assault course, chopping several obstacles on the way, from a watermelon to chunks of soft rock; this he did blindfolded. This tested his weapon's effectiveness and maintenance. He then shot an arrow into a target 20 yards away, the target being an orange. In the final test, the novice, armed only with his glave, needed to survive alone in the jungle for six days.

It was the first day of Jinn's trial. Khun Lignet had gone into the jungle two hours earlier. The other monks lined up in the combat area and stood in silent meditation. Vitchae stood with Jinn, his hand on the young monk's head as he chanted for strength. He then removed his hand and announced,

"Let the trial begin."

Jinn wai-ed the Prime Master, and took off into the jungle. He had just entered the jungle, when he heard something behind him. He spun around, removing his kendo stick from his sheath and looked upon the smiling face of Dam.

"I will run with you, my brother. I will hide while you beat Lignet." He laughed.

Jinn smiled, turned, and, at full sprint, took off, with Dam not far behind.

Seven days went by and Dam was anxious. He saw Jinn catch and fight Lignet and return to complete the assault course, but he knew that he could not go into the jungle with Jinn for his last trial, as that was forbidden. Dam paced up and down behind the Wat, where the other monks gathered. Then, out of the jungle in the distance, he saw his brother running towards them. The other monks formed two lines and Jinn sprinted between them to Vitchae, who stood at the head of the formation. Jinn stopped and wai-ed the Prime Master.

"Master," he said, "I have completed my task. I wish now to do my duty as, a Warrior."

The old master turned around to a marble altar and removed a red sash, which he put over the bowed head of Jinn. He then took Jinn's sword, glave, bow, and pitou, and placed them on his outstretched arms.

"You have earned the right to wear the symbol of our creed and from this day, you will hold the rank and title of Warrior."

Dam could not contain his excitement for his brother and dreamed of the day he too would stand there and receive the sash. Even though Dam did not have weapons, he made some out of wood, carving intricate patterns to mimic his brother steel or ivory handles. He'd never seen a pitou before, so he intended to look at his brothers, 'I will carve one later,' he thought, a proud day for the young villager.

Several more years went by. Jinn learned a new discipline, which he'd been told was a Duty. Tinju monks had been only called upon once in the last 50 years to perform a duty, which was to dispatch a rather nasty Japanese General. A young Vitchae concluded that duty. Nevertheless, it was something that they all needed to be proficient at. Jinn taught Dam some of the skills and when the curious youngster asked what a pitou was used for, he taught him how to use one. This he did in secret, unsure if allowed to do so or not, but he could not see any harm in teaching his baby brother.

Jinn undertook guard duty outside the cave that housed the holy relic. During his watch, Dam would sneak around to the cave and wait near Jinn. Dam was no longer afraid of the cave; he had beaten his fear, and although they never spoke while Jinn was on guard duty, just being near his brother made him feel safe.

Dam approached his 17th birthday. Although he was small, even by Thai standards, his small frame, like the other monks, was solid muscle. He felt ready to take the trial of the Warrior. 'Heck,' he thought, 'I did the first parts when I was 13 and re-ran it many times since with Jinn.' He knew his life would change when he became a Warrior. He felt ready to serve the King, Lord Buddha, Vitchae, and the Tinju, especially his beloved brother, Jinn.

On the day of his 17th birthday, he excitedly got dressed and ran over to the Wat. The monks were in morning meditation, so he waited for them to finish and went over to Jinn.

"Now," he said, "now, my brother."

Jinn got to his feet and he and Dam went to the temple. Vitchae was praying in front of the statue of the smiling Buddha when the young warrior and his familiar companion approached. He turned to face the boys.

"Master," said Jinn, "my young brother would like to take the 'Trial of the Warrior.' He is well versed in the trial and his service to our order would be invaluable."

The old monk looked at them, suddenly realising that he'd made a big mistake. Vitchae asked Jinn to leave the temple.

He beckoned Dam to sit. They sat crossed legged on the floor, while Vitchae explained that a Tinju monk had to be chosen. It was a birthright handed down through millennia from the time of the first Tinju monks, so it could not be changed. The old master became sullen as he gave other shocking news to the young villager. Dam listened, his head thudded, all emotion gone and the words that came out of Vitchae's mouth were just a garbled incoherent blur. He no longer paid any attention and was deep in his own thoughts, his own world, and his own depression. Vitchae never mentioned the sacred relic, and hoped that Jinn would not have told Dam about this. He was wrong.

Vitchae concluded by saying,

"I am sorry young Dam, but we will always be here for you."

Dam felt stunned. He got to his feet, wai-ed the old Prime Master and walked outside.

"Dam, Dam!" called out Jinn, but he was ignored by the young villager, who strode purposefully home.

Over the next few days, Dam was not seen around the temple area, or the village. Vitchae blamed himself for letting the relationship between Dam and Jinn go on for so long. He realised that he may have caused irreparable damage to the youngster, who should have been learning a village trade like his parents. Dam stayed in his room for two days, emerging on the third with his small homemade bow.

Banti, his mother, concerned about him, asked,

"Are you okay, my son?"

To which Dam replied,

"I am fine, mother, I'm going into the jungle to hunt. I will be back later."

He kissed his mother on the forehead. She never saw her son again.

Dam stayed in the jungle, just walking, hunting and sleeping, but mainly thinking. He knew that nobody had ever left the village before, and he thought that he would return once his head cleared. Feeling bewildered and confused, and unaware where he was, he didn't realise that he had entered into Cambodia and unfamiliar terrain. Eventually, he came upon a road, which confused him. He had never seen a road before, let alone the strange monster now heading toward him. He crouched back into the jungle as the monster roared passed him and then it came to a stop. An old man got out of the car and went over to where the now petrified Dam cowered. The man spoke to Dam in Cambodian, a language that he was familiar with. He had learned this with Jinn, along with Thai and their usual dialect, ancient Siamese. The old man took Dam over to his car.

"Where are you going? Are you okay? What are you doing way out here alone?"

Dam tried to answer the old man's questions, but he wasn't sure exactly where he was heading. The old man offered him shelter at his home in Phnom Penh, and Dam gratefully accepted. They drove north-east toward the capital, an eight-hour journey.

The old man and his wife took care of Dam for almost a year and he soon adjusted to life in Phnom Penh. Although he missed Jinn, his parents and his old lifestyle, he knew he would not return. His confusion now turned to anger, directed at the arrogant Tinju. Dam was a skilled artisan, but his real strength lay in his fighting abilities.

He had entered and won many illegal bare-fist street fights. These brutal contests often resulted in the death of a fighter, but Dam was good; he was Tinju trained and although he was small, his speed and strength overwhelmed his opponents. The fighters did not get paid much: only about five dollars per fight. However, a lot of money made from gambling at these fixtures. Dam earned a fearsome reputation, with his fights always well attended. He was a dynamic and ruthless fighter. It was at one of these fights that he gained the attention of Andrew Towhey, a well-known arms dealer from Ireland, now living in Cambodia.

Towhey watched Dam fight on several occasions and wanted this kid as his property; he knew that he could make a lot of money from the young warrior. Towhey went with Dam to see the old man who took care of him, gave him $100, reassured the old man that he would take care of Dam and moved him into his bungalow in Caw Kong.

The relationship between Towhey and Dam became like that of a father and son. Towhey was in his early fifties and he had no family. His only companion was a weasely looking Spaniard named Miguel.

Towhey was an arms dealer, who bought purloined weapons and ammunition from Cambodia and Vietnam, selling them on to Arab or Middle Eastern buyers, making a tidy profit. He was on the run from both Spain and Ireland. He'd made a fortune in his home country by selling his father's herd of cattle many times over to gullible, but rich, Irish farmers. Leaving his family to face the music, he fled to Spain, £2,000,000 richer. He developed property in Marbella, a tourist resort in Spain, where he ripping people off on property deals. His favourite trick was to getting Miguel to sell an apartment. After the unsuspecting customers parted with their hard-earned cash, Towhey would pop-up and say they owned nothing, as the apartment belonged to him and not Miguel.

He left Spain in the late eighties, due to the developing relations between the European communities. Moreover, the fact the IRA had nothing better to do, as they were no longer killing the British, they put Towhey on their shit list. Therefore, with a few £'s of the farmer's money as a reward, they decided to hunt Towhey, who fled and made his way to Thailand, accompanied by Miguel, where he set up an export business for arms and ammunition.

He stayed in Thailand for five years, until police got wind of his operation and their bribes became a constant annoyance to Towhey. Towhey and Miguel therefore left Thailand and settled in Cambodia, at the place they used to visit in order to satisfy his other great passion; Towhey was a paedophile. He loved young boys and girls; the younger the better. He loved to savagely pillage their innocence and it gave him a rush to hear their orifices pop under his large frame. The more they screamed, the more exited he became. He settled in Caw Kong, which was only a kilometre away from the notorious K11, which was a small community located 11 kilometres outside of Phnom Penh. It was a paedophile paradise, no questions asked. Kip, the unofficial headman of K11, knew Towhey and took care of him exceedingly well. Kip would phone Towhey when a new, young, lost waif would wander into the village. He would go to Towhey's house with the frightened youngster in tow, let in by Miguel, and be given some money, usually $10.

"Tell Mr. Andrew Kip is his good friend and will take good care of him," Kip always said.

The door would be closed, and while Kip waited outside, the young boy or girl was taken to a large room, where the bloated mass of blubber called Andrew Towhey waited on his bed. The bedroom door closed behind the frightened youngster and, after usually 30 minutes of squealing and grunting from the room, the tearful youngster would emerge. Their blood stained clothing was replaced with a sarong. They would be then be pushed out of the door where Kip would be waiting, lifted onto the back of his motorbike and driven away in tears.

Dam lived with Towhey for several years, but out- lived his usefulness. Nobody would fight him. He was too good, so no fights meant no gambling, therefore no money.

Towhey arranged for two Cambodians to kill Dam. They were local hoodlums who bragged they were assassins. One night after Dam dispatched another opponent who, although he knew of Dams reputation, fought him out of desperation for money. Meanwhile, the two would-be assassins waited outside the arena for Dam, who usually ran home. They ambushed him, brandishing pistols and daggers.

Dam sent them to the afterlife with lightning speed and ran home. Towhey and Miguel were both shocked to see Dam walk through the door. Dam had been a little surprised at them not coming to his fight. Towhey enquired what happened, as he had blood on him. Both Towhey and Miguel spoke Cambodian, although not fluently. Dam relayed the story, announcing the blood was not his. He told Towhey the previously untold story about his life in Salaburi, his training and the holy box. Dam suddenly became useful again.

****

216

Dam felt the pick-up slowing down as they approached Phnom Penh and the sights became familiar as night closed in. 'Good,' he thought, 'less conspicuous.' He needed to find himself some normal clothes. The pick-up driver agreed to take him to Phnom Penh centre and to one of his old fight stadiums where he kept some clothes. Although now he didn't fight on a regular basis, he still kept his hand in from time to time and trained fighters in return for some, usually half, of their small purse if they won. He would give them another beating if they lost.

The pick-up stopped outside a large wooden warehouse. Dam jumped off the back of the truck, thanked the driver, blessed him, and chuckled to himself for blessing someone. Dam went into the boxing arena and walked over to his locker space. His tracksuit was gone, so he took a pair of jeans and T-shirt that were lying around and went outside. It was hot and sticky; he hailed a mototaxi. The small motorbike headed off along the potholed Cambodian Road toward Caw Kong.

Towhey was overjoyed to see him. He knew what his pet assassin had for him, or hopefully had, which was a cool million dollars worth of history.

Miguel let Dam in and paid the taxi. Towhey sat behind a large teak desk. "Have you got it...have you got it?" asked an impatient Towhey.

"Yes, my friend," announced Dam, who put down his bundle of robes and reached into one of the tunic's pockets. He produced the small, golden, jewel- encrusted box and placed it down in front of Towhey.

"Excellent, excellent!" exclaimed Towhey as he leant over and picked up a digital camera. He took several photographs of the relic, then opened a large safe at the side of his desk, and placed the relic on top of several wads of dollars. He closed the safe and locked it with a key, which he then placed onto a chain around his neck.

"Okay," he said to Dam and Miguel. "It looks like you two will be going on a holiday. I will e-mail the photo off to our good friend Mohammed," he said with a sarcastic glint in his eye. "He will be waiting for this."

"Dam, go freshen up, we will go celebrate."

"Okay, Andrew." said Dam.

Dam knew that Towhey's celebration meant that he would be going to K11 to bring back a child and, while Towhey would be satisfying his sick lust, he and Miguel would be waiting and listening. He decided that once he got back from K11, he would slip away on his motorbike to, The Heart of Darkness, a large nightclub in Phnom Penh. He had money in his pocket, so if Fitta was there, he would give her a night she wouldn't forget in a hurry. He went in his room and unfolded his bundle. He hung up his homemade robe, washed the dried blood and spinal fluid off his pitou, and replaced it on its stand. He took out his folded S-16 respirator, having already dumped the filter in the jungle a long way from the village, and he put it in a drawer. Dam took his homemade metal glave from a shelf and sprung open the blades, knowing that he would need it for the next part of Towhey's plan. While sharpening the glave, he looked down at the table that had several sheets of a brown cardboard material placed on it, along with several containers that contained various coloured powders and jars containing syrupy solutions.

"You taught me too well, my brother," he said aloud, as if talking straight to heaven and Jinn. "Too well."

Remorse again crept in as he recalled seeing his brother Jinn, dying in a cloud of swirling smoke.

****

Getting to the village unnoticed had been relatively easy. Dam entered the jungle where the old man had picked him up several years earlier.

218

Although becoming disorientated several times, he kept heading in the direction of the mountains until he came across the familiar jungle surrounding the village.

He had spent weeks, preparing, planning and making cyanide flares, similar to what Jinn taught him.

He recalled how one day Jinn, now a new warrior, had said to him, "Look at this my brother."

He produced a hard brown candle shaped object.

"What is it, an essence stick?" asked the inquisitive Dam.

"Not exactly, something far deadlier," said Jinn. "I will teach you how to make one."

Jinn and Dam headed off into the mountains to a small cave they'd found. Jinn removed the contents of his tunic pocket and laid them on a flat rock at the mouth of the cave. It was early afternoon, so the hottest part of the day and when the monks took leisure time, or meditated. Jinn laid out two small round clay containers, a Sceet root, Aroona roots and several small, rolled, conical-shaped objects. Jinn unrolled the cigar-shaped objects into sheets, which were yellow-brown sandalwood, resembling oily marzipan.

Jinn explained that the contents of the jars were crushed graphite and sulphur. He poured this powder in the centre of the sheet and squeezed the mixed roots syrupy juices over the powder. He then tightly rolled the sheet, like a hand-rolled cigarette and put it in the sun to bake dry. Jinn sat down with Dam and told him that it was a 'Pai-non' sleeping stick. However, he did not fully understand their use.

"I just know," said Jinn with a menacing grin, "they're deadly."

Although when Jinn found out exactly what the sticks were used for, he never mentioned it to Dam again. However, there was no need, as Dam later figured it out and improved on the stick, with the addition of graphite and cyanide crystals designed for instant death.

Dam recalled making his way to the village; he knew what time the relic would be removed. He hid in his and Jinn's secret cave until nearer the time. Dam silently crept around the rocks to the mouth of the gated cave and waited behind an outcrop of rocks. He saw Somchay, the Prime Master, come from the meditation room, and approaching the guards, who bowed their heads on his arrival. He went to the golden gates, opened them, and went inside. One guard went inside with Somchay, while the other stood and watched. Like a leaping panther, Dam launched himself at the remaining monk. He put his hand over his mouth and inserted his pitou into the base of the guard's skull, engaging the catch. It was over in a fraction of a second. He then hid the body. He knew the Prime Master would be chanting within the cave, so had plenty of time. He removed the dead monk's bow and placed it on his shoulder. He put on his S16, pulling the robe's hood over his masked face. Having rehearsed this many times, his only worry was that his size would be noticed. The Prime Master and the other guard came to the mouth of the cave and walked past the hooded Dam, who joined on at the rear. They entered the temple and started the ceremony. Dam went unnoticed, easily replacing the harmless aromatic incense sticks.

****

Dam wallowed in his success.

'That was easy,' thought Dam, all respect for his old idols was gone. He was better than the Tinju, easily killing them all. He thought the only ones left were either too old or too young, so he knew the Tinju were finished.

He sniffed the air and said aloud, "Ah, smells good, the sweet smell of success."

220

His gloating was short lived, as a bellowing Towhey interrupted his thoughts.

"Dam, Miguel, come here!"

Miguel and Dam went into the living room. Towhey had a beaming smile on his face.

"Good news?" asked Miguel.

"Perfect," said Towhey. "I e-mailed the photos off to the Sheikh, who got back to me straight away. He sounded extremely keen to get the relic, and send out his aide, Abdul Rasid, to Thailand. He will e-mail with the details later, but he will be arriving in four days. I want you two there in plenty of time to meet him, so that will give you time for your hair to grow back, Dam."

Towhey and Miguel both laughed. Dam felt the stubble starting to grow back on his head and joined in the laughter.

"Come on," said Towhey. "Let's celebrate...Pop along to K11, Dam, and see what Kip has available. There's a good lad."

— Chapter Six —

The village of Salaburi now seemed like a ghost town with the villagers remaining in their wooden stilted houses, while the monks stayed in their living quarters or meditation room.

Pon had left the previous evening and, with him, not only went the hopes and honour of the Tinju, but the soul of the village. Even the jungle, usually full of the noise of birds and insects, was silent. It felt like the world was standing still.

The soldiers sat in the monks' training area. After making a rough Mah-jong set, they tried to occupy themselves. The batteries on their GPS tracker systems had gone flat, but with no electricity in the village, there seemed no way to get life back into their only contact with the outside world.

Vitchae sat alone pondering in his dark world the events of the past few days and his time as Prime Master. He thought that he should have handled the situation with Dam a lot better. He remembered thinking at the time that he may have been a little sharp with the lad, but he was worried about his failing eyesight. 'This must be Lord Buddha's will,' he thought. ' Maybe young Dam was right all those years ago. Why can't they earn a place in the scheme of things? After all, Lord Buddha never created the Tinju: men did.'

Trees shaking and swaying, and, clouds of dust thrown up in large whirlwinds of rotor wash abruptly broke the silence. A Sikorsky S92, helicopter roared over the treetops and came in low. It flared into a hover above the grounds behind the Wat. The soldiers cowered as the pieces of their game flew away. The pilot lowered the collective and, with a deafening roar, the helicopter gently touched down. The pilot cut the engines and the noise diminished slightly as the giant rotor blades came to a slow idle and then stopped.

The soldiers got to their feet, straightened their combat fatigues, and rushed over to the helicopter. All the commotion brought the villagers scurrying out of their dwellings and they walked toward the shiny white and gold monster from the sky. Most villagers had never seen a car, let alone a helicopter, as they never left the village. Only the remaining elder monks had seen any form of motor transport and that was whilst making the journey to Bangkok, but aircraft they had never seen.

Cenat assisted Vitchae and they and the other monks headed toward the helicopter, weapons in hand. The Sikorsky S92 was a large helicopter used by the Thai air force to transport small numbers of troops and supplies. This particular helicopter was certainly not regular; it shone white and was adorned in gold leaf and the Thai royal standard, skillfully crafted and in a high-glazed wax, making it sparkle like a new pin in the sunlight. The side door slid opened and six armed soldiers jumped onto the field, taking up a defensive stance around the helicopter. Six elder monks behind Vitchae and Cenat raised their bows. Vitchae and Cenat stopped about 50 metres away.

"Wait!" Cenat called out to the monks.

The five village soldiers came around the helicopter. The Master Sergeant ordered his men to form into a rank. An officer exited the helicopter and barked an order to the Master Sergeant, who saluted and gave an order to his men. The soldiers formed two lines on either side of the sliding doors, facing outwards. A few moments later, a figure emerged from the helicopter. He wore a smart white, crisply pressed uniform, with gold braiding and a thick golden sash with red tassels. His epaulets showed no rank, but had large pointed helmet crests on them. He looked over at the Cenat and Vitchae, who started to walk over. They met about ten metres from the helicopter. The figure gave a long respectful Wai to the two elder monks.

"Good afternoon Khun Cenat."

"Good afternoon Khun Taksin," replied Cenat.

224

Cenat introduced Vitchae to Taksin, who could see that the old monk was blind.

"I have someone I would like you to meet," said Taksin and looked over at the helicopter. Two more soldiers emerged, dressed in traditional Thai guard uniforms, with elegantly carved golden helmets that tapered off to a point.

They removed a small stepladder and placed it at the foot of the helicopter. A figure emerged, wearing a royal blue suit and wire rimmed spectacles.

A gasp went around the gathered villagers and they all knelt down with heads bowed, as did the monks and Taksin. This figure they all knew; in every Thai home hung a picture of the beloved King Bhumipol.

The seventy-eight-year old king walked over to the two monks and Taksin, who stood up and wai-ed. He spoke to them for a few minutes and then the four headed into the Wat, leaving the remaining monks and villagers awestruck.

The party remained in the Wat for several hours in deep discussion, only being disturbed by young monks taking in fresh fruit and water. The villagers remained in-situ, hoping for another glimpse of their beloved king. They discussed the atrocity that had happened. The King laid out his thoughts and plans and asked Vitchae and Cenat to accompany him to Bangkok to talk more, and to formulate a mutually beneficial plan. Although fearful of getting into the sky monster, they accepted.

They emerged from the Wat and headed toward the helicopter. Vitchae vomited as he got to the door of the beast and was given a drink of cool water. The King, Taksin, and the monks boarded the helicopter, followed by the soldiers, including the five from the village, much to their relief.

225

The pilot engaged the engines and turbines; the helicopter growled to life. Taksin explained to Cenat that his investigations had uncovered very little. He said that his friend had called him the previous night, and had thought he had seen a Thai monk in a boxing stadium in Phnom Penh. He did not know if it was relevant. However, he'd already relayed this information to someone named Pon.

"He said he was Tinju, so I presumed that he was one of yours," said Taksin.

Cenat, looking shocked, asked,

"Pon?

"Yes," said Taksin. "He called me during the early hours from a mobile phone and I never give out my number. Only a few people have it, with you being one of them, Khun Cenat. Although I wasn't sure that he understood. It was difficult to hear him. I think he was talking through the earpiece."

The large helicopter's rotors threw up swirling clouds of dust and debris, sending the villagers into a panic, and drowning out the conversation between Taksin and Cenat. The pilot set the throttles and watched his instruments. With the dial indicators in position, he looked around for any obstacles or debris that might get sucked into the intake. Seeing it was clear, he gently raised the collective and the large aircraft rose off the ground. The pilot aimed the helicopter at a clump of trees in the jungle and pushed the cyclic stick forward. The nose of the helicopter dipped, and moved forward, gaining height and clearing the jungle canopy, it disappeared from view.

— Chapter Seven —

Nick had a restless night. He had bought back the woman who he was drooling over at the bar in front of Champion a-go-go. After drunkenly arguing with the mamasan, he left alone, without paying the bar fine. He accompanied Spock and Lek and, as the three walked down the street, Von caught them up.

"Mai pen rai, no problem," she said. "Bar closed now; I go with you, no bar fine."

Nick slurred. "Good"

The four got on a mototaxi, went to the hotel and up to their rooms. Nick's interest in Von quickly waned. She was fairly old and unattractive, so he did not want to pay her for sex, 'a waste of money,' he thought, so gave her 20 Baht for a taxi and told her to leave. She mumbled something in Thai, stormed out and slammed the door. He showered, the cold water felt good on his now re-stinging sphincter. He felt between his butt cheeks; with the hairs scorched off, he could feel blisters starting to form. 'This'll sting,' he thought. He was right, and he spent the night tossing and turning in bed, at times administering ice to this rather sore area. Nick eventually nodded off around daybreak. A loud hammering thump on the door woke him up.

"Are you awake matey? It's five o'clock."

"Yeah Spock," he said, "come in."

A cheery Spock entered his room.

"That's a bit dangerous leaving your door unlocked," said a concerned Spock.

"No," said Nick "it's okay,"

Nick thought for a moment about his door and the damage Spock's thumping could do.

"Don't knock next time, just tap and walk in," said Nick

They talked about the events from the previous night, which Spock found difficult to believe or fully take it in. Spock told Nick that Stu was in his room, but didn't know who with. He explained, he'd woken Stu well over an hour ago, and just spoken to him again through the door, but he said that he was in the middle of doing something and mentioned that he was on the 'vinegar stroke' so told him to go away.

Spock asked about Von. Nick told him that he paid her and sent her away, although not mentioning he had only paid her 20-Baht. Nick enquired about Lek, and Spock explained that she started work in the bar at 6pm and wanted to shower and change.

"I told her I would see her later," said Spock,

"And will you?" Nick asked.

"Unlikely. She was a sturdy old shag, but a bit of a horror."

Nick laughed and said,

"You're learning, mate. There are plenty more. Now sod off while I get dressed. I'll meet you in reception."

At six o'clock, they all met up in the hotel reception, Nick, Spock and Stu, who was the last to arrive, arm in arm with Dao. The other two looked at them. Spock had seen Dao in the happy world bar, but hadn't paid much attention to her. 'So that's where the little bugger disappeared to and why he acted so strange, The daft twat has fallen in love,' thought Spock. He looked at his happy friend.

228

"What happened?' Asked Spock.

Stu explained he had no idea. He gave details about how he remembered leaving the Happy World Bar, but couldn't get Dao out of his mind. He vaguely remembered the go-go, and the next thing he remembered was when he woke up next to Dao. Then, after he came around a bit, they showered together, and made mad passionate love. Dao spoke a little English, but the words she would use to describe what they did, was not mad passionate love, but 'boom boom.'

Stu wanted to keep Dao, but was unsure how. He asked Nick, who explained he must pay a bar fine of 200 Baht for every night he took her away from the bar. Stu thought this a little seedy, as this was love and not just a fling, but gave Dao 200 Baht to go pay the bar. She wanted to go change and shower again in her room. Nick told Stu they would see her at her bar later.

"She can't go anywhere with anyone else because the bar has been paid...she's been reserved."

Stu kissed Dao and told her that he would see her later.

The lads headed into the hot sticky night air. It was 6:30 pm, and starting to get dark. They stopped at a clothes shop and Stu and Spock bought some vests and shorts. Spock bought some thick camel shorts, which both Stu and Nick thought he would be too hot wearing. They ate at an outdoor restaurant, ordering a full English breakfast. Although late, it was their first meal of the day and the first real food since they ate on the plane the previous day, apart from the street barbecue, which Stu thought had given him rather loose stools...The shits.

Now fed, they changed into their new clothes back at the hotel and decided to go explore this magical place some more before they met up with Dao at the Happy World Bar. Stu already missed Dao; it had been almost two hours since he last saw her. They made their way to Soi 2, a lively Soi situated at the top end of North Pattaya. There were about 50 bars in a covered area, many with live music. The lads settled in one bar, where a band consisting of three Thais blasted out a not too bad version of 'I shot the sheriff.' They ordered Singha beer and settled in. Disliking the taste of beer, having sunk copious amounts the previous night, they had to force it down.

They moved around Soi 2 for a few hours, now juiced, they groped the happy bar girls en-masse behind and in front of the many bars. Every time Stu or Spock took out a pair of breasts from a giggling girl's bra, they would buy them a drink. Nick, they noticed, kept his hands well away from his wallet.

Having a great time, they soon crept toward spannered. They came across a quiet bar and, although it had many girls, it was not as noisy as the others. They sat down and Stu could see Spock with his 'time for the trick' face on. 'That's why he bought thick cotton shorts,' thought Stu.

Sure enough, true to form, Spock made his way off his stool and positioned himself on one of the small chairs around the bar. The people at the bar fell silent and watched as Spock got into his position, legs up, lighter ready. He felt his methane supply bubbling, and gave one good push. He furrowed his brow for extra push power.

A look of relief, followed by horror, came across Spock's large face. He put his legs down, put the lighter back on the table and nonchalantly picked up his drink. There was no flames, no entertainment, nothing.

Everyone looked puzzled and went back to their conversation and drinks. Spock looked bemused and shocked. Stu got off his stool and went over to his large friend.

"What happened mate... And what's that awful smell?"

Then Stu realised what had happened.

Nick then leaned back on his stool and said,

"Lads, shall we start drinking shorts? I am fed up with beer."

"Yes, mate, order me a vodka and coke," said Stu, and trying to keep a straight face, continued,

"And you better order Spock a size XXL. It smells like he has pooped in his."

Stu then fell about laughing. Spock felt embarrassed. He looked at his old friend in tears of laughter and said,

"Yes matey, very funny, now get up, and go buy me some new ones."

'Never trust a fart in Thailand'

Spock changed into his new shorts and cleaned up in the toilets. 'Best five Baht ever spent,' he thought. The cost for using some public conveniences.

While they waited for Spock, Stu noticed a hotel, with a large sign that read: 'Sabaiiland body massage.' It was on the corner of Soi 2, which made it look a little out of place.

"What's that?" He asked Nick.

With a smirk, Nick informed him that it was a 'soapy massage' and they could go tomorrow.

They reached the Happy World Bar. The girls whooped at them,

"Welcome Nick, welcome Spock." They looked at Stu and laughed. "Hello Stu."

Dao was sitting behind the bar, reading her book. She saw Stu, took their drinks over and sat down.

"What happened last night?" Stu asked.

"You don't remember?" asked Dao, smiling.

"No," said Stu.

"Better you don't remember, stupid man," she said.

Dao was 22 years old and, like most *bar girls in Pattaya, had been lured there with the dreams of finding a farang, foreigner, to take care of her and her family. Many 'bar girls' were country girls, usually from the Isaan region, a poor area in the north east of Thailand. Most have children. Dao, being no exception, had a son.

Stu was Dao's second farang experience. Her first was an old German man. Mamasan told her,

"The older they are, the better. Can't get it up. They only want company and usually fall asleep. A real catch."

Dao, having been at the bar now for two weeks, had seen the foreign men come and go, and she was no longer afraid of the large foreign invaders. She decided it would be okay to go with Kurt. Dao got her bag and went around to the other side of the bar. Kurt bought her drink after drink, which was good for the bar because she only drank orange juice. Kurt paid 120 Baht a glass, of which Dao got a cut of a 'lady drink,' usually 20 Baht.

Kurt was 75-years-old; older than her granddad. By the time they left the bar, Kurt was well wankered. They got back to the room and, as mamasan told her, he went off into a loud snoring slumber. The old man awoke in the morning, gave Dao 1000 Baht, which would have been two weeks' salary in her village picking rice. She showered and left. 'Easy money,' she thought, and never saw Kurt again.

Her second experience was now with Stu.

The previous night, he had left the bar with his friends, but returned later and made a terrible noise that Charlie said was a foreign song. Stu, with a rose in his mouth, went behind the bar, grabbed a bemused Dao, and asked Charlie to play a record that had been playing earlier, 'Wonderful Tonight.' Stu twirled and serenaded Dao for 10 minutes, before collapsing into a chair and, like a fat novelty Buddha statue, fell asleep. Charlie's wife asked Dao if she liked Stu. She looked at the heap in the chair.

"Yes," she said, "he makes me laugh."

"Well take him home and take care of him," ordered the mamasan.

They found the card from the Sawasdee hotel in Stu's shirt pocket, so bundled him into a baht bus and Dao took him to his room. She put him in the shower and turned the water cold, at which point he shook himself, looked at Dao naked in the shower along with him, pointed at her and slurred,

"You're lovely." A stupid drunken grin then came over his face. Getting out of the shower, he flopped onto his bed and promptly fell asleep, drooling.

The next day they awoke, Dao expected to be paid and sent back to the bar; she didn't think anyone found her attractive. Many Thai women think this as they see models on TV wearing makeup and on catwalks or in movies. They believe all foreign women are beautiful, and Thai women humbly think they are ugly. Dao was surprised when Stu told her he wanted to keep her, although wasn't sure how, but he would find out. This made her feel happy. Dao quite liked this funny little man. She enjoyed her first real snog and sex was no different to that with a Thai man, it just took longer.

Now in the Happy World Bar, Stu decided to go home early, after he and Dao finished their drinks. Spock and Nick decided to head off to a go-go in Soi 7 to search for the lucky woman who was going to get a damn good rattling that night. Spock knew what kind he wanted for that evening and she would have to be sturdy; he was in the mood. Stu asked Nick if they were going to see that place 'Sabaiiland' tomorrow. Nick said a very elated, "Oh yes," but was shocked when Stu asked if Dao could come, whereupon he gave a firm, "Oh no!"

A knock on the door by Stu, wanting to know if he was going for breakfast, woke Spock the next morning. Spock said that he would meet him downstairs. Spock, having a strange taste in his mouth, moved his tongue around and felt something odd. He pulled out a small, thin, serrated leg.

"How did that get there?" He said, remembering that once again he had been wankered. Lek turned over and saw Spock inspecting the leg. She rolled over, taking a bag from under the bed and gave Spock a half-eaten bag of fried locusts.

Nick had another sleepless night. After losing Spock in Soi 7, he'd returned alone. 'Never mind.' he thought, 'Luanne will be here later and maybe my arse will have stopped hurting.'

Luanne was between boyfriends. One had just gone back and another was due out in a few days. Nick had known Luanne for several months and been with her a few times. He called her on the off chance that she was free and she'd arranged to come later and spend a day and night with him. Luanne liked Nick, but he never paid as much as her other men, so he was a stopgap every now and again. This arrangement suited them both.

They all met in the reception at around noon. Stu and Dao had already eaten. Stu mentioned that Dao wanted to go to her room as her friend had returned from her home village and she wanted to see her, which would give the lads a chance to go to Sabaiiland.

Dao's friend, Moo, had not been home; she had been with her 'boyfriend.' Moo came to work in the bar with Dao, and took to bar work like a duck to water. Whereas Dao had been timid and shy around the men, Moo was outgoing, spoke, and flirted in broken

234

English with everyone. She was taken her first night and every night since. Her latest conquest, an English man, had taken her for a week and took her to stay in Jomtien, a beach resort about 10km from Pattaya, which was much less raucous. The English man left during the early hours of the morning to fly home, so Moo would be back in the room she shared with Dao.

Dao wanted to see her friend and tell her about Stu, and also see what trophies and gifts Moo acquired this time, gold, and mobile phones being the preferred items.

Although Moo was not beautiful like Dao, she was cute and outgoing, and men loved this.

Lek and Dao left the hotel together mid afternoon, so the lads headed to Sabaiiland. They went into the swish hotel. Stu and Spock were looking forward to a massage, as both of them had aching backs from too much shagging.

The reception area of Sabaiiland was huge, with a bar on one side, tables set out around the floor area, and a large flat window on the other side. Behind this window sat very elegantly dressed Thai women, about twenty in all. It looked like a giant fish tank. The lads sat down and ordered a coffee. All the women wore small badges with numbers written on them, and Nick smirked.

"These are the err...masseuses," he said.

A smartly dressed Thai man came over to their table.

"Which one would you like, sir?"

"Hang on, matey," said Spock, "we're just looking."

The man backed away.

235

The lads spent several more minutes observing the women. Spock noticed a large woman sat on the back row. 'She'll do,' he thought, 'she would be able to give me a good sorting out.' He called the Thai man back over.

"Give me number 34."

The Thai explained the price was 1800 Baht for 90 minutes. The man went to the fish tank and called out number 34 and number 26 for Stu. Nick said he would go later, which didn't surprise Stu or Spock as they realised that Nick was even thriftier than Stu.

The pair were then taken to very smart rooms, with Spock's room being next door to Stu's. Spock noticed a large bed and an even larger round bath. He couldn't see a massage table, but noticed that there was a large inflatable bed propped up near the bath. The woman went over to the bath and turned on the taps. She went over to the confused Spock and motioned for him to remove his clothes, handing him a towel. When the bath was full, she told Spock to get in. She then undressed and got in, facing the big lad. Taking soap from the liquid container at the side of the bath, she gently caressed the foam sensually over Spock's body from head to toe.

"Marvellous," he said blissfully, and after she bathed him, the woman stood up. Spock looked at her Amazonian figure, never imagining that Thais came in XXL sizes too. The woman put the airbed on the floor and motioned Spock to lie on it. He did as instructed, and the woman opened the top of a large plastic bottle, squeezing its oily contents onto Spock, and herself. She then lay down on top of Spock, rubbing her body along and up and down Spock's back. Several minutes later, she rolled Spock over and noticed that she had done a pleasurable job as a large proboscis stood firmly to attention. She repeated the process on his front and listened to Spock cooing. 'He was happy,' she thought. After a few minutes of this performance, she pulled a weak-kneed Spock to his feet, flopped him onto the bed, placed a condom on his erect member and proceeded to give him the most sensual blow job he'd ever had. A few moments later, after doing her job too well,

236

she replaced the condom and attempted to bring life back into his flaccid tool.

It didn't take her long. She mounted Spock, gyrating and thrusting herself rapidly up and down. Spock soon deposited his second spoonful of 'man fat.' She then took him back to the bath and bathed him again. They went back over to the bed and turned on the wall-mounted TV, She patted the space next to her and Spock lay down beside her. Forty-five minutes passed and not a word was spoken between them, mainly because it was a boring routine for her and Spock was too gobsmacked and blissful to speak. They lay down and watched an in-house porn movie, and in a soft voice she whispered, "If you want to go again, it'll cost you more money."

The phone in the room buzzed to signal 90 minutes. The woman and Spock both got dressed and made their way back to the reception, where Nick and a smiling Stu waited. Stu had finished about two minutes earlier, and he giggled and cooed like a schoolboy. Spock sat down and looked at Nick.

"Did you enjoy your first soapy?" Nick asked with a smirk.

"Yep," said Spock, "but my back is still sore."

They made their way back to the Sawasdee hotel, and popped into a few bars on the way for an afternoon libation. They arrived back at the hotel early evening and felt squeaky-clean.

Luanne had arrived at the hotel earlier and had been waiting for Nick. He introduced her to Stu and Spock, and told them he would meet up with them later in the Happy World Bar. He and Luanne headed up to his room. Nick was like a dog that just sensed a bitch on heat.

Stu and Spock sprayed themselves with mosquito repellent, and headed to the Happy World bar. On their arrival, they saw Dao sitting behind the bar playing Connect-Four with her friend, Moo, and two men sat opposite them. Stu and Spock sat down at a table. A bit of jealousy crept up in Stu, but he felt relieved when Dao got up, went to the fridge and brought over two bottles of Singha beer. She kissed Stu and sat down next to him. The two men at the bar glared at Stu. Spock returned the stare and the two immediately returned to their game. Moo kept looking over at the giant sitting with Dao and Stu and smiled. Spock returned the smile and the woman cheekily stuck out her tongue, and smiled again.

Stu and Dao talked, while looking gooey-eyed at each other. Spock concluded a deal with a street seller for a fake Rolex 'Yacht Master' watch. He paid the man and showed his purchase to Stu, who looked, and agreed on it being a fine looking timepiece.

"It looks like the real McCoy," said Stu.

The two men who were at the bar exited, careful to avoid nudging Spock as they scuttled out. Moo came to the table, pecked Spock on the cheek, and sat next to him. Dao introduced Moo and Spock ordered her a drink. Moo took Spock's new watch from the table, looked at it, and then showed Dao. After speaking Thai to each other, Moo turned to Spock.

"You ting tong, stupid," she said and started counting, using her fingers to demonstrate 1-2-3-5 and holding up four fingers. She could see Spock seemed confused, so repeated, "1-2-3-5."

Spock thought, 'Bless her, she's trying,' and said,

"No, it's 1-2-3-4-5,"

Moo held the watch up in front of Spock, exasperated.

"Look!" She said.

Spock looked at the watch, looked at the numbers on the watch, and then realised 1-2-3-5-5.

"Little bastard has ripped me off."

It wasn't late when Stu and Dao, walked hand in hand, back to the hotel. Spock followed, with nobody by his side but a petite Moo hanging around his shoulders like a fox stole. 'I hope I don't break her,' thought Spock.

Spock thumped on the door to Nick's room, who had been absent all night. Spock knocked again and walked in. Nick and Luanne were in bed watching TV. Spock asked Nick if he was okay and told them about his watch. He left the room with Luanne moaning to Nick about locking his door.

Spock returned to his room. Moo was taking a shower. He bought whisky at the mini-mart on the way home and poured himself and Moo a glass.

'The bloody woman drinks like a fish,' he thought, remembering she'd kept up with him at the Happy World Bar. Moo finished showering and told Spock to take one, which he did, mainly to get cold water on his worn out todger.

He finished showering and got into bed, where a naked, smiling Moo was eagerly waiting. 'I will just give her a quickie,' he thought. He thought wrong. Spock finished after about two minutes, but Moo was having none of it. She wanted a climax, and that was that. With great strength for such a little woman, Moo shunted Spock into position after position, mounting him and widely thrashing and thrusting on his now sore and swollen tool until, after about twenty minutes, she came. She had broken Spock. He lay there for several moments, too worn out to move. Moo sat up, watched a movie, and drank whisky. Spock looked at Moo, 'She was cute' he thought, and Wow! What a great shag'

'What can we do now?' he thought, as it was still early. Spock noticed something about Moo that he wasn't keen on. He stroked his head. 'Hmmm getting a bit long,' His hair was about 2mm long, but he

239

usually liked to feel his scalp. 'I'll show the cheeky little monkey,' he thought.

The 'thunderbolt' had struck again.

Nick had a great night just relaxing with Luanne; she bought him flamazine cream and applied it to his now recovering burn. They talked, made love, and chilled out all night, and then they fell asleep holding each other. In the morning, Luanne got up and dressed. She had to get ready to meet a boyfriend, who was due in later that day.

Thai women became good organisers regarding the visits of boyfriends so they would not clash. Sometimes, however, it was unavoidable. The woman tended to take one away, usually the one who sent her the most money. Then, she will get her friends to tell the other man she has gone home for a few days, 'baby sick,' being the usual excuse. They usually got away with this, but occasionally lost the man to other bar girls. They never got concerned about this, as they could be replaced with ease. Moreover, this was an acceptable practice between bar girls, as it was, after all, a business.

You never lose your girl; you only lose your turn.

Nick felt sad at Luanne's departure. 'But at least she was free,' he thought. He got out of bed and went over to the small window next to his door. The corner rooms had a patio door that led out onto a balcony and a small window that was about the same size as a normal window in the UK. This window opened inwards and looked out onto the hotel entrance and small courtyard. Nick leaned out of the window and watched Luanne get on a Baht bus. Nick wished he earned more money. Although he did work in London, it was only for a few weeks at a time to earn money to come to Thailand, about six times a year. He subsidised his money by selling counterfeit goods, which he bought in Pattaya. The arrangement he had with Luanne was okay, but he would like a more permanent relationship. A loud rap on the door, followed by Spock bursting in with a big grin on his face, violently interrupted Nick's thoughts

"Morning, matey."

Stu, Dao, and Moo sat on the bed in Stu's room. Moo had been explaining about the previous night with Spock, sometimes speaking in Thai when she did not want Stu to know the details. She started speaking in her broken English, explaining they had just had sex. Spock got out of bed and produced a Remington rechargeable razor. He went to the bathroom and asked Moo to shave his head, even though she had trouble reaching around his massive frame. When she finished, he thanked her, removed the towel wrapped around her, and tugged at her pubic hair. Spock did not like this because it was a small but long tuft of hair, and he liked either a nice bush or nothing, so she was to have nothing and off came the tuft. Stu and Dao laughed, but Moo said she didn't like it because it itched.

Spock came in the room and joined the others and, after realising what they were laughing about, said,

"She won't be cheeky again or next time the hair on her head would fall victim to the Remington."

"Is Nick coming for breakfast?" Enquired Stu.

"I don't know, mate. I went to his room, and his door was unlocked, but he wasn't there. Perhaps he was seeing off Luanne." said Spock.

"Oh yeah, that's right, but he's stupid leaving his door unlocked," said Stu.

They laughed and joked more. Stu hadn't seen his old friend so happy and contented in many years and, as Spock and Moo went on, he felt like he was watching a comedy duo.

Dao went onto the balcony to hang out the towels, and noticed a commotion below.

"Come look!" she said.

241

The three joined her on the balcony and noticed people gathered around a white Toyota Hiace ambulance, with its back door open. A nurse was escorting a hobbling man to the vehicle. The man was supporting his arm gingerly. They reached the rear door of the ambulance. The man looked up at the balcony, giving Spock a contemptuous glare

"What's Nick doing down there?" Stu asked, bemused.

— Chapter Eight —

The brightly lit stadium was full to capacity with people shouting. Large amounts of money changed hands as Cambodians and Thais jumped up and down on small, tatty wooden benches to get a better view of their fighter. They cheered each time the man who they'd bet on scored a punch on his opponent. Two fighters stood in the centre of a makeshift ring lined with sand and splattered with blood. Their hands were covered with thin gauze that blood seeped through. Both their faces were swollen and bloody as they punched and kicked each other in a ferocious frenzy, each one trying to kill or maim the other. It was brutal, but the crowd loved every moment. One fighter landed an elbow on the side of his opponent's temple, which stunned the other fighter, allowing blow after blow to be thrown against the now defenceless man's head. He was finished him off with a viscous roundhouse kick. The crowd went wild, some cheered, some booed, while others yelled at their fighter to defend himself; this was futile. The man had been knocked unconscious by the kick. He dropped face first to the floor. His opponent raised his hand and chopped at the back of the fallen fighter's neck, ensuring he wouldn't get up. Victorious, he waved to the raucous crowd, who had now lost interest. Two men dressed in shabby jeans and t-shirts came and dragged the fallen fighter out of the ring to the back of the stadium. He would soon recover and live to fight another day; he was one of the lucky ones. Two more fighters made their way into the ring and stood to the side while the sand got raked over. The victor walked around the audience trying to get a tip from the crowd of people. 'Slim pickings tonight,' he thought.

The fighter went to the changing area, cursing and muttering under his breath, with the noise of the next fight ringing in his ears. He took a bowl of water from a large plastic drum and poured it over his head. The changing area was outside of the very basic stadium. A corrugated iron fenced area with a 60-watt bulb hanging over it. The fighters changed and warmed up there, punching, and kicking sand filled sacks hanging from makeshift beams, their clothes piled up in rows. There was usually no theft here because they had nothing worth stealing. However, four nights ago, one of the fighters had his clothes stolen. The fighter took another bowl of water and washed the dried blood from his mouth and nose. He spun around and came face to face with a man wearing jeans and a white T-shirt, his head shaven and a rucksack on his back.

"What do you want?" Snapped the fighter.

"I am looking for this man," replied Pon in Cambodian, showing him the charcoal drawing of Dam. "Do you know him?"

The fighter looked at the picture. He recognised a young Dam, whom he'd known for several years and fought many times, with Dam always coming off the victor.

"Yes," said the fighter and, not asking the reason behind Pon's search, asked, "How much money will you give me?"

****

Pon reached the meeting point in Pong-Nam-Rom in the early morning. He sat down, took the mobile phone from his bag, switched it on and it beeped into life. He dialed the number on the card given to him by Cenat.

A sleepy Taksin answered.

"Hello?"

"Hello... my name is Pon and I am..."

"Hello!" repeated Taksin.

Pon, realising that Taksin couldn't hear him, hung up, and tried again.

244

One of the stall owners went over to see what the noise was and noticed the monk holding the phone upside down. The stall owner took the phone, turned it the right way and Pon replied to the now agitated 'Hello's' from Taksin.

Taksin explained that he had a friend living in Phnom Penh who worked for the Thai consul and had seen a Thai monk near a boxing stadium several hours earlier. Taksin didn't know if the information was relevant, but he gave Pon the location and details. Pon thanked him and put the phone in his bag. The stall owner gave him food. He sat on a bench, looking again at the picture of Dam.

****

It had been a long hard trek for Pon to reach Phnom Penh. He walked from the food stall to the market directly in front of the border crossing, swapping his mobile phone for jeans, a t-shirt, and a rucksack from a bemused market trader. He put his robes and other items in his rucksack and tied his sword onto the back. He knew he could not cross the border without papers, so he walked around the back of the market to where a small stream meandered under a bridge at the border crossing. Wading through thick river foliage downstream for about six kilometres, he entered Cambodia and unfamiliar ground. Pon got out of the stream and walked a short way through a jungle He came across a road, which he decided to follow, hoping it would lead to Phnom Penh. Staying in the shade of the jungle to rest from the searing afternoon sun, he travelled during the early morning and night, when it felt cooler, resting in the afternoon and early evening.

During the hot afternoons, Pon stopped in shaded areas of jungle and the outcrops of rubber plantations. He ate the dried food and drank the liquefied King Cobra liver, mixed with oranges and mango for energy and to quench his thirst. He never slept much; his thoughts often returned to Salaburi, his brothers, his masters, and Dam. While resting in the afternoon, he carved a gold nugget from his bag. It was a half-finished image of a large winged serpent. His mind was empty of past events as he concentrated on his work. Pon had no money, as a

245

Salaburi resident had no need for money; they grew or killed everything they needed. The monks and villagers loved to whittle and carve intricate statues from the minerals they found in the many caves and potholes in the nearby mountains, and sometimes spent years on these small carvings. Pon brought along his ornaments, thinking they could be useful for trading. After seeing the reaction of the soldier to his mobile phone trade, he thought they might be worth something. He had brought along one finished golden nugget, two red stone, one blue stone carving, and the unfinished gold nugget, which he was now working on.

Pon arrived at the stadium after four days. He hoped that Dam was the monk Taksin's friend had seen, and that someone would know him. He watched a fight finish and followed the victor to the changing area. He felt elated when the fighter said that he knew Dam. Pon took his ornaments from his rucksack.

"I don't have any money," he said, "but I have these. You are welcome to one if you can tell me anything."

The fighter took the objects in his gauze-covered blood stained hands and stared at them. He noticed two were gold nuggets, so keeping the four-inch gold unfinished one, handed the others back to Pon.

Now feeling elated, he told Pon,

"His name is Dam. He lives with a man named Andrew Towhey, who has a large house in Caw Kong."

He then gave Pon directions to Caw Kong and Toohey's house. The fighter finished the conversation with a warning,

"Be careful of Towhey; he is a bad man, very dangerous."

Pon thanked the boxer and left the stadium, leaving the fighter examining his newfound wealth.

Pon got onto the road that the fighter told him would take him to Towhey's house. Feeling he was getting close to his target, he hoped that Dam still had the relic. He ran the 12 kilometres along the unlit, pot-holed road. His thoughts focused on revenge.

— Chapter Nine —

After getting off the phone with Mohammed, Towhey sat at his large teak desk. Dam and Miguel were on their way with the relic to meet Abdul for the exchange and get his million dollars. Towhey took a mouthful of his imported Bushmills Irish whiskey. He savoured the flavour of the smooth velvety amber fluid as it slipped down his throat.

The phone rang.

'What does that stupid Arab want now?' he thought and answered.

He assumed wrong.

"Hello, Mr. Andrew," said Kip.

Kip made small talk about his health, his business, etc. Towhey let him ramble, because he felt that nothing could upset him today. He stared at his racks and drank his whisky while Kip talked.

"What?" he asked, suddenly becoming interested in the conversation.

"Yes, Mr. Andrew, she only came today, eight-years-old, so she will squeal good for sure."

"Bring her straight over, Kip," an excited Towhey ordered.

"Yes, Mr. Andrew, straight away,"

Dam and Miguel were due to meet with Sheikh Mohammed Del Alaz's most trusted aid, Abdul Bhunto. The meeting was to take place in Pattaya, an area Towhey knew well. He hated Pattaya after losing a fortune while living there from having to pay off corrupt police, both

249

for protection of his dubious business dealings, and his sordid personal pleasures. He vowed to never return.

He had sent Dam and Miguel away that morning to give them plenty of time to set up the meeting point and give Miguel time to prepare for an extra little task. Miguel and Dam left early to make the eight-hour drive from Phnom Penh to the border at Poi Pet. They would get to the border that night and stay at one of the many hotels around the border town. Miguel would then walk across the border first thing the next morning. Dam, not having a passport, would go across on the back of a load cart.

Once across the border, Dam and Miguel would meet up in the market area, where a car that Towhey pre-arranged with one of his old acquaintances would be waiting. They would drive the four hours from Aranyaprathet to Pattaya, where they would have a two-day wait until Abdul arrived.

Towhey poured himself another glass of Bushmills and waited the arrival of Kip and his night's entertainment. He played with the safe key hanging around his neck and thought about his new friend Mohammed, who had just made him wealthier, therefore, more powerful. He was satisfied with how easy he had managed to con the stupid Sheikh.

****

Mohammed Del Alaz was rich, obscenely rich, one of the richest men in the world. Not a ruthless or evil man, he made his money from oil and, like other Sheikhs, enjoyed the trappings of the wealth his liquid gold provided. Mohammed lived with his family in Saudi Arabia, with servants taking care of his every whim. He was a collector, who loved collecting artefacts from other religions. Mohammed's twisted train of thought was that if he possessed some artefact from other gods or prophets, on his death Allah and the prophet Mohammed would welcome him into heaven with open arms.

250

This strange way of thought already cost him dearly. He had many significant artefacts from religious history. His prized possession was the Holy Grail of Christ. He paid $2,000,000, to his now good friend Julian Grimes for the Grail. Mohammed had advertised over the Internet, looking for artefacts, and although he'd had many replies, only two intrigued him enough to pursue, so sent his experts to check the authenticity of the claims.

After his team reported back about the man who claimed to know the whereabouts of Christ's holy grail, he had Professor Julian Grimes flown out to Saudi and present the Sheikh with the exact location of this long lost treasure, showing him an ancient text. Grimes laid out his evidence and convinced the Sheikh that he could obtain the Grail, for a price.

It was, of course, an elaborate hoax. Professor Julian Grimes, also known as Mr. John Crawford, claimed he lived in Cambridge, England, and was a tutor at Kings University. Crawford did live in Cambridge. He was an assistant curator at the university's museum, and a con-man. Grimes photocopied old books and maps and dubiously obtained a chunk from the stump of a column from the ruins in Glastonbury Abbey, which he knew was a building block from the late 10th Century.

Crawford then took his fake evidence to Saudi Arabia. While at Mohammed's palace, he convincingly told his story, showing unreadable and partially damaged papers. He explained that the missing chunks of the originals were the reason everybody searched in the wrong place. He went on to explain that the Knights Templar found the Grail during the 11th century and sealed it into a building block, the same way as the mythical Excalibur became sealed in a rock. The knights then built it into a pillar within Glastonbury Abbey over 900 years ago. Crawford said he knew, pointing to the evidence, the location within the guarded ruins of the Abbey, in the South West of England. Mohammed excitedly paid him a large deposit and gave him instructions to obtain the Grail.

On his return to England, Grimes asked one of the Cambridge art students to make him a wooden model based on what the student thought the Grail might look like. Grimes then employed a stonemason to cut a bung out of his ancient masonry. Placing the model in the hollow and sealing it in with concrete, the stonemason then scraped a minute hairline crack around the stone, away from the seal, making it appear as if the rock magically split in half.

Grimes then set off a small explosion at the ruins that everyone blamed on a Methane gas build up, and a vagrant being clumsy with his matches. Then he obtained a copy of the article from the local press, which he scanned and e-mailed to Mohammed. After providing the proof, he told Mohammed to transfer the remainder of the money to him so he could pay off his accomplices.

Several weeks later, Grimes arrived at the Sheikh's palace with a stone block, which, when x-rayed, revealed the Holy Grail. The stone was then carbon dated and its age revealed. Delighted that he possessed the Grail and convinced that he now owned the symbol that Christians had searched so long to find, Mohammed gave Grimes more money.

However, Grimes appeared terrified and claimed that a radical group of Zionists, who were the secret guardians of the Chalice, were now pursuing him. Grimes implored Mohammed never to mention him, or the Grail, The Sheikh bought his tale, not wanting to get his good friend Professor Grimes into any trouble, locked the Grail away in his private vault and gave his word never to divulge anything about it.

Grimes then told Mohammed that he also knew the whereabouts of some missing parchments from the *Gnostic gospels. Excited by this, Mohammed commissioned his new and trusted friend to find this artefact. "Spare no expense Julian," he said. "Money is no object."

Grimes explained that they had been buried somewhere in a desert and he was going to head there, straight away, to give his fugitive status time to cool, stating that he might be gone for some time.

Grimes went to the desert...Caesars Palace Casino, Las Vegas, in the Nevada dessert.

****

Mohammed, pleased with his Grail acquisition, then turned his attention to his next project. The dental remnants of Lord Buddha. His advisors spent several years collecting proof and documentation to support the fact that, indeed, such an artefact did exist. They presented the findings to Mohammed who dialled a number. The voice at the other end answered.

"Hello."

"Hello, could I speak to Mr. Towhey?" asked Mohammed

"Towhey speaking."

Mohammed introduced himself, and told him that he wanted the Buddha's relics. Towhey, taken aback, replied, "The price is still $1,000,000 dollars."

"Yes," said Mohammed. "No problem."

Mohammed's researchers obtained ancient drawings of the box, so he requested photographs proving that Towhey knew where it was.

"Okay, I will send you proof and call you when I have it," Towhey said, excited.

Towhey put down the phone and shouted to Dam.

A few days later, Towhey sent Mohammed a photograph of a monk holding the jewelled box outside a Wat. The photograph was of Dam, dressed in monk's robes, clutching a phony, homemade relic, standing outside Wat Phnom in Phnom Penh.

Towhey received the call from Mohammed wanting to buy the relic three weeks ago. Towhey was now only days away from adding more wealth to his already full pot, thanks to his employee, but soon to be ex-employee, Dam.

A tap on the door was Towhey's signal that Kip had arrived with his quarry. He went to the door, where a happy Kip stood outside with a young girl. The girl had been sobbing and her dirty tears left black smudge marks around her cheeks. She wore a dirty faded floral dress and looked up at the big Irish man as he opened the door. Gripped with fear, she started to sob again, but was sharply checked by Kip, who squeezed her hand.

"Good evening, Mr. Andrew, I trust she is okay for you?"

Towhey grabbed the girl, dragged her inside and, closing the door, instructing Kip to wait on the porch. Kip went over to a table, sat down, and lit a cigarette. The door opened again and Towhey gave Kip a packet of five King Edward cigars and a bottle of Samsong whiskey.

"Thank you, Mr. Andrew," Kip snivelled.

Towhey slammed the door shut, wanting to get on with the night's proceedings.

He dragged the sobbing girl towards his bedroom. She was terrified, but noticed the safe.

"Don't look bitch!" He snapped in Cambodian and pulled her into the bedroom. Aroused to bursting, he pushed the youngster into the bathroom.

"Shower!" he hollered.

The girl ran into the shower room, locking the door behind her. Towhey, agitated, undressed and got onto his bed, thinking of how he intended to push himself into that tight little orifice and thrust when the girl screamed. That was the part that he loved; the popping and then the screaming. The more he thought, the more aroused he became.

"Hurry up! Hurry up!" he yelled, "Come on, or I'll break down the fucking door."

The door slowly opened and the little girl came out.

"Come here, come here now!" growled Towhey.

The terrified child shuffled over to Towhey, who leapt up, ripped her dress off, grabbed her arm and dragged her with him onto the bed. The little girl sobbed frantically, which excited Towhey even more. He put his hand between her legs and felt a warm liquid hit his hand. He looked down and saw a stream of urine coming from the frightened young girl.

"Dirty little whore!" yelled Towhey in his broad Irish accent and threw her off the bed. "Clean it up and get back here."

The girl ran back into the shower room and washed herself, while an angry, but still aroused, Towhey waited impatiently. He switched off the main light and turned on the bedside lamp.

"Come here, come on!" screamed Towhey.

The door opened and the young girl walked nervously out of the bathroom. She glanced at Towhey and then looked over at the figure now standing in the shadows by the door. Towhey, seeing the girl looking, glanced over in the same direction.

"What the fuck...Kip, get out, you little fucker," hollered an angry Towhey.

The figure moved forward into the light.

255

"Who the fuck are you?" Towhey yelled in English and then repeated in Cambodian.

The figure wore the same monk's robe that Dam had made, complete with sword attached to a red sash. Pon, who had changed outside earlier into his Tinju robes, threw Towhey the picture of Dam and said,

"I am looking for this man. He has something that does not belong to him, and I want it returned." Pon spoke slowly in Cambodian, so Towhey could understand.

"He isn't here, now get out." Pon looked at the girl, who ran to the monk and desperately held onto him

"Please help me, holy monk," she pleaded.

Towhey, annoyed by this intrusion into his sordid world, leapt out of his bed and rushed at Pon. The monk held the girl to him, removed his sword and sliced it across Towhey's throat. The Irishman stopped in his tracks, looking shocked. Pon turned his back on Towhey and, shielding the girl from the carnage, they left the room. Towhey fell to his knees and slumped forward, his head thumping loudly on the floor, followed a few seconds later by the rest of his torso.

Pon held no remorse about killing. Vitchae and Somchay had told the monks to remember that they weren't the judges of these duties, that was between them and their god. They were only commissioned to arrange that appointment.

Pon arranged two appointments that night. The first he now carried over his shoulders. He placed Kip's lifeless body, who he had dispatched earlier with his pitou, with Towhey's corpse. He laid Kip on top of Towhey and placed Towhey's head on the top, like a cherry on a cake.

The little girl picked up Towhey's safe key, which had fallen off his neck, due to having no head to hold it in situ. She opened the safe. Her eyes widened as she took out bundles of crisp dollar bills.

Pon looked around for clues to the whereabouts of Dam.

The little girl put back on her ripped dress. She went over and told Pon about the money.

"You keep it," he said.

She split the bundle,

"You take half. You will need it, holy monk. There's enough for me and my family to start a great new life. With this, I can go home and my parents will be pleased and let me stay," she said, with a note of hope now in her voice.

Pon accepted. He thought it could be more useful than his ornaments. He found a photograph in a frame on Towhey's desk, which showed Dam holding the relic. Pon stared at the picture, then placed it in his rucksack.

There were many papers on Towhey desk, but he couldn't understand them. He would take them to Taksin's friend, thinking that maybe he could help. He still had one more task to complete. He went back into Towhey's bedroom and over to the two bodies.

He opened his jar of sunblaze powder and poured a thin line over the centre of the bodies, and then spread a thin liquid over the powder, leaving a blob on the bodies that hardened. He took out another pot that contained gold dust, black, blue, and white fine filings, which he sprinkled in a circle around the bodies. This would, when the sunblaze ignited, react with the heat and direct the force upwards. He took out his tinderbox, went back to Towhey's desk for some paper, and grabbed a bundle of tissue. A ringing and vibrating came from the top of Towhey's desk.

"It's his mobile phone," said the girl and handed the phone to Pon. He pressed the receive button and a voice at the other end, a voice that Pon had not heard for over eight years, answered.

"Andrew, it's Dam, we have arrived at Poi Pet, so just checking in."

Pon looked down at the little girl.

"The man who brought you here, what was his name?" he asked, covering the mouthpiece.

"Kip," replied the girl, screwing up her face in disgust.

"Dam, it's Kip. Andrew's taking a shower," said Pon.

"Oh, Kip," said Dam, "you've brought him another child, have you?"

"Yes," said Pon

"Are you okay, Kip? You don't sound your usual self."

"Yes, I am fine," said Pon. "What's your message?"

"Tell Andrew we are now in Poi Pet, and we will check in tomorrow when we get across the border, before we leave for the Dolphin hotel in Pattaya."

"Yes," said Pon, "I'll tell him."

The phone clicked off and Pon stared at it. "Soon, my friend, very soon." he said as he placed the phone in his bag and switched it off. He asked the girl if she knew Pattaya. She didn't, so he thought, 'Now I have another phone, I will call Taksin, maybe he knows.'

Pon felt relieved and thanked Buddha for his continued help by saying a prayer. He then blessed Towhey and Kip's bodies and, along with the young girl, walked outside.

Pon lit the tissue and tossed it through the open window into Towhey's bedroom. There was a sudden whoosh! with a blinding white light and intense heat, and then the darkness returned. All that remained was a fine gold line around where two dead bodies had lain moments ago, and a gaping hole in the roof of the late Andrew Towhey's bungalow.

Pon and the girl walked into the hot dark night and caught a passing tuk-tuk.

— Chapter Ten —

Cenat squeezed Vitchae's hand.

"Are you okay, old friend?"

Vitchae felt elated. He turned his head and looked at Cenat, "Yes, I feel fine."

The Royal Bangkok Hospital was a modern and luxurious medical facility. The rooms in the royal wings were the best in the country. Along with its high-paying patients, it also catered to royalty and high-ranking government officials. Although a relatively small hospital, it housed state-of-the-art operating theatres and some of the country's, if not the world's, top surgeons.

Nurses came in and out to check Vitchae's vital signs every 30 minutes. The events of the past few days would be unforgettable for the two old monks.

****

The flight from the village to Bangkok had taken about an hour in the helicopter. The flight had been uneventful, which surprised Vitchae. He had heard the roar of the engines, felt the aircraft move, and heard a slight hum after an airman closed the door. He then felt a slight bump when landing. 'Not too bad,' he thought, trying to imagine the view if he wasn't blind; birds flying past, bumping into clouds, and maybe even crashing into the sun.

The interior of the helicopter resembled a hotel room with its plush upholstered interior. A large seat rose higher than the others, where the King sat, with two seats at the front for the personal guards and four rows of three facing the cockpit for soldiers, airmen or the other members of the royal family. Large intricate carvings, and gold leaf covered etching covered the velvet velour sides, which made it sound proof once the airman closed the side door.

The five soldiers in the village mumbled about fearing they would be stuck in the jungle and the King's escort guards quietly sniggered. Cenat and Taksin were talking. Vitchae listened, while he held onto his friend's hand for dear life.

They arrived at the Imperial Palace and were escorted to the Temple of the Emerald Buddha. Vitchae and Cenat felt strange, as they had not been to the temple for many years. The last time Vitchae was there was when he was Prime Master. He hadn't seen the temple since his sight completely failed, but still felt in awe at the atmosphere created by the holy temple, which sent a tingle down his spine. They both went into the temple and up to the statue of the Emerald Buddha arm in arm. They stood and prayed, asking Buddha for guidance, before being taken to the monk's quarters and housed for the night. Early the next morning, the two monks ate, studied their scriptures, meditated, and were later summoned to the royal residence.

The King was in the stateroom standing around a table, along with five men and one woman, with maps and photos spread out.

The two elderly monks entered the large room and Cenat led Vitchae over to the King. The party gave them a respectful wai, which Cenat returned.

"I am truly sorry for the loss of your brothers, Khun Vitchae and Khun Cenat," said the King.

Vitchae had grown up alongside the King, who was six years his junior. He remembered seeing him as a boy. He came to the temple with his father and watched the ceremony. Vitchae was only on his second cycle as a novice monk, twelve-years-old. When the King ascended the throne in his early 20s, Vitchae blessed and chanted with him. When Vitchae was made Prime Master 30-years-ago, apart from

262

the last four years, he and the King had developed together, although with different lifestyles. On his birthday, the King would worship the relics alongside the Tinju monks, chanting at the side of the Prime Master. The King would then leave to perform his other royal duties, while the monks would blend into the background and follow the King throughout the day as his bodyguards. At the stroke of midnight, when it was no longer his birthday, the monks would return to Pong-Nam-Rom and trek through the jungle back to Salaburi. The King would never speak to the monks. He was the ruler, the living Buddha, and they were his servants and finest warriors. Although, the King often wondered what happened to the old Prime Master. He'd noticed Vitchae's sight failing year by year, and then four years ago, Somchay had taken up Vitchae's role as Prime Master, so the king presumed that the old monk had died.

The King beckoned them closer to the table. The six people around the table shuffled to make room for the monks, so they could see the papers laid out. The King asked him if the aerial photo of the village laid on the table was the village of Salaburi and surrounding area. Cenat had never seen the village from the air and stared at the photo. He could make out the Wat, and other things he started to recognise.

"Yes," Cenat replied, at which point the King ordered the group out of the room. The six gathered up the papers and photographs from the table, bowed, and left. When they left the room, the King and the two elderly monks went to sit on three chairs next to a large picture window, looking out onto the vast grounds of the royal palace. The King then explained his proposals, while the two monks listened with great interest.

"We will draw up some plans, and you can go over them. Then return to the village and see what the villagers think," said the King.

The King was like a shepherd, wanting his lost sheep returned to the flock, and into the 21st (Gregorian) century. The same as he had done with the rest of his beloved country and people.

The King then went on to explain that as he became older and approached the end of his cycle of life, he would soon have to hand power over to his son Crown Prince Maha Vajiralongorn. The middle-aged prince was not a traditionalist. He liked all things modern, and had no time for the past.

"Maybe after this tragedy, we need to rethink the customs of the past," explained the King, "Nowadays, technology outweighs the old ways. I don't want another tragedy to happen again. There's too much greed in our world now."

The King outlined his plan.

Vitchae and Cenat sat, listening to this wise old King. They had tears in their eyes, but knew the King was right. These had also been Vitchae's thoughts over the last few days, and now that the living Buddha confirmed it, they must accept it.

Vitchae knew he was also close to the end of his life, but would embrace this challenge, and enter into this strange new world with the people of the village, his flock.

The next three days were hectic for the two elderly monks, but they had more energy and strength than most people did in their twenties and wanted to be consulted on everything. The King left most of the decisions to them. They would take the ideas to the village. On the third day, the King returned to the discussions; he looked over plans, drawings, and projections with the monks and a team of surveyors, architects and geologists, who worked closely with them.

Vitchae gave his thoughts and ideas for the continuation and survival of the Tinju, but with changes in their structure. The King agreed and plans were formulated, with everyone happy and pleased with the outcome. Vitchae presented the King with the last ornament he'd carved, which he finished after losing his sight, so it was of great significance to him. The King had never seen anything cut and shaped with such precision as this four inch red stone. The King spent several moments admiring it before thanking Vitchae. He then gave it to the woman in the group, who looked at the ornament and, with eyebrows raised, looked at the smiling King. She held onto the ornament, and then left the room. The King said that when the holy relic was returned, it would be placed with the Emerald Buddha, safe in the Imperial Palace for all, not just royalty, to enjoy and worship. Pon would be rewarded in the way befitting the kingdom's greatest warrior. There was no doubt about Pons success, as he was on the side of right. When business in the stateroom had concluded, only the two monks and the King remained. Vitchae and Cenat wanted to get back to the village and relay the exciting news. The King gently took Vitchae's arm.

"Master Vitchae," he said, "You have faithfully served me as a boy and man, now let your King to repay you."

The private hospital room door opened. A Swiss and a Thai doctor entered. They went over to Vitchae's bedside and the Thai doctor said,

"How are you, Master Vitchae?"

Then, without waiting for a reply, he sat Vitchae up. A nurse, who followed them in, pulled the backrest out and propped Vitchae against it.

Doctor Wansuk Tapakit and Doctor Fritz Hienbach had been summoned to the Imperial Palace two evenings ago. The Swiss doctor was recognised as one the best at his field, ophthalmology. On their arrival, the doctors were shown to the stateroom, where the confused monks were waiting. The King asked if anything could be done to help with the monk's vision. Dr. Hienbach examined the old monk's eyes, mumbling about cataracts and lens damage caused by the cataracts. He moved the scope around asking Dr. Tapakit to translate. After spending ten minutes examining Vitchae, he looked at Dr. Tapakit and, speaking English with a Swiss accent, announced,

"Schedule the surgery for tomorrow afternoon, okay."

The Thai doctor, who was used to this abrupt, but brilliant eye surgeon, nodded.

"Have him prepped and ready for surgery at two o'clock sharp. Okay." continued Fritz.

He bowed at the King and strode out of the room.

The surgery went smoothly. It was a simple but effective procedure to remove the severe cataracts, and replace them with new lenses. The following morning, Doctor Tapakit removed the bandages wrapped around Vitchae's eyes and stood back. Slowly, Vitchae opened his eyes and looked around the room. Cenat was at his bedside, somebody unfamiliar to him entered, but he ignored him, becoming engrossed with his new, clear, world. He took hold of Cenat's hand.

"I can see again, old friend, I can see!"

Cenat cried with joy. Vitchae looked around the room repeatedly.

"Ready for discharge," instructed the Swiss doctor. He strode out of the room and on to his next patient, with the small Thai doctor rushing to keep up.

 Vitchae gazed at everything and then focused on the man who had come in.

"Hello, Master monks," said Taksin.

"Hello, Taksin" replied Cenat.

 Vitchae smiled and said,

"It is very nice to finally see you, Khun Taksin"

Taksin wai-ed the monks and said,

"I have good news for you." He looked at Vitchae. "Well," said Taksin, "more good news. Pon called last night, so I arranged for my friend at the Thai consulate in Phnom Penh to take him to the airport. He told me that his duty went to Pattaya, so he was in pursuit, confident that the Holy Relic would be returned in the next few days. My friend called me several hours ago, confirming that he dropped Pon off at the airport. He is now on an aeroplane and on his way to Pattaya."

The two old monks looked at each other.

"Come on, Vitchae." said Cenat excitedly. "We have to get back to the village, to make ready for our warriors' return and start on our new mission."

The two monks thanked Taksin, who had arranged for a helicopter to fly them to the village. Vitchae didn't mind the prospect of flying, feeling confident that the pilot would miss the sun again.

"Excuse me, Khun Taksin," said Cenat, asking, "What is an aeroplane?"

— Chapter Eleven —

Pon was learning about aeroplanes. He sat bolt upright, clinging onto the armrest of the Boeing 737, on his way to Utapao airport, Thailand.

****

Pon, along with the little girl, had taken a tuk-tuk to Phnom Penh. He called Taksin en-route and explained what he had discovered. Taksin told him where Pattaya was, and explained that the quickest way to get there would be to fly. Pon sounded confused, so Taksin explained that his friend would collect him and take him to the airport in the morning.

Pon and the girl arrived in Phnom Penh and she caught a night bus back to her village. She thanked the monk, and, with tears, she now wept, holding hope in every teardrop. Pon went to a hotel recommended by Taksin and paid five dollars from his bundle, courtesy of Mr. Andrew Towhey. He went to his room, meditated for several hours and then slept on the floor next to the large bed.

The logistics of getting Pon to Pattaya by plane was difficult. Taksin discussed at length with his friend how they could do it. Pon had no papers, but Taksin's friend assured him that it wouldn't be much of a problem in Cambodia, but that Taksin would have to arrange for his arrival in Utapao. Taksin could mobilise armies, so should have no problem dealing with immigration.

Pon spent the morning meditating, carving one of his ornaments, and staring at the photograph of Dam. He thought about Towhey, who was the first white man he had ever seen. He decided that he did not like these foreigners. 'These people are strange,' he thought and hoped that he would never meet another one. Towhey's phone had been constantly ringing since the early morning, so Pon turned it off.

Taksin's friend arrived mid-afternoon, dressed in a smart immigration uniform. He drove Pon to the airport, about a 20-minute drive. He gave him two brown envelopes with 'Diplomatic Papers,' written across the front, one in Cambodian, and one in Thai, officially stamped 'Royal Thai Consulate.'

Pon saw an aeroplane land as they approached the airport and he felt scared.

"Don't worry," said Taksin's friend, noticing Pon becoming nervous. "It is the safest and fastest way to travel."

Pon looked up at the sun, which looked a bit low today, and thought, 'I hope we don't crash into it.'

They went into the airport and Taksin's friend took Pon straight through to check-in, where a Cambodian customs officer waited to greet them. Taksin's friend gave Pon strict instructions that once he left the terminal, he should give the official one of the envelopes, with the other for a Thai official on arrival at Utapao.

Pon and the official got waved through check-in. The official nodded to the staff and went through the detectors, which rang as Pon went through. Pon sword, though covered with paper, was still easily recognisable as a sword. He went through the departure lounge and got onto the back of a small supply vehicle waiting on the tarmac.

"Okay," said the Cambodian, holding out his hand. Pon gave him the envelope written in Cambodian.

The man folded it and placed it in his pocket. Pon sat on the small truck, which drove to the waiting aeroplane. Nervously, Pon went up the small stairway, entered the fuselage, and was greeted by a smartly dressed Thai woman, who showed him to a seat at the rear of the plane. She could see Pon was anxious, so reassured him by telling him that he had the safest seat on the plane.

"Aeroplanes don't back into mountains," she chuckled.

This bit of light-hearted banter didn't help, leaving Pon terrified as she buckled him into the seat. He stared out of the window, not daring to move. After sitting on the plane alone for about 30 minutes, a bus pulled up and other passengers started filing on. Still afraid, Pon stared out of his window as the jet's engines started up. The plane taxied down the runway. 'Not too bad,' thought Pon, as the plane hurtled down the runway and went airborne. Pon was fluent in Thai, Cambodian, Burmese and ancient Siamese languages and was screaming in all four at the top of his voice, "STOP! STOP!"

The plane touched down 90 minutes later at Utapao airport, with Pon still clutching onto his armrest. The flight attendant had closed the window blind, so he could not see outside. That didn't help, but at least he'd stopped screaming. He felt a bump when they landed, which made him jump and, as he was just about to scream again, thinking they'd hit the sun, the flight attendant came over and opened the blind.

"Look," she said, "we've landed."

An immigration official then got onto the plane, and he and Pon remained there until the other passengers disembarked. He then led Pon off the plane and onto another small service vehicle, which drove the short distance to a small hut at the side of the small terminal. They entered through one door, went through a door opposite and straight outside to the front of the airport. Pon handed the man the other envelope. The man smiled and went back inside the office.

Pon sat down under a tree, studying the map that Taksin's friend gave him of Thailand's eastern seaboard. He noticed a straight road marked going from Utapao to Sattahip and through to Pattaya. Pon had never read a map before, but after a quick lesson in the Phnom Penh airport car park by Taksin's friend, he thought it looked easy. He was right, but the road, which was only about an inch on the map, was in reality about 40 kms. He decided to walk.

— Chapter Twelve —

"Seven days. That's 168 hours...10080 minutes," Stu announced

"Yes, alright matey, we know, so shut up, and watch the show," said an irritated Spock.

"But Spock, we only have a week left," said an anxious Stu.

The dancers came onto the stage, so Stu shut up and watched. The first performer out, dressed in a sexy Tina Turner Basque and a large wig, started to mime to 'Simply the Best.' She strutted about the stage like the real Tina, but a Thai version. Four scantily clad back-up dancers came out from behind the stage and joined Tina in perfect sync. They all mimed along to the queen of pop. Tina wound up for the big finish. Her back-up dancers whipped off their bikini tops, revealing their breasts, perfectly round and well-proportioned. The crowds around the stage cheered and whistled.

"Nice tits," shouted Spock.

"Yeah, pity they're all blokes," said Nick, who picked up his drink with the hand that wasn't in a plaster cast, finished the last drop, and asked,

"Three more, lads?"

****

Nick had broken his arm in his tumble out of the window. He was taken to a hospital and x-rayed, which revealed a small crack in his left ulna, the smaller of the two bones in the forearm, and a few bumps and bruises. They wanted to keep him overnight, but when he found out how much it would cost, he demanded to be put in a plaster

273

cast and released. The doctor advised him to return before he went home to England, to have the plaster split prior to his flight. He would get it removed in England six weeks later. That was five days ago.

He had now forgiven Spock, who hadn't realised that he'd bumped the door into him, resulting in him falling out of the window. When Nick told him what happened, he grovelled and begged forgiveness. Nick, of course, played on this, even though he knew he was partly responsible because he never locked his door. However, he always did now.

Nick phoned Luanne while he was at the hospital; she agreed to visit him later.

Luanne dumped her current boyfriend when Nick called her. The middle-aged Englishman, who had been saving up for months, often at times with difficulty, due to having to send Luanne money, after she told him that her baby was sick. He gladly sent her 10,000 Baht a month. When the Englishman arrived, Luanne had been waiting at his hotel. She hugged and kissed him and he was as happy as a sand-boy. They went to bed and made love twice. He had not seen his love for many months, and was never unfaithful in England. He never went anywhere, mainly because he had no money to go out with after paying Luanne. She told him that she never went anywhere, just stayed at home with her sick baby, and just arrived back from Udon Thani, North East Thailand, that morning to see him. She professed her undying love and told him that she didn't care about his money. This was, of course, a load of old bollocks, but it was the Thai way and, although many men fell for this, nobody ever really got hurt. There were only a few broken hearts, which were soon mended in the carefree land. They were making plans for his two-week stay when Nick phoned. Luanne rushed into the bathroom with the phone and told Nick not to call her. Nick pleaded with her, claiming that he was on his deathbed and the doctor had given him only days left to live. Luanne weighed up her options. 10,000 Baht a month, or Nick. Nick was a Pattaya-wise foreigner, she knew he was bullshitting.

However, she also knew this new man to be a stupid foreigner who would believe anything, so she could do as she pleased. She had known Nick for a long time. She liked the cheap Charlie, and maybe he would pay her something this time. Luanne walked back into the room, where the Englishman laid on the bed.

"Is everything okay, darling?" he enquired.

"No," she sobbed. "My mama call to me, my baby is very sick, so I have to go home...I will call you later."

She picked up her handbag and left for the Siam Sawasdee hotel, leaving the poor Englishman to wonder what happened. He thought he would give her more money when she contacted him.

Nick's mood changed when he arrived back at the hotel after getting discharged. Luanne was waiting in the reception with Dao and Moo. Nick's whinging stopped, and he started to hobble and pull pathetic pained expressions. Luanne came over, asked if he was okay, and started fussing around him like an old mother hen. They disappeared up to his room.

Since it was getting late, Stu, Spock and the girls went for something to eat. The lads stayed with Nick at the hospital all day, listening to him grumble and whinge, much to the annoyance of Stu, who told Spock

"You pushed the idiot out of the window. You stay."

Spock pleaded,

"You're my mate and I would for you."

The guilt trip worked and the two stomped around, listening to Nick droning on about how much it was going to cost, how much his arm hurt, and how it was all Spock's fault.

275

The next morning, Stu and Spock decided to hire a motorbike to discover what else there was to see around the eastern seaboard. They decided to try the Tiger Zoo at Sri Racha, about a 40-minute drive from Pattaya. They set off on Honda CBR 400cc's motorbikes. With Dao navigating on the back of Stu's machine, they headed off on the Bangkok Road to the zoo. The bikes were fast, 'like shit off a shovel', and they soon reached the Tiger Zoo. The animals were kept in large open enclosures, so they drove around the vast zoo.

The lads felt uncomfortable because the bikes' engines got hot and were positioned in the wrong place. They stopped at a small cafe and, while they ate ice cream, packed their now roasting testicles with bags of ice. They now understood what a boil-in-the-bag fish felt like, from the fish's point of view. The zoo was busy, but the cafe where they sat was deserted. People seemed to be avoiding that area, which puzzled all four of them. The waitress in the cafe spoke to the two girls, who looked up.

"What did she say?" Spock asked.

"Kookie Ling," replied Moo, and she and Dao moved away.

"What?" asked Stu?

The two girls started talking amongst themselves about the English translation...There was no need, as a large, liquefied, brown blob landed on Stu's half-finished ice cream. The two lads looked up, seeing three or four monkeys scurrying around on wires in trees above their heads.

"Monkey shit!" shouted Moo.

They arrived back at the hotel in the early evening and decided that the following day they would try the 'Million Year Stone Park and Crocodile Farm,' which they would get to by taxi.

They returned the bikes and spent the evening in Spock's room, playing dominoes. They bought two bottles of Samsong whiskey, some orange juice for Dao, and two bags of ice for their still throbbing, swollen and well-cooked bollocks.

Million Year Stone Park was the largest crocodile farm in Thailand. It had a stone that had been carbon-dated as over a million years old. There was a large pond with giant catfish and several tiger and bear enclosures. However, the main attractions were the crocodiles. Thousands of beady eyes peeped out from an enormous lake. The four watched a show, where a Thai man put his head in a large crocodile's mouth, doing what most people would consider suicidal stunts. Stu, Spock, Moo, and Dao had their photographs taken sitting on a croc, which eyed a rather nervous Spock up and down. The trainer had to remove the crocodile, as big Spock told the croc that if it moved again, he would be going home with a pair of fresh crocodile skin shoes. The reptile must have understood this and shot off around the arena, with an angry Thai in hot pursuit. They went to a small restaurant next to the show and ordered four crocodile steaks.

"And make it snappy," added Spock.

Stu groaned at his pathetic attempt at humour, but Spock didn't care. He'd seen a good show and was now eating the cast.

Over the next few days, with Nick feeling better, they all went to a small island about a 40-minute ferry ride from Pattaya, called Koh Larn. They caught the ten o'clock ferry. Nick was happy as it only cost 20-Baht. They drank a few beers on the chugging old ferry, and arrived at the Koh Larn jetty forty minutes later. There was no beach were they docked, so they went and asked at the restaurant/resort on the jetty opposite. They met the proprietor, an Englishman called One-eyed Steve, due to the fact he only had one eye, and his loud, slightly crazy wife, 'Non' He directed the lads to one of the four beaches on the island, and said he would see them upon their return. They hired a tuk-tuk for the day and went to Samae Beach. It was hot and sticky on the beach, so they put on high factor sun block. They frolicked on the beach and Stu dragged a giggling Dao into the sea.

"I'm going in for an aqua shag," he proudly boasted, followed by Spock and Moo, who was soon up to her shoulders in the water, which only covered Spock's waist.

Stu lifted Dao's legs up around his waist. He slid his hand between her legs, slipping her bikini to one side. She tugged at the front of his shorts, releasing the animal from its slumber. He pressed himself forward, entering a willing, and now familiar, moist world. He slowly kissed her. They heard rapid high-pitched, unfamiliar speech behind them. Dao looked over Stu's shoulder and pulled herself closer. A black rubber ring floated past the couple, with three young children and one old Japanese woman inside, who happily chatted and drifted along, watching the couple engaging in their nuptials. The annoying Japanese floated around between both couples, much to the annoyance of a frustrated Stu and Spock. The two girls chuckled as the two lads enquired as to whether the floating Japanese enjoyed sex and travel.

"Fuck off!"

The Japanese just smiled, nodded, and continued to float around for ten minutes, by which time the lads' ardour had worn off. They straightened themselves up, got out of the water grumbling, and went over to where a laughing Nick and Luanne had been watching the drama from their beach chairs.

They decided to stay the night and went to One-eyed-Steve's to book a room. They sat and ate at deck chairs on the pier restaurant. At six o'clock, with the island left deserted after the last ferry departed, Nick said that his arm felt sore, so he and Luanne went to their room. Stu, Dao, Spock, Moo, and One-eyed-Steve sat and talked. Steve suggested they go to watch the sunset at the small beach that was only five minutes away. They thought this was a good idea, so ordered two motorbike taxis and went to the small deserted beach. They sat down, cameras in hand and waited.

The sunset was spectacular. They could see the tall towers and outline of Pattaya clearly against the backdrop of the horizon. The sky blazed in a golden glow and then turned into a fiery blood red along the horizon as the sun slowly made its nightly descent and the darkness drifted down to meet it. There were a few midnight blue clouds that just ambled along with, it seemed, no particular place to go and in no particular rush to get there. The darkness won its nightly battle and the sun withdrew completely, leaving a dark starry sky behind. The odd light grey-blue patch remained, which made the sky appear like a dark, cobalt blue quilt, with the lights from Pattaya lighting up the horizon. Nature's spectacle astounded them.

The beach was in darkness, apart from the odd glow of a star making a late appearance and, after about ten minutes, Spock let out a long sigh, followed moments later by Stu.

"What an awesome place," said Stu.

"Yeah," agreed Spock, feeling in a Philly mood. Moo coughed and swallowed hard. Dao coughed and spat several times. A relaxed Spock looked over to the dark shadowy figure of Stu and said,

"Dao doesn't swallow then, matey?"

They returned to One-eyed-Steve's. The girls went to their rooms for a Listerine gargle and sleep. The lads went to the restaurant. Steve and Non sat on the small jetty overhanging the ocean.

One-eyed-Steve had lived with his wife, Non, on the island for four years.

The restaurant and rooms were on a pier, opposite the ferry jetty. The T-shaped pier had five rooms along the jetty and a restaurant at the end. It was a large open restaurant with a roof supported by beams. It

279

had a small bar in the centre and twenty tables around it. There was also an extra uncovered overhang at the front, approximately twenty meters long by five meters wide, where you could fish or just sit and relax.

Spock and Stu ordered beers and joined the couple. A few hours later, feeling spannered, the four sat around a table. Stu enquired about how Steve lost his eye. He explained that he had lost it in an accident several years earlier whilst wankered, and then, pointing to a scar on his shoulder, said,

"That's nothing, I got this after I falling off the pier," and pointed to the spot. Things then started to get like the scene in Jaws where Hooper and Quint started comparing scars.

"Take a look at this one."

"That's nothing; I got that beat."

This went on for what seemed like hours. Stu and Spock decided they were there to judge who had the best scar between Steve and his wife. Every time one of them showed a scar and explained the story behind it, they would then point to the spot where it happened. Always at the restaurant and always spannered, which explained why they never had any customers staying the night. Stu recollected the time he'd spent in the Royal Navy, when he visited HMS Victory, Nelsons flagship, where a brass plaque placed on the quarterdeck read: Nelson fell here. Stu thought, 'If these two had a plaque for every time they had an accident, the floor would be worth a fortune in brass.' Spock just thought, 'I know another walking calamity asleep in one of the rooms.' Nicks ears must have been burning.

One-eyed-Steve and his wife Non, now shitfaced, ran out of scars to show and looked to Stu and Spock to announce a winner. Stu mentioned that although Non had some impressive scars, the majority came from the same place: a hole in the kitchen floor, which went straight into the ocean or onto rocks when the tide was out. Non's exit from the restaurant was therefore not as ambitious as Steve's, so Steve, in their opinion, won. Non wasn't very happy and stormed off to bed. Stu and Spock wondered how this light-hearted banter turned so serious and imagined being murdered in their sleep. They staggered back to their rooms.

The next morning, they awoke and went for breakfast, following the girls to the restaurant. Non smiled and shouted,

"Good morning."

Spock and Stu's heads throbbed from the night before, but not as much as Steve's shins. As they approached, they noticed large scratches and dried blood. He had sealed his victory by falling down the hole in the kitchen floor while making himself a late night snack.

"Not too bad, the tide was only just out," he said.

They spent another day on the beach just relaxing and drinking; it was idyllic. They decided to try another island tour in the next few days, but on a different island, thinking this one unsafe.

Catching the 6 p.m. ferry back to Pattaya, they had a quiet night playing dominoes. Stu and Spock had paid the bar fine for Moo and Dao until their day of departure. That way, they didn't have to go to Happy World Bar every night and could go and see Stu and Spock off at Bangkok airport when they went home. Charlie was happy, but didn't like the thought of his two big drinkers being loose in Pattaya, with other bars taking his Bahts. Dao and Moo felt ecstatic; they were having a great time with wages at the end.

Bar fines got paid by customers who took a girls out of a bar. The fine was usually 200 Baht per day. It is a system used at every bar in Thailand. The girls receive a small percentage of this fine and a percentage from drinks bought for them. Most bars also paid a small basic wage and the girls negotiated with their customers how much they want to get paid to spend the night with them. However, most of the new girls wanted a steady boyfriend and were happy with the man only paying the bar fine. They knew that if taken for a long time, especially by new and unwise foreigners, there was a good chance that they and their family would be taken care of. Therefore, money was rarely mentioned. They were, in the eyes of the customers, a girlfriend. This stage, if a man took them, it would usually end with marriage.

****

With one week left of their holiday, Spock, Stu and Nick decided to have a boy's night out. They left the girls in Spock's room to watch T.V. and compare notes and trophies. Dao now had a mobile phone, courtesy of Stu, and the already telephone-owning Moo now had a gold bracelet, courtesy of Spock. Luanne said nothing. She had worked in Pattaya bars for two years and thrown away, or given away, more trophies than the two newcomers owned. Luanne smiled at the two happy girls.

"Don't worry ladies." she said, "There's more to come."

The lads went out early. The plan was to have a few drinks and watch the Tina Turner katoey (lady-boy) show. Intending to only get juiced, but as with the best laid plans of mice and men, as they watched the show, they soon became spannered, making their way up rapidly to shitfaced, and it was only eight o'clock.

The katoeys were elegantly dressed it was difficult to tell the difference between them and women, especially when they danced and mimed to Tina Turner, Diana Ross, and Barbara Streisand numbers. They finished their first set and background music started to play. A now shitfaced Spock turned to Nick.

"Where's the toilet, matey?"

"Yeah, I want to go too," said Stu.

Nick pointed to the toilets, where the lady-boys stood chatting, fixing their make-up, and adjusting todger position.

"You have two hopes of me going there; Bob hope and NO hope," announced Stu

Spock agreed, so they decided to pee their pants. Nick saved this embarrassment by suggesting they go outside and pointed to an alleyway a short distance away at the side of a hotel. He said that they could have a slash against the side wall.

Getting off their seats, they staggered toward the alley.

— Chapter Thirteen —

Towhey planned the meeting well: he was always suspicious and leaving no room for error. He chose Pattaya because he still knew the corrupt police there. Even though he left under a shadow, he knew forgiveness would come in the form of Baht notes. It was the easiest place to get away with anything, from stealing a national treasure to, even murder, for the right price. He'd made his two henchmen drive across the border, as there were no searches at these borders and no detectors, unlike airports. He chose the hotel of one of his old acquaintances, the Dolphin, for the meeting. Towhey knew that his friend paid the police to ignore the goings-on there. It was a favourite venue for many underhanded activities, mainly picking up street-walking prostitutes. These girls could not work in the bars as they had the reputation for stealing from, or abusing customers.

Mohammed wanted a neutral place to meet and this, Towhey told him, was ideal. Towhey had planned for every contingency, except his premature death.

Dam and Miguel became concerned after unsuccessfully trying to call Towhey for two days. 'Very unlike Andrew, something must have happened,' they thought. They considered postponing, but knew that Abdul was arriving shortly and did not want to risk incurring Towhey's wrath if his deal didn't go through. So they went ahead with the schedule. Unbeknownst to Dam, Miguel had already booked his return flight to Cambodia for right after their meeting with Abdul. He also planned to transfer the funds into to his bank account in Gibraltar, just in case something had happened to Towhey.

Everything was set. The inspection of the relic and transfer of funds would take place in their second floor room at the Dolphin. Miguel's extra task was already set up and planned: the murder and disposal of this now unnecessary Thai, Dam. They booked Abdul at the Marriott

Hotel and arranged a safety box for the relic. Abdul was to stay there one night and fly back the next day to Saudi with the holy box hidden in the base of a metal statue of the prophet Mohammed holding a copy of the Quran. The relic would be wrapped in a thin lead sheet, to make it appear hollow on x–ray. Dam and Miguel had the statue made on their arrival in Pattaya.

They collected Abdul, a small chubby Arab, from Bangkok airport. He carried with him a large suitcase.

'Much too large for a one-night stay.' thought Dam.

They headed to Pattaya. Miguel and Abdul made small talk in English about Towhey and Mohammed. Dam drove, as he couldn't understand English.

They arrived at the Marriott Hotel. Abdul went to freshen up, while Dam and Miguel waited in the reception area, which they thought a pleasant change from the seedy Dolphin.

The three then went to the Dolphin Hotel and up to the second floor, room 205. They sat down at a small table. The hotel had a musty, urine-y odour and the rooms were dank. Dam opened a window to let some of the smells from the street filter in. Abdul, who was used to the high lifestyle, felt uncomfortable. He opened his suitcase, removed a Toshiba A8-P440 laptop, and plugged in an antenna. He connected to the internet. Dam took the metal statue from his rucksack, unscrewed the base, and removed the small jewel encrusted box, placing it in front of Abdul. Dam started to get an odd feeling in the pit of his stomach. Abdul did not appear as if he was from a museum. He wore large gold bracelets, rings, and a genuine gold Rolex watch. Dam knew something was definitely not right. Miguel glanced at his watch and patted the small bulge by his rib cage. A Walther PPK handgun.

A smiling face appeared on the computer screen as Abdul removed more items from his suitcase.

286

"Hello," said Mohammed.

He and Abdul had a conversation in Arabic, but then reverted to English to speak with Miguel about Towhey.

"No problems," said Miguel. "Andrew needed to go away on business. He had another artefact to look at in the jungle and won't be able to get a signal on his phone."

"Okay," said Mohammed, "send him my regards."

"I will get him to phone you on his return," said the relieved Miguel, glad that the Arab believed his story.

Abdul removed two enlarged A4 size photographs from his briefcase and studied them against the box. The photographs were of ancient pastel drawings. One depicted a young smiling King Bumnalonkorn, sitting in the lotus position, with the holy relic placed in his spread out hands, surrounded by fierce looking devil-headed warriors on armoured elephants.

The other photograph was an enlarged segment of the first that showed only the box. Abdul compared this against the box in front of him. He grunted and started to operate the machines. He scraped off small shavings, placing them on various pads and sensors.

"This will only take a moment," he said.

Lights flashed and noises emanated from the machines for several minutes. When a device completed its diagnostics, Abdul turned to the computer screen and announced to the smiling face of Mohammed,

"I will have to carry out a *Carbon 14 test on the contents in Saudi, under better conditions to be 100% certain, but by the age of the box's metal, I am confident that it's genuine."

287

Mohammed beamed and said,

"Excellent! Let's get on with the transfer."

Dam stared at the pictures of the holy relic that Abdul had left lying on the table. 'These were the first Tinju,' he thought, remorse now coursing through his body.

Abdul passed the computer over to Miguel, who spent a few minutes typing in his bank account details.

Mohammed focused on something off screen for several moments and then announced,

"Transfer complete."

Miguel let out a sigh of relief.

"One million dollars. I'm a rich little Spaniard, thanks to these stupid Arabs," he said aloud in Cambodian, so the two Arabs couldn't understand him...however, Dam understood.

"No! I won't let you double-cross Andrew," screamed Dam.

Miguel shouted at Dam to shut his mouth, or he would never see Andrew again. A heated exchange then took place between the two. Abdul, unable to understand, nervously reached into his pocket for a handkerchief. Dam, presuming Abdul was going for a gun, quickly reached into his jacket, unsheathed his glave, and in one smooth, flowing movement, removed the top of Abdul's skull. He grabbed the holy box as Miguel fired his PPK at him. A bullet entered Dam's left shoulder. He threw the glave at Miguel, but it missed and stuck firmly into the wall behind the now determined Spaniard. Miguel aimed again. Dam, seeing only one way to escape, leapt out of the open window.

"Mierda! Shit!" Miguel raged.

288

Mohammed's voice screeched and wailed in English and Arabic from the computer.

— Chapter Fourteen —

The sound of three zips opening, followed by three high streams of liquid hitting a wall with three Ahhs! signalled that Nick, Stu, and Spock had made it to the alley at the side of the hotel, and were relieving themselves of excess fluid to make room for more beer.

A thud, a groan, another loud thud, and then a yelp quickly followed.

Stu, leaning with one hand against the wall, turned to face Spock and casually enquired,

"Did somebody just fall on your head?"

Spock, wiping his piss-sodden hand down his shorts, slurred,

"Yes, matey...it would appear so."

They both glanced to where Nick had been standing moments earlier. They looked down upon a laid out Nick, who had a small Thai man lying prostrate on top of him.

Spock glanced at Stu.

"I suppose I'll get the blame for that, too."

Spock and Stu rapidly finished with their squirts and went to help the two fallen men. Spock picked up Dam, who was conscious, but shaken and confused.

Stu went over to assist Nick. He noticed something shining on the floor, so he picked up the object, slipped it in his pocket and asked Nick if he was okay.

291

"No, I am not bloody okay," Nick grumbled, spitting a white object into his hand. Spock and Stu helped the two injured men to their feet. Nick had a large gash on the back of his head from it hitting hard against the floor.

Dam groggily mumbled in Thai. Spock and Stu couldn't understand the Thai, but noticed a large dark stain over the shoulder of his jacket.

"Come on," said Stu.

He supported Nick and along with Spock carrying a weak, but light Dam, headed out of the alley and into the nearest bar.

Miguel came rushing out of the hotel as the four turned the corner, still cursing and with gun in hand. He stared at the group and took aim. He lowered his weapon as they disappeared around the end of the alley.

The two injured men were sat down. The girls at the bar came over to help, but avoided the Thai man after seeing the blood on his shoulder. They guessed it was drug related, so did not want to get involved.

Now that they were in the light and could see that the dark stain on Dam's jacket was blood, they looked at each another, unsure what to do. An anxious mamasan told them to get the injured men to hospital as soon as possible. She said that she would call the police and told them that Pattaya Bangkok Memorial Hospital was only a few Sois away. The girls tended to Nick, easing his todger back into his sodden shorts. They dabbed at the urine that covered the front of his shorts with tissues. Nick took a clean tissue from one girl and wrapped up his denture knocked out by Dam's fall. He put the tissue wrapped package into his shirt pocket. He looked like a vampire with front teeth, and the small metal rods that held the denture showing.

To break the sombre mood, Spock removed his upper denture and offered it to a rather unimpressed Nick.

"Here matey, you can use mine." He smiled.

Nick just moaned about how much they had cost and that they would be expensive to replace.

Miguel thought about what to do next. He did not want to leave any loose ends, which is what Dam had now become. Although things had not gone according to plan, his main fear was not that Dam would talk to the police; he was not scared of them. He was however, terrified of Dam. Miguel knew once Dam regained his strength, he would come to hunt him down and kill him. 'So I need to finish him now,' he thought, deciding to walk up to the bar, shoot Dam in the head, and in the ensuing panic, run back down the alley into the Dolphin Hotel and lie low until the dust settled. He had $1,000,000 and knew that even a fraction of that would buy his way out of anything. 'Yes', he thought, 'that is a good plan.'

It was the last thought he ever had.

****

The mamasan flagged down a Baht bus, and gave instructions to the driver. Spock carried Dam onto the bus and laid him on a bench. Stu helped Nick, who complained about feeling sick and dizzy.

'So do I,' thought Stu, 'it's called being spannered.'

They climbed onto the bus. People gathered around them, curious by the on-going activity. Nobody noticed that from the alley, a large, brilliant white plume shoot up into the night sky for an instant and then, like a lightning flash, was gone.

The Baht bus arrived at the Pattaya Bangkok Memorial Hospital accident and emergency department. Stu went inside and returned a few moments later with a nurse and ancillary staff. They helped get the two injured men off the bus and into the casualty department. The casualty staff took the two injured men behind large swinging doors

293

into a treatment area, while Spock and Stu stayed outside in the waiting area.

Approximately thirty minutes later, a doctor came out. He introduced himself and asked what had happened. He spoke English, so Spock and Stu had no problem understanding. They couldn't be of much help, but told the doctor what they had seen. The doctor went on to explain that the Thai man had a bullet in his shoulder that would need removing when the emergency theatre team arrived. He then informed them that Nick had a nasty laceration and a concussion, explaining they needed to be admitted to the hospital. Nick required sutures and observation, although he would probably be released the next day. The Thai, after being treated for his gunshot wound, would then be turned over to police custody. He told Stu and Spock that they would have to pay for two private rooms, as the Thai didn't have any money, and their friend kept passing out when money was mentioned. Stu handed over 4000 Baht, which they both thought the right thing to do. They felt sorry for the Thai man and it would stop Nick whining so much when he was released.

"Oh, and by the way," said the doctor. "Your friend asked me to give you this. He asked if you would keep it safe."

He handed Stu the tissue paper containing Nick's denture, so Stu slipped it in his shirt pocket. They left the hospital and caught a bike taxi back to the hotel.

The girls had spent the evening laughing and joking about foreigners, food, and shopping. They were spannered on the whisky and wine coolers that the lads had left them.

Spock and Stu entered the room, which went from raucous laughter to a guilty silence.

"Where's Nick?" slurred Luanne.

Spock explained that a Thai man fell on his head, bounced off him and landed on Nick, who was now in hospital. There was a stunned silence. Then the girls burst out laughing, joined in by Spock and Stu.

After the merriment died down, Luanne said that she would go to check on Nick. She left the room, still chuckling.

The others planned what to do next. Stu put his hand in his pocket and pulled out the golden, jewel- encrusted box. They all stared at it for a moment and then Dao asked,

"What is it?"

Stu turned the box over, looked, and fiddled with it.

"I don't know; I found it where the Thai fell. There's a lid, but it doesn't seem to open," said Stu.

He handed the box to Spock, who looked. He started pushing the gemstones, which, because of the time period, weren't faceted or polished.

"Maybe there's a catch somewhere?" Spock said, pushing the stones. He pressed a ruby on the front of the box.

For the first time in 2000 years of being undisturbed, the lid popped slightly open. Spock lifted it fully open and, like an over-full vacuum cleaner bag, a small cloud of dust escaped. The four gazed at the contents. After a few minutes silence, Stu announced,

"It's a portable ashtray."

The four teeth were in a bad state of decay when they arrived in Siam 2000 years ago. Prior to King Bumnalonkorn making the golden box, they had been kept in a simple clay pot for 500 years. Now, with time and the sudden introduction of air from the outside world, the teeth degraded, leaving only small hard ash and dust, which crumbled under the large poking finger of Spock.

"Get your finger out of their mate and I'll give it a wash," said Stu.

Stu took the box and emptied out the remains of the Buddha's teeth into a small waste bin. He rinsed the inside of the box under the tap. He repeated this a few times with liquid soap and tissue paper, until it was ash free.

"There," he said, "I will give that to my mum and tell her it's a priceless relic."

"You're as tight-fisted as Nick." said Spock.

The lads laughed and the girls joined in, though not knowing why.

A thought occurred to Stu. He took Nick's tissue- wrapped denture out of his shirt pocket and placed it in the box.

"There you go," he said. "That'll keep them safe till Mr. Moaner gets out of hospital."

He clicked the lid back shut and put the box in a bedside drawer.

They came up with a plan.

"Right," said Stu. "We leave for Koh Samet Island first thing in the morning."

"Too right," said Spock. "I don't want to get stuck at a hospital all day again, listening to Nick moan. We can see him in a couple of days, which should give him time to get over it. Besides, we are on holiday and only have 164 hours left. That's less than 10,000 minutes and," continued Spock with his stern, but slurred voice, "we're going to another island, so girls, pack your Listerine."

296

They retired for the night, leaving the mouthwash bottle a little emptier the next morning.

— Chapter Fifteen —

Silence returned to the hospital after the earlier flurry of activity, with Dam and Nick each taken to private wards. The operating theatre staff prepared for emergency surgery, with x-rays of Dam's shoulder, and Nick's skull, taken and processed. Dam was given a pre-medication of Omnopon and Scopolamine, which would not only relax him and relieve his pain, but would dry his secretions, readying him for the operation to remove the bullet.

Dam felt drowsy from the effects of the narcotic Omnopon. He heard voices outside his room, where a heated discussion was taking place between a doctor and a police officer. The police lost the argument and was told to wait until Dam was stable, and then he would be able to answer any questions. Dam heard the conversation, which seemed centred around a dead Arab with the top part of his head removed. 'Miguel must have run away,' thought Dam. The room was quiet except for a slow constant beep from a bit-map E.C.G monitor, which showed his heart rhythm.

Dam sat up in bed. His shoulder had been dressed to stem the flow of blood, with a bandage placed around it to keep it in place. The nurse had left the room after taking his vital signs and writing them down on the chart at the bottom of the bed.

"Just have to wait for the surgery team to get ready, then we will get you down to theatre," she'd told him.

Due to the narcotics Dam was now in a euphoric state. He'd thought a lot over the last hour or so about his youth in Salaburi. His thoughts now drifted back to Vitchae and the last conversation that he'd had with the Prime Master. He recalled how he had pleaded with Vitchae to let him fulfil his destiny and become a warrior. He remembered the hurt that he had felt at being rejected. However, the worst pain of all came when Vitchae told him that Jinn, who he always believed to be his brother, wasn't related to him The heartbreak washed over him again, spurred on by the face now staring at him from the bottom of his bed.

The figure was dressed in a Tinju monk's robe with a sheathed sword held in his hand. Dam stared at Pon for several minutes.

"Have you come to send me on my final journey...my brother?" he asked.

Pon stared at Dam and then moved closer into the light at the side of Dam's bed. Pon had realised a connection with his 'duty' when he met Banti, the old woman in the village. He'd stared at Dam's drawing and photograph many times, but now his suspicions were confirmed as he stared into Dam's face. The hate and lust for revenge still burned deeply in Pon; he knew that this man must be sent on the journey to atone with Buddha for his sin against his warriors.

"Yes, Dam, I have. Where is the sacred relic?" asked Pon.

Dam closed his eyes as the pre-med drugs bit deeper. He shook himself alert and said,

"I don't know, brother. I remember being betrayed and taking the sacred item before I escaped out of the window. Perhaps it fell onto the floor."

Dam fell silent.

Pon had been hiding in the alley and had seen Dam tumble from the window. He had seen Stu and Spock aiding Dam and Nick, and searched the alleyway after dispatching Miguel, but there was no sign of the relic. He therefore assumed the foreigners must have it.

Dam cut off his trail of thought and asked, "Will you forgive me, my brother?"

300

Pon solemnly replied,

"You know I cannot. Only Lord Buddha can do that."

Dam remained calm and said,

"I am ready to atone for my sin against my family."

Pon took his sword, flipped the lid on the handle, took out his pitou, and removed the dressing from the silent Dam's shoulder. Dam put his arm around Pon's neck as Pon moved closer.

"Pray for me, my brother," whispered Dam.

Pon remained silent as he thrust the pitou into Dams open wound, directing it towards his heart. He pierced through myocardial muscle and felt a pop as the pitou punctured the arterial chamber. He felt the pressure of Dam's heart as the blood forced against the pitou. Pon did not engage the blades and, after a few seconds, the pressure on the pitou ceased. Dam's arm fell limp from Pon's shoulder. He removed the pitou and whispered to the lifeless body of Dam,

"You could never live as a Warrior, but you died like one...my brother."

Pon said a silent prayer for his brother's safe journey to the afterlife to make his peace with Buddha.

Alarms and lights emanated from the monitors, to alert the emergency teams that the patient's vital functions had ceased. Pon replaced the pads and bandages and left the room.

The hospital came alive, with nurses and medical staff converging on Dam's room. Pon ducked into the shadows; he knew that he needed to find the foreigners. He had seen Nick brought in with Dam, so he walked along a corridor.

301

Pon went into Nick's room. The air-conditioner was on, making Pon feel cold for the first time in his life. Nick's sidelights was on, but he was asleep with his head bandaged, looking like he was wearing a thick white turban. By the side of the bed, a woman slept in a chair, her head resting on the mattress. Pon made his way to the foot of the bed and noticed the medical charts written in Thai. Pon picked up a chart and noted the address, Siam Sawasdee hotel, Soi Buchouw. He replaced the chart and eased slowly out of the room.

Nobody paid much attention to the monk as he made his way out of the hospital. Monks usually visited the sick and dying, and there was too much activity going on in Dam's room for anyone to pay much heed to Pon. He stood outside and looked skyward. He thought about what higher purpose had allowed him to survive, with his duty, his own brother. Was this a test from his god? He would continue until his duty concluded and the holy relic was returned. He hoped his brother's journey to the afterlife would be swift. Pon prayed for guidance and set off for the Sawasdee hotel, in the wrong direction.

— Chapter Sixteen —

Salaburi dissolved into a frenzy of activity as people descended upon the village like wolves on a foal. They walked around with cameras, theodolites, clipboards and various types of electronic equipment, measuring and probing the village and surrounding jungle.

It had been like that way since Vitchae, Cenat and Taksin returned a few days ago, bringing with them the five men from the stateroom, along with the lady the King had given Vitchae's ornament to.

****

It was mid afternoon when the large Sikorsky helicopter from the Royal flight landed. As the large aircraft approached, the villagers gathered in hope of catching another glimpse of their king. The side door slid open and out stepped Vitchae, Cenat, Taksin, and the others...but no King. Although disappointed, the villager's were happy to see the two monks. Still, they were unsure about the strangers unloading electronic equipment from the chopper.

Vitchae, Cenat, and Taksin approached the remaining monks and wai-ed them. The monks noticed, as did the villagers, that Vitchae walked unaided from the helicopter. He addressed each one individually and looked directly at them, noticing the look of surprise on the older monk's faces, and a look of horror on one young monk who used to pull faces at the once blind Master. A murmur went through the gathered villagers. Vitchae faced the crowd and gave a long respectful wai.

"Vitchae can see," somebody said, followed by a crescendo of noise.

"Vitchae can see; the King cured Vitchae."

303

They felt jubilant, although not surprised that the king had given back Vitchae's sight. After all, he could make *rain, so curing blindness would be easy for the great king.

Taksin told the villagers that the king ordained a new direction for the village. He arranged to meet with them all again the following morning, which would give the team of researchers time to prepare. Cenat requested the villagers assist them.

The woman with the team was the head geologist and mineralogist at the Bangkok Department of Agriculture and Development. She gathered her belongings and, along with some equipment, headed off into the mountains with a local man to act as her guide.

Vitchae and Cenat knew it was time for them to lay out the plans for the Tinju's survival. With heavy hearts, but positive about the outcome, he and Cenat went into the temple, along with the surviving elder monks.

Sitting by the Buddha statue, with his smiling golden face looking down upon them, Vitchae laid out his and the king's proposal.

"The Tinju will carry on as a separate order of monks, but with some changes. We would still be a combatant force, used in cases of emergency. However, the assassination side of the training would cease. Our new monks would not be chosen as a birthright, but positions in the order granted based on the merit of volunteers who want to devote their lives to serve Lord Buddha and the ruler. The best Muay Thai fighters in the kingdom would be brought in to train and support the monks until they become competent enough to become instructors."

Vitchae reminded them, "This was how the original Tinju started millennia ago."

The old Master continued,

304

"Our surviving youngsters will be re-united with their parents, and given the opportunity to stay with their family or continue with the Tinju. It would be the family's choice."

The elder monks remained silent, until Vitchae finished outlining the plans.

After several minutes, one elder monk asked, "When does this take effect, Master?"

"Immediately," announced Vitchae. "His majesty has put the word out amongst other Wats, so we should have a willing group in a couple of days."

"And when will the little ones be returned?" another monk asked.

"If you agree, we can start now," said Vitchae.

The monks looked at each other and nodded their agreement.

"Let's make it so."

That evening, the village was filled with merriment as some families were reunited with their sons. The villager's congregated in the meeting area on the side of the Wat. *'Sato' and 'urban whiskey' went down well among the villagers and the newcomers.

The monks stayed inside the Wat to meditate and pray.

The bleary-eyed villagers gathered the next morning at the large village altar. On the large stone table plans, drawings, photographs and laptop computers, with 3-D images on the screens were laid out. The woman geologist had returned the previous evening and joined in with the celebrations, but left again at first light.

Taksin spoke to the gathered villagers. He told them of the King's proposal to make a roadway to connect the village to Pong-Nam-Rom, with mains electricity and running water supplied to the village. They would lose virtually no jungle to construction and the surveyors were planning the best route to ensure this.

He told them that it would bring prosperity to the village, whose crafts, carvings, and jungle produce could be sold to make money to improve their lives and bring them in line with the rest of the country.

The villagers were given brochures of cars and pick-ups, which amazed them. The pictures got ripped out of the brochures to be framed and hung in their home later. They would all be given ID cards and therefore able to borrow money from banks anywhere in Thailand. The King would personally provide four pick-up trucks for the village to transport fruits and other produce to the border market. The jungle herbs and medicinal remedies would be researched for the benefit of the world, with any profit from discoveries given to the village.

The villagers listened. They tried to take in the information while being shown images of what it could look like through drawings and simulations on the laptops.

Taksin concluded by reading out a message from the King that ended with, 'My beloved people of Salaburi. The decision is yours to make.'

Silence descended, followed by murmuring amongst the villagers, who were confused and apprehensive about any change to their lifestyle. However, change had already taken place with the return of their young Tinju, and if the Tinju could change, so could they.

One villager asked, "What do you think, Master Vitchae?"

Vitchae thought and then replied,

"Our King, the living Buddha, has thought about this and decided that it will be good for us all. We must change in order to survive."

The villagers became silent again, until one of them asked,

"Where can I get one of these?" and held up a picture of a gold Toyota Vigo D4D.

The villagers burst into roars of laughter, holding up the pictures removed from the now torn and discarded brochures.

"I want one too," said another villager.

"Me too," came the shout from individual villagers. Vitchae turned and looked at Taksin.

"I think that's agreed then, Khun Taksin."

Taksin dialled a number on a digital satellite phone.

"Hello, Khun Taksin".

"Hello, your majesty. The village wholeheartedly agrees."

Over the next few days, people and equipment were brought in. Small surveying helicopters flew around, mapping the area between the village and Pong-Nam-Rom. The villagers either helped with feeding the newcomers or carried equipment to and from helicopters.

The elder monks stayed in the Wat, preparing for the arrival of the new Tinju. Vitchae and Cenat spent many hours together, mainly discussing Pon. They prayed he would be safe in fulfilling his duty, which would be the last duty of the Tinju. Vitchae felt troubled about sending this brave warrior monk to kill his brother and recover the holy relic.

Vitchae still had one family left to visit. He went into the Wat, prayed, and then went into the village.

The geologist returned to the village and went over to Taksin. She looked excited about something. She laid out machines in front of Taksin, who studied the information.

Taksin smiled and thanked the geologist, who looked fit to burst. She gathered up her equipment and headed back into the jungle.

Taksin tried to find Vitchae, so went to the Wat. Cenat told him that Vitchae was in the village at the home of one of the monk's families, and when he mentioned whose home, Taksin decided to delay his news for now. He told Cenat that he needed to leave for Bangkok shortly. Taksin smiled.

"Master Cenat, can you please tell Master Vitchae that the village is about to become extremely prosperous."

— Chapter Seventeen —

Taksin informed the King on his return from Salaburi of the findings made by Miss Ratray Sesilin, the geologist and mineralogist, along with the group of specialists in Salaburi. After doing laboratory tests on Vitchae's ornament, she confirmed that it was a large unfaceted 60-carat ruby and inclusion free, making it very valuable.

Ratray surveyed the area where the monks usually found the stones for carving and found a vein of ruby, although she could not yet determine the size. However, where there was ruby, there was usually sapphire and, sure enough, with the village guides' assistance, she also discovered a large sapphire pocket deep within a cave.

Taksin informed the King that they were still unsure as to the size and route of the veins, but Ratray remained confident that the veins would be large and bring prosperity to the village. It would only be a one-hour drive to Chantaburi with the new road built. She'd also found Rose Quartz deposits, which usually denoted gold, so it was possible there was also some of that precious mineral.

Ratray was thrilled when she told Taksin that she'd never come across anything as exciting as this before. She intended to continue investigating the area for several more days, until a complete and thorough report could be made to the King.

Taksin was in his office at the Imperial Palace, organising and co-ordinating the improvements and developments of Salaburi, when his phone rang.

"Major General Nalaphon Chinawat, the Pattaya chief of police, is on the line, Khun Taksin," announced his secretary.

The two exchanged morning greetings and then Taksin enquired,

"Have you any news from the investigation?"

"The body of an Arab was discovered with the top of his skull cut clean off by a sharp, double-bladed instrument found embedded in the wall. My officer's took fingerprints off the blade, which belonged to a young Thai man, about 25 years of age, who was taken to Pattaya Bangkok Memorial Hospital with a bullet wound. The man died in the night, rather suspiciously," said the chief, but continued, "We found a computer in the hotel room, which had been receiving messages from another computer. We are trying to trace the person it linked to. My officer's also retrieved several pictures of what appears to be the object that you are searching for, Khun Taksin."

Nalaphon went silent as he looked at his notes.

"Have you any further leads?" enquired Taksin.

"There was blood on a window, so we assume that the Thai lad jumped out. We also received reports about three foreigners who accompanied him to hospital. We tried to interview the one injured, but he seemed a little confused. We do not know where the other two went. We found which hotel they were staying at, but the receptionist informed us that they had left with two girls early that morning. It also appears that somebody else was in the room. There was more than just the young Thai and the dead Arab. The Dolphin's receptionist told my officers that the Thai man checked in a few days ago with another foreign man, who they recognised as a friend of a Mr. Andrew Towhee, an unsavoury character that left Thailand some years ago. However, they could find no trace of this other man anywhere. They did find a scorched area and a slight gold outline on the floor of the alley at the side of the hotel, although I'm unsure whether that is relevant."

Taksin thanked the police chief, requesting that he monitor the situation and continue investigating.

310

Taksin felt confused, so decided at this stage just to wait and see what developed. He hoped that the sacred relic had not already left the country and that Pon was safe and would contact him soon.

— Chapter Eighteen —

Spock, Stu, Dao, and Moo were now on their way to Koh Samet, a small island and marine reserve on the eastern seaboard. They had caught the morning bus to Rayong. The lads told the girls to turn off their mobiles, and to leave them off. The bus would take three hours to travel from Pattaya to Rayong, followed by an hour on the ferry to Koh Samet.

'Koh' precedes all islands' names.

While on the bus, the girls tried to teach Spock and Stu a bit of the Thai language. Thais liked foreigners to learn a little, but not too much of their language. The lads didn't appear interested. They knew the basics:

Sawasdee krap - Hello.

Tow Lai krap? - How much?

Hung nam, ti nay krap? - Where is the toilet?

Aw bia sing, koat song krap. - Two bottles of Singha beer please.

'Krap' being the polite ending to a sentence for a male, 'Kah' the polite ending for a female.

They knew the essentials. Besides, their ladies spoke English, even if not fluently, they understood.

They surveyed the other passengers on the bus, who were a mixture of foreign and Thai. Stu pointed to a small, bald Thai man, wearing a T-shirt and jeans.

"Look Spock, there's your Thai brother, he's also bald as a bell-end."

Spock chuckled.

"Yeah, the economy size."

The four arrived at the Rayong jetty and bought ferry tickets. They then went to one of the tour desks and booked two bungalow style rooms at the Malibu Beach Resort, which looked reasonable and was located on the beach. They walked around a small market and bought masks and snorkels.

They boarded a small ferry 30 minutes later. Stu noticed a familiar figure sitting a few rows in front of them.

"Look, Spock, there's your economy size brother from the bus. It looks like he has a sword tied to his rucksack, ready to chop off your useless head," said Stu, chortling.

Spock took this comment with as much dignity as he could, giving Stu a short sharp clip around his ear.

Pon had never seen the sea close up, and had never been on a boat. But he'd conquered the sky, so the water should be easy, he thought.

The old ferry pulled out of the harbour and headed towards Samet. Pon felt a little scared for the first few minutes, but hearing laughter coming from Stu for some reason put him at ease.

They arrived on Samet and caught a Tuk-Tuk to the Malibu Beach Resort. They passed Pon along the way.

"Your brother looks lost, Spock," said Stu. Then, noticing Pon following in the same direction, continued, "No, it's okay; he appears to be going our way."

314

They arrived 15 minutes later at the Malibu Beach Resort, a large resort with 50 rooms, a swimming pool, restaurant and small mini mart right on the beachfront. They checked in, changed into their swimming gear, and went out onto the hot, golden sand. The girls had bought food from the market and happily munching on their dull, yellow-coloured fruit that gave off a pungent aroma.

"What's that?" asked Spock

"*Durian," said Moo. "You try, alloey, delicious,"

Spock, pulling off a chunk, sniffed it.

"Smells like crap." He took a large bite, and then spat it out."Tastes like crap too."

The girls ranted about him wasting food, so Spock picked up the chewed lump of Durian, washed the sand off with bottled water, and offered it back to the girls.

They spent a lazy afternoon chillaxing and looking out at the clear blue, still water of the South China Sea. The beach was busy. People lay on sun-loungers or swam in the warm ocean.

That evening, they ate, showered, and took a stroll along the beach. Malibu Beach wasn't large, but other beaches were easily accessible from there. It was a central location. They found smaller beaches with small resorts and bars nearby, owned by both Thais and Europeans. They stopped at Inga's Bar, which had small bamboo sides and a thatched, dried banana leaf roof. Inga, the owner, was from Norway and an amenable chap, but once he started talking, he never seemed to want to stop. They ordered cocktails as Inga told them that they were the best on Samet.

"Why don't you try the Long Island Ice Tea?" he suggested.

His small, haggard-looking wife mixed the cocktail and, although the lads had seen her put in at least seven spirits, the lads assured Dao there was very little alcoholic content because it had a cocktail umbrella. She believed this, drank it straight down, and ordered another. Inga told them that he'd owned the bar for several years and high season was good, which allowed him to survive throughout the low season. He said that he lived at the back of the restaurant, in a small bungalow which, when the lads investigated on one of their voyages of toilet discovery, turned out to be a shabby, run-down shack. Stu asked Inga if his bungalow was behind the dog's kennel. Inga looked indignant and went to speak with other customers.

They moved along the beach, stopping at several more bars and bought shellfish from the many half oil-drum barbecues. It was the freshest seafood they had ever tasted.

They returned to the resort around midnight, carrying a wankered Dao. Stu put her to bed, and Spock and Moo staggered to their room.

****

Koh Samet, like most islands in Thailand, was covered in jungle, rocky outcrops and mountains. The larger islands had been developed to a stage where very little jungle, only sporadic spots, remained. Large islands, such as Phuket and Samui, had been modernised, with any spare piece of land turned into a hotel, resort, or other building to attract the hoards of foreign visitors and their money. The smaller islands remain relatively unscathed, with tourist developments only in the flat areas around beaches, leaving the harder-to-develop hillsides and still lush jungle untouched.

It was in this small jungle terrain overlooking Malibu Beach Resort where Pon made himself a small shelter to observe his targets.

316

He gathered edible roots and tree snakes, which he ate raw as he did not want to alert anyone to his presence with a fire. He noticed fish in the crystal clear water alongside the boat, but these didn't look the same as the ones he had caught in the shallow streams surrounding Salaburi, so he decided not to catch or eat them. Using the illumination of the resort, he saw the four go out. He meditated and continued with his carving. His plan was to make a move that night, but when he saw the four returning to the resort, with one woman looking sick, he decided it would be wrong to do anything now. Besides, he would need her to translate for him in order to get the relic before dispatching them to their respective gods. He thought Spock was a Phra farang Kaw, a foreign white monk, because of his shaven head and hoped that Buddha would forgive him for killing another monk.

****

The next morning, the four awoke around 11 a.m. They ate breakfast and went down to the beach. It was a hot, sunny day. Dao had a hangover, blaming Stu and Spock for feeling unwell and not believing Stu's excuse of, "You must have eaten a bad prawn."

The lads wanted to go snorkelling, so brought their masks and snorkels. They had to pluck up courage because the previous night, they had asked Inga about sharks in the ocean. Inga told them that there were sharks, mainly Leopard Sharks, but they were harmless to humans, being bottom feeders and only feeding on small crustaceans.

This panicked the lads, as the words Leopard and Shark in the same creature's name certainly didn't sound harmless.

After spending the morning chilling out, the girls went to their room to watch television, leaving the two brave explorers alone. They eventually plucked up the courage to go beyond their ankles. Spock and Stu entered the warm clear water with the sound of the Jaws theme-tune in their heads. They swam out over a coral reef. It was low tide and they were in about two meters of water. They saw the

317

undersea kingdom and soon forgot their fears. Large longhorn and fire corals littered the seabed, soft and fan corals all swaying with the current. The reef was alive with sea life: schools of neon blue tetra and butterfly fish were all around them. They pointed out to each other different species. A large, brightly- coloured triggerfish swam past, and a Crown of Thorn starfish caressed the hard coral, taking its lunch out of the living rock. They snorkelled along, not noticing the crouched figure on the rocks, watching their every move.

They were watching a cute-faced, small, box puffer fish, when suddenly there was a loud splash in the water close by. Their first and only thought was, 'Shark!' They popped their heads out of the water and swam in a panic toward the shore. They swam a short distance, stood up and looked back at the rocks. They saw thrashing arms, legs and a body, which kept disappearing under the water, only to re-surface and thrash more.

"Look," said Stu, "someone's drowning."

Pon had never learned to swim. The streams around the village were too shallow, so nobody swam, and now he was learning the hard way. He had slipped off the rocks into the sea and thrashed about in panic, with his arms and legs slapping the water in an unsuccessful attempt to keep afloat. He swallowed seawater and felt it going into his already weakened lungs. After a few minutes, totally exhausted, he stopped thrashing and sank beneath the surface. He felt tranquil; everything was still and silent under the water. He imagined that he would soon be in Nirvana. He was ready to meet Buddha for guidance about the journey beyond.

Pon felt a tug on his T-shirt and was lifted to the surface. He broke the surface, coughing and spluttering.

Spock carried Pon to the beach and placed him on the sand. On all fours, he coughed, spluttered, belched, and vomited out seawater; he felt exhausted. After a few minutes, he rolled onto his back, looking into the smiling faces of Stu and Spock. Pon felt unprepared and an easy target. He rolled onto his front, got unsteadily to his feet and ran off into the jungle. Stu waved sarcastically and said,

"Yes! Well, don't mention it, no thanks required."

Spock responded, "What a rude little shit. He gives bald people a bad name."

Pon got to his shelter and collapsed, his lungs felt on fire.

A few hours went by and Dao and Moo joined the lads on the beach. They went snorkelling again, but decided it was time to shower, change, eat, shag, and go out. They decided to leave the snorkelling gear in Stu's room.

They entered. A familiar face, dressed in monk's robes with a sword pointed at them, stood with his back against the wall. Shocked, they moved forward. The monk cut through the air with his sword as a warning not to come any closer

"Where is the sacred relic?" Pon snarled in Thai.

Dao and Moo, unsure of what he meant, became scared and confused. Stu was angry and confused. Spock, angry by somebody pointing a blade at him, reacted.

He threw the masks and snorkels at Pon, who slashed a mask clean in half but, not responding quick enough to return to his guard, received a bone-crunching left hook from Spock that could have felled a horse. Stunned and rattled to the bone, Pon dropped his sword. Spock felt shocked at not knocking the little man out. He grabbed him by the throat and lifted him against the wall. Pon felt dazed and tried to shake the effect of the blow off. He now dangled off the floor, with an angry Spock staring at him. He became subdued and looked at the four.

Stu instructed Dao and Moo to ask him what he wanted. Spock released his chokehold slightly to allow the monk to reply. Pon tried to think of a way to reach his glave. Moo then asked him what he wanted and he croakily replied.

Dao and Moo then understood.

"The little gold box belongs to him and he wants it back," said Dao.

Stu thought for a moment and said,

"The portable ashtray...Why didn't he just ask?"

Dao relayed the message to Pon, who fell silent, deep in thought about the events over the past weeks, of his murdered brother monks and his brother, Dam. He now felt confused about these two white men, realising that his lust for revenge had blinded him from the path of enlightenment. He thought. 'Surely it cannot be as simple as just asking.'

He looked at the serious face of Stu, and the frightened and confused faces of Dao and Moo. He glanced to his side and looked up at Spock. These people didn't appear the same as the other foreigners who he'd dispatched previously. They saved his life and he owed them that, so he quietly asked,

"Have you got the holy relic...and could I have it?"

Dao translated this to Stu, who said,

"Tell him I found it. It is safe in Pattaya, and of course, if it means so much to him, he can have it. With pleasure."

Pon, feeling confused, couldn't decide his next course of action.

'What do I do?' he thought.

Spock lowered him to the ground. Pon, looking startled, nervously started laughing. His hurt, misery, anguish, and lust for revenge had built up like a pressure cooker and now, with his thoughts conflicted, his release was laughter. Spock looked at the laughing monk and smiled. Putting his arm around Pon's shoulders and looking deep into the monk's eyes, he said, "You, my small friend, are a nutcase."

Stu then started laughing, making Pon laugh louder. Spock joined in, followed by the girls. Spock picked up Pon's sword, tapped him on the head with the handle, and gave it back to him, which kept the laughter going even though nobody in the room knew what was so amusing. It felt good and continued for several minutes.

Once the laughter died down, Pon sat on the bed and briefly told his story via Dao and Moo. Although their English wasn't so good, the two lads got the gist. They noticed that the two girls looked sheepish when the box got mentioned. They lied when asked whether the box had been tampered with.

"Well at least they have new teeth now, last another 2000 years easy," said Spock.

Stu and Spock laughed again and Pon, who did not have a clue what Spock said, laughed anyway, which bought scowls from the girls. Pon was careful not to mention the demise of his previous duties, including his brother.

After Pon related his story, Stu told Pon of their plan to spend two more nights on the island and then return to Pattaya. They assured Pon that the relic was safe and he was welcome to stay with them. Pon, although cautious, agreed, as he did not want to spoil their holiday. Besides, he could learn more about these strange foreigners.

Spock went to the mini-mart and returned with a large bottle of Sangthip Thai whisky, four glasses, and a fruit-based drink for Dao. He poured the whiskey and asked Moo to tell Pon that it was an English tradition when new friendships were made. Pon had never

321

tried alcohol before and the first taste hit sharp in the back of his throat. By his third glass, he found quite a liking for this new liquid; by the fourth glass, he was wankered and fell fast asleep. Spock booked him into a room and carried him to his bedroom, laying him on the bed. It was only seven o'clock.

The four went to Inga's. Pon woke up once during the night, rolled onto the floor and fell back to sleep.

The next morning there came a knock on Stu's door. He opened the door to a very angry looking security guard and a sheepish looking Pon, who had woken up alone and presumed that he'd been duped. He had been running around, swishing his sword, and causing mayhem. The resort staff eventually subdued him and told him that his friends had put him in the room. After calming down, the security guards took him along to Stu's room.

Stu brought Pon into his room; he didn't think that he had slept long, but according to his watch, it was five o'clock. He left Dao and Pon in the bedroom, while he showered and dressed. He wanted to do a bit more snorkelling, so he decided to wake up Spock and grab a bite to eat first. He walked back into the bedroom, where Pon and Dao sat watching television. Dao was showing Pon how to work the TV remote-control.

"Come on," said Stu, "We'll go get Spock and Moo and then grab the last of the sun, before it gets dark."

Dao smiled and said,

"It's five o'clock in the morning, stupid man."

Pon, the assassin, who could easily kill a man in the blink of an eye, whose fighting skills could, on a good day, take out a small army, was led with his ear gripped firmly between the finger and thumb of an irate, small, fat Englishman and placed in his room. Stu sat him on the bed, turned on the TV, gave him the remote and his watch and pointed to ten o'clock.

"Come back to the room then," he said, and made gestures in the hope that Pon would understand.

Stu went back to his room. Dao lay naked on the bed, smiling. 'That's a bit of luck,' thought Stu, 'she appears to have left her legs open.'

They had fun during the day with Pon, who was an amusing little chap under all that seriousness. Stu and Spock taught him to snorkel in the shallows after buying two more sets of snorkelling gear. He was scared at first, but the two lads held onto him. He marvelled at everything he experienced. He brought the rest of his meagre belongings to his room. Stu and Spock taught him a few traditions, like the normal English greeting of placing your hand into a fist and displaying the middle finger. The lads had fun watching him perform this greeting especially at Inga's, but they received a bollocking from the girls, who told Pon it was a joke and not a good thing to do.

They ate at a barbecue. Stu and Spock thought Pon could eat the contents of a small ocean. He tried everything that had been cooked and finished it all: bones, shells, everything. He drank a couple of beers after being informed it was a harmless liquid, but after being put straight by the girls, stopped after the first few.

They had a good time on the island with their new friend. The next day, Stu and Spock decided that when they returned to Pattaya, Pon had to stay the night, as it was time, and indeed their duty, to get him laid. They caught the two o'clock ferry the following afternoon and headed back on the bus to Pattaya. Pon turned on Towhey's phone and called Taksin.

Taksin informed him of the investigation, but Pon told him that the relic would be in his possession soon. Taksin told him about the two suspect foreigners who had vanished. However, the other one had been discharged from hospital, so could lead the police to the other two. Pon realised they he was referring to Spock and Stu, so he told Taksin that he had everything under control, asking him to inform the Pattaya police to back off from the investigation. He informed Taksin that he would be getting the relic later that day and return with it to Bangkok the following morning. However, Taksin told him that he would travel to Pattaya first thing to meet him and escort him back. Pon thanked him and turned off the phone.

Buddhist monks devote their lives to the teaching of Buddha, with male and female monks distraction free; hence, both sexes shave their heads, as grooming is a distraction. The Tinju were a male-only order, so knew nothing about women; they were a distraction and never entered into their lives. Therefore, what they have never had, they never missed. Pon, having spent time in the company of two attractive women, had suddenly and without warning developed a new and exciting sensation. For the first time in his life, he felt horny.

— Chapter Nineteen —

They arrived back at the Sawasdee hotel at twilight. Dao, having switched on their mobile phones while on the bus, had called Luanne. Luanne told her that the police were searching for them and Nick had been questioned over their disappearance. Pon, overhearing their conversation, smiled.

The girls relayed the news to Spock and Stu, who felt bemused and worried, until Pon told the girls,

"Please don't worry. The police won't trouble you, everything is fine"

Dao relayed this to the lads.

Stu and Spock realised they knew nothing about this funny little monk. Maybe they would gain better knowledge in the next few days, which sadly was all the time they had left of their holiday.

Nick and Luanne sat in the hotel lobby. The group returned and Dao and Moo went over to Luanne.

Stu, Spock, and Pon went over and sat down with Nick to get his moaning out of the way. Along with his plaster cast, he now had a bald patch, a small gauze dressing taped to his head, covering ten silk sutures, and no front teeth. The lads assured this gummy vampire that his teeth were, 'somewhat safe.' Nick moaned about how much they would cost to replace, and how expensive his treatment had been. Pon, not being able to understand the conversation, went to join the women. Nick whispered,

"Who is he?"

"He's an assassin, matey, and our bodyguard," Spock joked.

Spock did not realise how right he was about the first part, until Nick mentioned that the Thai man who they had taken to hospital had subsequently died, which was why the police were looking for them.

Stu and Spock felt shaken by this news. They asked Dao, who just nodded and said,

"I know, Pon already told us that he was in the alley when his brother jumped out of the window. He told us that his brother was attempting to retrieve the holy relic from two foreigners in the room, which was how he knew you and Spock must have found it."

"What about his brother?" asked a concerned Stu.

"Pon felt sad about his brother, but told us that he was a brave warrior, which was why he needed the ashtr...relic to restore order, and in memory of his brother." Dao explained.

Pon had told the girls a small white lie. The lads believed it and presumed that Dam must have died from his bullet wound. They thought it best not to dwell on it too much and, as the police were no longer involved, it was surely true.

Pon spoke to Dao, who asked,

"Can Pon see the relic?"

Nick looked bemused.

Stu thought fast.

"I have an idea," he said.

They told Pon that Spock, the great white monk, would bring down the relic. However, Pon said he would rather receive it in the room, for a private ceremony. He would go to the toilet and change into his monk's robes.

326

"Quick Spock!" said Stu and they rushed toward the lift.

"Don't forget my teeth." said Nick, still bewildered.

They took the elevator to their floor. Stu went into his room and took out the box from his bedside drawer. He sprung open the lid. Spock came from the lift with a plastic cup filled with sand, taken from the ashtray outside the elevator. They placed some sand around the tissue paper with Nick's denture, shook out the excess into the sink, and snapped the lid shut. They then causally sat on the bed, shaking the box to make sure it sounded, and felt, similar to the original and placed it on the bedside table.

Ten minutes later, Pon, Dao, and Moo came into the room. Pon was dressed in his robe, with his sheathed sword on his red sash. He entered the room and caught a glimpse of the holy relic, looking slightly dented from the fall. He spoke to Moo, who asked Spock if he could hold the box while Pon prayed. Spock picked up the box and presented it to Pon, who knelt down and lit essence sticks he'd obtained from the hotel reception. Wafting the wisps of scented smoke around the room, he chanted his mantra. The girls stood in silent prayer. Stu sat on the bed, smirking, as Spock bent down like the pope, with the golden box in his hand and a stupid smile on his face. Stu took a few photographs to finish off his film, which give him something to do to stop him laughing.

Pon's ceremony lasted about 15 minutes. When it was over, he took the holy box, carefully wrapped it in a silk cloth and placed it in his robe pouch. He then turned around to give a quick blessing to the girls and smiled. He mentioned something to Dao, who scowled at him and said to Stu,

"He wants to go out now."

Stu booked a room for Pon on the same floor. Pon was a little concerned about the relic's safety, until Stu assured him that the girls would be staying in the room, so it would be well taken care of until they got back. Pon showered, then neatly and ceremoniously folded his robe and put his glave on top for protection. He went to Stu's room and handed the bundle to Dao, who placed it in the wardrobe. Stu and Spock returned from the mini mart and stocked the girls up with fruit-based alcoholic drinks and other provisions for the night.

Nick, Spock, Stu, and Pon went into the hot, sticky night air.

"First on the agenda," said Spock. "We'll buy him new clothes. He's been wearing the same jeans and T-shirt for three days now...then," he continued, "I think Soi 6 would be a good place to start on our mission to get the mad monk laid."

It was a good night, with the entertainment mainly provided by the shy Pon. Although the language barrier proved to be a bit of a problem, they overcame this with gestures. Pon translated through the many female muggers who, like before, swarmed the lads. The Thai women were not that receptive to Pon, and although he did not mention that he was a monk, just the fact that he was a Thai man, was enough to put the girls off, as they knew they would not receive any money from him. That problem was soon overcome when Spock and Stu offered a rather buxom Thai woman 1000 Baht to take care of their friend and work colleague.

Pon and the woman disappeared into a room above the bar. They returned several minutes later, with a glazed look on Pon's face and a smile on the woman's, who had just made the quickest 1000 Baht she'd earned in a long time.

Pon went along for a 'soapy' at Sabaiiland and by the end of the night, he was 'one of the lads.' They got him drinking beer, informing him that Heineken beer contained no alcohol because the bottle was green, unlike the Singha on the island. He fell for this and quickly became spannered, working his way to shitfaced. The lads decided they'd had enough laughs for one night and returned to the hotel at one o'clock.

328

Embarrassed, Pon went along to Stu's room, trying to act sober. He bowed to the girls, took his robes back to his room and flopped onto the bed. Having already spent most of the night on beds, he thought he might as well sleep on one. With a satisfied grin, he fell into a blissful sleep. For 29 years, this little Tinju warrior had devoted his life unselfishly to the causes of wisdom, courage, and, the path to enlightenment. It had taken men from a strange country, with their strange non-religious habits, three days to lead him astray and he was enjoying every minute.

The other three went to Stu's room. Nick took Luanne back to his room because she was spannered, as were the other two girls. Stu suggested a game of dominoes, but Dao felt in a romantic mood. She gave Stu a long, lingering kiss and started to rub his todger over his shorts.

She whispered, "Are you sure you want to play dominoes?" She then nibbled his earlobe.

After being shoved out, Moo looked at Spock, smiled, and asked,

"You want boom-boom?"

Spock thought for a millisecond.

"Shame not too," he said, and they rushed to their room.

— Chapter Twenty —

Dao's voice followed a loud sawing noise that emanated from her and Stu's room.

"Stop snoring, pig William."

Then silence. That had been going on for the past few hours. It started again, but stopped when there was a loud rap on the door. Grumbling, Stu got out of bed, put a towel around his waist, and opened the door. Two armed, uniformed soldiers stood in the doorway. Stu drowsily looked at the soldiers, whose angry, expressionless faces glared back at him.

Behind the two soldiers stood a man wearing a smart white uniform with gold braid and next to him the mad monk, Pon.

"What do you want?" a sleepy Stu asked.

The man in the white uniform spoke in English, and asked,

"May we come in?"

Stu asked them to wait and closed the door. He went back inside the room, opened the curtains and windows to let in some air, and told Dao. He then re-opened the door and invited them inside. The two guards remained outside, while Taksin and Pon entered the room.

Pon, who followed behind Taksin, got a clip around his ear from Stu as he entered, which made him chuckle. Taksin wai-ed Dao who, trying to hold on to the sheet, returned the wai. Stu removed clothes off chairs and invited them to sit. Taksin introduced himself and told them that he was a representative of the King. Dao felt awestruck.

Pon asked Stu to go to get Spock. Stu left the three in the room, and walked past the guards who saluted him as he went to Spock's room. He rapped on Spock's door and a sleepy eyed Moo opened it. Spock was still festering in bed. Stu told him about the events of the last few minutes. Spock slipped on his shorts, Moo put on a dress, and they went along to Stu's room. The guards saluted the party as they entered. Spock could not resist the opportunity, and looked the guards up and down to inspect them. He then saluted them and announced they should stand at ease and carry on. Not understanding a word he was saying, the guards remained stony-faced. Spock joined the others in the room. Taksin and Pon wai-ed the new arrivals and Moo gracefully returned the greeting, while Spock made a clumsy attempt at this simple manoeuvre.

Taksin went on to explain the significance of the holy relic and express his gratitude for their assistance in the recovery of the sacred item. He gave the lads his business card, just in case they needed to contact him. He informed them that the relic would be taken to the Imperial Palace, and they could visit as his special guests. He said that he and Pon would now be going to Bangkok, and thanked them both again. Taksin stood up, wai-ed the girls and then the lads, who again clumsily returned the gesture. Pon said something to Taksin, who wai-ed the monk and left the room, hearing a slapping sound as Spock gave Pon a clip around the ear. However, Taksin didn't look back.

Pon faced the four and, through Dao and Moo, thanked them for everything. He now considered Spock and Stu his brothers, and the girls his sisters, a great honour for the four.

Pon then reached into his cloth bag and brought out a small gold ornament, which he handed to Dao.

"For you, my sister," he announced.

Dao took the ornament and wai-ed Pon. He then brought out a blue ornament and gave it to Moo, who did the same. He removed his two remaining red stone ornaments and gave one each to Stu and Spock.

Stu smiled at Pon and shook his hand. He felt a lump in his throat and could feel tears welling up in his eyes. He had grown fond of this funny little monk. Spock grabbed Pon, picked him up, squeezed him gently, and replaced him on the floor. Pon smiled and went into his bag again. This time he brought out the wad of dollars that he'd shared with the small girl in Cambodia. He gave the wad to a startled Spock.

"He had money all this time. The tight-fisted little sod kept that quiet," said a smiling Spock. They all smiled at Pon, who bowed and walked over to the door. He turned and said in pigeon English,

"Goodbye, my friends." He then held up two clenched fists and extended the middle fingers on both, pointing them at Stu and Spock. He smiled and walked out of the door, leaving the four stunned by the cheeky little monk.

Dao broke the silence by clipping both Stu and Spock around their ears, saying,

"Your fault...You teach monk no good."

They stared at their gifts. Dao knew hers was gold, so couldn't wait to show Luanne and brag about it. Moo looked at her intricately carved sapphire, unaware of its value. The lads stared at theirs, noting the skilled workmanship of the carving. They all felt sad by Pon's departure, but something made them feel sure they would see him again.

"Oh well," said Stu. "I will give this to my mum and tell her it's a ruby worth a fortune."

"You will as well," said Spock, knowing that his friend always told his mum small Porky pies, lies, about gifts.

Unbeknownst to them all, Stu was correct. It was a 67-carat flawless ruby and it was worth a fortune.

333

They looked at the wad of dollars, which Spock laid out on the bed.

"What should we do with this?" asked Spock.

Dao counted out $2600 in $100 bills.

"I know," said Spock. "Remember that article we read in the local newspaper, 'Pattaya Today?'

Stu recalled the article and said,

"Oh yeah, good idea."

Spock mentioned his idea to the girls, who agreed and pecked the boys on the cheek.

"You are Jai dee, kind-hearted," said Moo.

Spock and Stu were now in good books with the girls. The four decided to go eat breakfast and then go to Pattaya Park, a water theme park.

Nick then came and banged on the door. He had seen Pon leaving.

"What happened?" Nick asked, agitated.

Stu told him,

"The King wanted his best assassin back because he needed to go on another secret assignment."

"Bullshit," said Nick. "Have you got my teeth?"

Spock sniggered and said,

"Not exactly...but don't worry, they're safe."

The two lads laughed and the two girls looked at each other, quickly changing the subject.

"Is Luanne awake?" Moo asked. "We want to show her something."

— Chapter Twenty-One —

A tranquil feeling of majesty and reverence was felt within the Temple of the Emerald Buddha. A bamboo scaffold had been erected around the golden Buddha statue, which smiled down on the three figures knelt below.

After an hour of chanting and prayer, Pon took a small glass case and ascended the scaffold. He reached the head of the 50' statue and slotted the four rods on the base of the glass case into four newly drilled holes on the head. Pon then looked at the contents, bowing to the small, jewel-encrusted box. He glanced at a large green emerald, housed alongside the holy relic. The two treasures would remain together until the end of time.

Pon looked down at the two men below. He felt honoured to be the one who would sit the most holy of relics into its final resting place.

The two figures looked up at Pon and the holy relic. A beam of sunlight shone through a small skylight in the temple, hitting the emerald and the new addition. The gemstones and gold box gave off a radiant glow, throwing spectral lights around the top of the statue's head, appearing like a halo. Those present felt that Buddha was gracing this holy ceremony.

Pon climbed down from the scaffold and joined Taksin and the great Thai King. They stared at the wondrous light show going on above their heads, feeling in awe of the spectacle.

After leaving the temple, Pon went to the monks' quarters to freshen up before joining Taksin and the King in the stateroom and being brought up-to-date with the happenings in Salaburi, and more importantly, the Tinju. After making his way across the vast grounds of the royal palace, Pon went into the stateroom.

Taksin, King Bhumipol and Crown Prince Maja Vijiralongorn were looking at 3D images on a computer. Pon wai-ed the party and the King beckoned him closer.

The King enquired about his journey to recover the holy treasure. Pon gave his account to the King, who sometimes looked shocked and horrified, even though he knew that to a Tinju, it was all part of his credo. Pon didn't mention his antics from the previous night, but smiled when he thought about them.

Taksin told Pon of the work carried out in Salaburi. The original plan to transport fruit and medicines to markets had been greatly enhanced by the discovery of large mineral deposits nearby. Salaburi would now become the most important mineral mining area in Thailand. Prospects for the future of Salaburi were excellent. The village would be wealthy and develop into a small, modern town with hospitals, schools, and gemstone laboratories. Thailand would once again have its own ruby and sapphire mines, which would be the envy of the world.

The King decided that only a few outsiders would go into the village, so there would be minimal disruption to the surrounding jungle. They intended to use a new mining technique that the King had developed.

Taksin told Pon about the plans for the new Tinju, informing him that all the elders had agreed. He also told him that all of the surviving young monks had returned to the Tinju to carry on with their calling. Several new monks and instructors had already arrived and all they were waiting for now was their head instructor and new Prime Master... Pon.

The King proposed that Pon continue to be a Tinju, but as the Prime Master. He also wanted him to be the royal bodyguard to his son, the Crown Prince. That meant travelling around the world with the prince as an envoy, representing Thailand and its monarchy. Pon would be given a residence at the palace, befitting his new rank, if he chose to accept.

338

"The invitation," said the King, "is also extended to your family."

Pon looked confused by the King's last comment, but let it pass. He had plans of his own and hoped that the King could offer him guidance and wisdom on his decision.

Pon thanked the King for his gracious proposal and told him and the other two about his ideas. The three listened to Pon as he relayed his thoughts, ideas and the reasons behind them.

The room went silent. The King thought about the information, and thanked the monk for his honesty. He agreed to grant his wish, but first he wanted Pon to return to the village and discuss the matter with Vitchae and the other elders before making his decision final. Pon rose, wai-ed at the party, left the room and returned to the monks' quarters. The King, Crown Prince, and Taksin chatted amongst themselves. Taksin got on his Sat-scan portable phone and rang Khun Penmark, the chief surveyor in the village. He gave him a message for Vitchae; informing him that their warrior would return to the village the following morning.

A white Bell Jet Ranger helicopter waited on the helicopter pad the next morning with its rotors idling. It waited for its passenger, who was standing well away from the rotors, ignoring the constant waving of the pilot for him to board. Pon was afraid to get on the helicopter, so was gently pushed in by the aircrew and seated in one of the four passenger seats. An airman strapped Pon into his seat. Pon started to relax, until the pilot opened the throttle and the gentle idle turned into a loud roar. The airman closed the door, so all that he heard was a gentle hum and the yells of their passenger.

The helicopter flew around Pong-Nam-Rom and the previous meeting point. Pon eased a little, as they were not as high as the aeroplane had been and he could clearly see the land. The pilot banked the aircraft and the airman pointed out to Pon the large build-up of heavy machinery, bulldozers, road-rollers and cranes.

The helicopter levelled off and the airman explained that they would fly the route that the road would take to the village. Ten minutes later, the pilot did a circuit of the village and Pon noticed the amount of activity going on below. They flew over the Wat and came to a hover. A large crowd had gathered. The helicopter slowly descended, touching down with only a slight bump. The pilot disengaged the engines and the rotors slowed to an idle swing and then stopped. The airman slipped off Pons safety belt and opened the door.

Pon stepped off the Jet Ranger's low fuselage to the sound of a massive cheer erupting from the gathered crowd. He was overwhelmed and wai-ed and bowed to the people. A small group started to walk toward him. Pon noticed Vitchae walked unaided, looking directly at him.

He walked forward and the party met about 20 yards from the helicopter. They all stopped, and Pon recognised the tearful old women with Vitchae. It was Banti, his mother, along with his father and sisters. The old woman couldn't contain her excitement any longer and went to hug Pon, sobbing uncontrollably. His father and sisters joined in and hugged their new prodigal son and brother. Everyone was in tears, including Pon. After a few moments of constant chatter and hugs, Vitchae said,

"Welcome home, Prime Master. There is a lot to tell you. But for now enjoy this moment with your family and we can meet up later."

"Master Vitchae!" Pon exclaimed. "You're sights returned."

"Yes Pon," said a smiling Vitchae. "The Kings' miracle."

The family went to the temple, which seemed the most appropriate place for another miracle. They chatted, cried, and prayed for a few hours and then Pon discussed his plans. He wanted to get their thoughts before he spoke to Vitchae, wanting his family to make plans together.

340

Pon did not mention Dam. He thought best that the old woman should continue to think her son had perished in the jungle eight years ago, so there was no point in muddying his memory as Dam had repented and atoned for his crime. Moreover, Banti, who thought that she had lost both her sons, with Jinn, now found her real son was the bravest of Tinju warriors. Pon decided to let her enjoy this moment and every moment from now on.

Pon and his family left the temple after a few hours, with his father having to prise Banti off him, saying,

"Don't worry woman, he isn't going anywhere."

Pon walked to the monk's quarters and went into Vitchae's room. The old Master, sitting with Cenat, beckoned for Pon to join them. He sat on the floor along with them and they prayed together, thanking Buddha for his protection and wisdom.

Vitchae outlined the plans for the village to Pon. He then took him to the arena where the new instructors were putting the new monks through their paces. They saw Pon, stopped what they were doing, faced him, bowed, and gave him a long respectful Wai.

"Welcome back Prime Master," said one young monk.

The other students echoed the sentiment. Pon thanked them and told them he felt honoured to be their teacher and to be instructing them on the way of the Tinju, telling them that they should look

forward to the day when they achieved the honour of wearing the red sash and title Warrior.

Pon was perplexed about his decision. He turned to Vitchae and said

"Master, I need to discuss something urgently with you."

"All in good time, Prime Master," said Vitchae. "Let's look around the village and see what was happening."

Vitchae, Pon, and Cenat left the arena and the monks went back to their training.

Vitchae had a suspicion about what Pon wanted to discuss, nevertheless, he first wanted to show him everything and try out his new role as Prime Master. They walked around the village. Vitchae introduced him to all the new arrivals, telling him what they did. "This is Khun Kitwat, he is in charge of the electric supply." He then pointed at a newly erected wooden hut and lights.

"Look, we have a generator and power. We now have electric lights in some of the houses. Your family has it already...Have you ever seen a television?"

The old master rambled on excitedly for the rest of the day and into the evening. He introduced Pon to Ratray.

"Ratray found out that our ornaments are valuable precious stones."

When there were no more people to meet, Pon turned to Vitchae as they sat along with Cenat, inside the Wat.

"Master," said Pon. "I need your wisdom on a decision that I feel I must make."

A reluctant Vitchae looked at Cenat, who rose and suggested that he should leave.

"No, master Cenat, please don't leave. I would also like your thoughts," Pon said.

Cenat sat back down. Pon stared at the statue of Buddha, recalling the fateful day when all he could see were his brother monks surrounded by deadly smoke. He slowly inhaled, looking for spiritual guidance.

342

"What troubles you Prime Master?" Vitchae enquired, placing his hand on Pons shoulder.

— Chapter Twenty-Two —

The dreaded day arrived. The day when they had to go back to the place where only a few weeks ago they fondly called home, but now referred to as the freezing cold, depressing, shit-hole... England.

Spock and Stu thought that the time went far too quickly. A sentiment not shared by their new friend, Nick, who thought it could not have come soon enough as he was running out of pain-free extremities and money.

Their flight was due to leave at 3:00 p.m., so with the time zone difference, they would arrive in England later that same evening. They booked a taxi for 11:00 a.m. to take them to the airport, giving them plenty of time to check-in.

They woke up early and silently started to pack, joined by Dao and Moo, who had moved several items into the room that they'd called home for the past few weeks.

There was a sombre air in both rooms as they slowly folded their belongings and packed them into their suitcases. Each item held a memory of the last few amazing weeks. They lads had never been so happy or contented. They knew apart from Chunky, nobody would believe their tales. They had been told by a friend prior to leaving, and later by Nick, not to try to explain Thailand, because nobody would believe them. At the time, Stu and Spock thought he had been talking rubbish, but now they weren't so sure. It certainly wasn't normal to go out in England, be surrounded by beautiful oriental woman who took the greatest of care, eat delicious food any time day or night, get drunk 24 hours a day and stay cheaply in a four star hotel.

They were used to going out with over a £100; getting spannered, buying loud, obnoxious, drunken slappers drinks in loud obnoxious places and then going back to their cold flats with a bag of cold food, alone and skint.

"Mate," said Stu, as he made his way into Spock's room "I think we'll buy Chunky a packet of digestive biscuits when we get home and she can listen to our tales. She's a good listener and it will only cost us a packet of Mc.Vities."

To which Spock replied,

"I'd forgotten about that stupid dog. All she will get is my foot up her arse."

There was a love hate relationship between Spock and Chunky, but deep down the big gentle giant had a soft spot for the old dog. Many times she would trot upstairs to Stu's flat with a mouthful of chocolate, followed by Spock who accused her of pinching it off his table.

"Likely story," Stu used to say. "You never leave chocolate uneaten long enough to reach your table."

Spock was seen holding a drunken man by the throat and shaking him for kicking Chunky, who was outside the salon minding her own business. Yes, this gentle giant had a soft spot, although he would never admit it.

They all went for breakfast at their new favourite spot. The Yorkshire rose, a small restaurant, which did a full English breakfast, better than any in Cleethorpes.

Nick booked later that day to have some temporary plastic crowns put on until he got home to England, where he could use the NHS. He ate soup.

They ate breakfast and returned to the hotel to pay and get their belongings. Dao and Moo wanted to go to the airport to see the two

346

lads off. Stu and Spock gave the girls 10,000 Baht each the night before, which they hoped would take care of them for a while. The grateful girls gave them their treat in return. Neither of the pair had a seed left between them. The Listerine share price also took a tumble as sales declined

Stu and Spock stood at the reception, waiting for their bill. The hotel manager came to the desk and wai-ed the pair.

"You two don't have to pay, that had already been taken care of," said the manager.

The two lads looked at each other confused.

"Pon must have had something to do with it, the little shit," said Spock.

Stu chuckled.

"Yeah, I hope someday that we run into the amusing little chap again."

They signed Nick's plaster cast and Spock asked,

"Who's going to take care of you now?"

'Certainly not you two f*****g m***er f****r b*s**ds,' thought Nick

They waited in the courtyard of the hotel.

A large, white chauffeur driven car drove into the car park. The chauffeur got out of the car and asked the waiting group,

"I'm looking for Mr. Stuart Wilson and Mr. Peter Harris."

"That's us," said Spock and Stu. "But we ordered a taxi."

"Courtesy of the King," the driver announced, smiling.

Spock and Stu were surprised, but not as gobsmacked as Dao and Moo.

Stu and Spock put their bags in the boot and Stu asked the driver if they could bring the girls along.

The driver bowed and said,

"Of course, sir."

Spock and Stu shook Nick's good hand. They got in the car, telling him to take care.

The car drove out of the courtyard, Stu asked the chauffeur to make a quick detour en route, to which the driver happily agreed.

The four sat in the back of the plush vehicle. They felt like royalty. They laughed and joked with the girls, and like royalty waved behind the darkened windows, at the people walking down the road.

"Peasants," Stu joked.

Nick and Luanne went to the edge of the courtyard to wave them off. The car had only gone a short distance, when Luanne went back inside. Nick stood and watched as the car slowly made its way along the road. He wanted to make sure these two, who he felt sure jinxed him are gone. He leant out into the road. 'One last wave,' and through grated teeth thought, 'Thank god, they've gone.'

A passing Baht bus then hit him.

The side of the bus hit Nick hard, spinning him around like an atomic slinky into the courtyard. He landed hard on his shoulder, which thudded and he felt his bones snap on the hard stone floor.

Dao looked out of the car's rear window and saw Nick hit by the Baht bus, which didn't stop. They never do. It just sped up and drove away.

"Baht bus hit Nick," said Dao.

The others looked back, but saw nothing.

"Stupid women, speak English, what do you mean?" said Stu, who received a sharp slap around his head.

The car drove out of Pattaya towards Bangkok. Ten minutes later, they pulled into a place in Banglamung town. A sign above the drive read 'Baan Jinjay.' The car pulled up to some small buildings, which resembled a tatty resort. All four got out and went into an office.

A large German priest sat behind a desk, along with a Thai Christian nun in deep discussion. They went silent as the four walked in and Stu placed an envelope in front of the priest. The four then turned, walked out of the office and got back into the car.

The flabbergasted priest looked inside the envelope and showed the nun. They both smiled and looked out of the window as the car reversed. They tipped the money onto the desk and stared.

"There must be a few thousand dollars here," announced the priest.

The sign on the wall behind him read 'Baan Jinjay. Pattaya orphanage.'

The journey to Bangkok airport along the motorway was swift. However, the mood in the car was solemn and silent.

Moo had seen boyfriends off before, but never in this style and never with the same feeling being with Spock. This was Dao's first time and she felt strange. Although she and Stu had only been together a short time, she could not imagine being with anyone else.

349

"That'll pass once they've gone, and we go back working in the bar," Moo told her.

Stu and Spock felt gutted and just held onto the girls. They wanted to take them home with them, but knew getting a visa was virtually impossible.

The car stopped outside the doors of Terminal One at Don Muang international airport. The chauffeur removed Stu and Spock's bags from the boot and they went inside the airport.

They stood holding onto their respective partners and arranged to phone regularly. Stu already planned to book another flight out as soon as he got home.

"I will wait for you," said Dao.

Stu assured her that she would not be waiting long.

Stu realised that she would still be working the bar and sleeping with strangers, but hoped that when he returned to Thailand, she would finish with whom she was with and go with him. This, although Stu and Spock found hard to accept, it was the Thai way. The girls had to earn money and the only way was to sleep with foreigners. Stu and Spock both offered to send money to them, but unlike most girls, they turned down the offer.

"And next time I will take you to England," said Stu. "I never want to be without you, and Duengdao Wilson has such a nice ring to it."

After final hugs, Dao and Moo walked towards the door. Stu and Spock watched them go outside. They thought the departure lounge at the Bangkok international airport must be the saddest place in the world. They felt like bursting into tears, but composed themselves as they walked into the departure lounge. Their lives would never be the same.

— Chapter Twenty-Three —

The lone figure stood in the temple in front of the 50' foot gold statue of Buddha. Previously named 'The temple of the Emerald Buddha,' and now known as the 'Temple of the Sacred Light'. Here stood someone else whose life had also changed over the past few weeks. Pon stared at the two holy relics side by side on top of the statue's head. He knew that in a short while, the afternoon sun would shine directly through the skylight. For about two hours a day, a dramatic and fantastic display of dancing, spectral lights would surround the top of the statue as the two treasures bounced sunlight off each other; creating a holy bright aura.

The temple was due to re-open to the public the following day, after a ceremony by the palace monks. New and old Tinju were on their way to Bangkok and Vitchae would perform the ceremony. The Royal family would attend, so it would be an awesome spectacle. Pilgrims would flock from all over the Kingdom to pack out the temple. People from around the world, from every walk of life, would be able to gaze upon the new wonder of the world, the 'Buddha's light.'

Pon would have his hands full with his new positions. His thoughts turned to the quick transformation in his life, which he knew would take time for him to adjust. With his new family already housed in large quarters in the palace grounds, he discussed his ideas with Vitchae and Cenat. He wanted breast implants and to become a ladyboy.

Only joking!

He would accept the King's offer and become bodyguard to the Crown Prince. He felt honoured to be able to instruct and guide the new monks on the path of enlightenment and ways of the Tinju as their Prime Master. However, this was a role he would share with

Vitchae as he realised a Prime Master needed to be in Salaburi full time.

Pon and his new family would relocate to the palace. His mother and father were given paid duties around the palace, and his two sisters attended university. The family felt thrilled. It was a dream for them. They had never left Salaburi before, let alone travelled in a helicopter.

Pon would travel to Salaburi when his palace commitments allowed, helping train the new Tinju. His palace duties came with a title; 'Defender of the Monarch.' This meant that he would accompany the Crown Prince around the globe on state visits. He would be an ambassador for the Thai people, as well as the prince's bodyguard.

Pon told Vitchae of the more private parts of his journey. He expected Vitchae to be angry with him for breaking his vow of celibacy, but all Vitchae said was,

"What was it like...Tell me more about foreigners?"

Cenat looked shocked.

'Maybe my old friend and Master accepted this new order and life change too readily,' he thought.

Things would take time to adjust. Pon needed time to re-think his life, which changed in such a short space of time, hoping that he was worthy of the trust and duty now bestowed upon him. He stared up at the ever-smiling face of the Buddha's statue.

Pon felt a little uncomfortable wearing his new uniform, gone was his monks robes, replaced by a smart white uniform, his new attire whilst at the palace. His epaulets displayed the royal heraldic crest with shiny golden buttons, again with the crest on them. His red sash had been embroidered with a golden border, sewn with traditional Thai emblems, and at the base was clipped his sword.

352

Pon thought about his family and the love they had shown him, which would be unwavering. He also thought about his new friends, Spock, Stu, Dao, and Moo, hoping that it would be not the end of a friendship, which taught him the most valuable lesson of all. The most effective weapon that he had in his arsenal was 'Laughter.'

The sun now hit the skylight. The light show took on its spectral dance as the sun's rays bounced around and created the Buddha's halo. Pon stared as the lights gained in brilliance, until the halo surrounded the Statues head. He could imagine how the spectacle would amaze the throbbing masses who would witness it and feel the same tingle of excitement that he did, being touched by 'The light of god.'

He said aloud,

"Thank you my Buddha for allowing me the privilege to serve you."

He looked up, shielding his eyes and, for just a second, he thought that the light made a small vortex, a swirling opening. He could clearly see the golden box containing the Holy Relics: 'Nicholas Godfrey of Brighton's expensive ceramic false teeth.'

Pon turned around, walked towards the door of the temple, and went outside into the hot sticky Bangkok air; his duty concluded.

— Epilogue —

Spring arrived, releasing the icy grip from the fingers of a long, cold, English winter. On a mild sunny morning, the birds sang in the trees, the lambs jumped and frolicked in the fields, fish splashed around in the babbling brooks and a euphoric feeling abound in sunny old Blighty. It felt a good day to be alive.

Everything was happy. People were happy. Animals were happy. The plants and trees were happy, and Nick was happy, as he sat in the departure lounge of Gatwick airport.

He smirked as he thought, 'Bimen airways, Bangladesh airlines; never in a million years, and Gatwick airport, no chance it's too far for them.'

Taking a long gulp from his pint of lager, he recalled the events from his previous encounter, remembering the pain from his arm, mouth, head, arse, and finally his broken clavicle. He ran his tongue over his new crowned teeth. 'That last holiday cost me a fortune, and most of it I spent in bloody hospital.' he thought. 'Not again... No sir.'

He planned to fly to Bangkok on an inexpensive return flight with Bimen Airways. He would then go to Pattaya and, if they were not there, he would stay. However, if they were in Pattaya, he would head to the now re-developed Phuket. He had left instructions with his sister, should they call, she was to tell them that he'd gone to work in London.

Nick, feeling pleased with himself; moved his stool closer to the small brass table and took another gulp of lager, watching the world go by as he enjoyed his refreshing pint. He held the glass to his lips and suddenly felt an icy chill course through his body. Looking over the rim of his glass, he saw two figures approach him. Fear gripped him

355

like cold steel. He tried to stand, but hit his knees on the bottom of the small, but heavy, table. He fell forward, hitting his head and mouth, with full force on the edge of the table.

Stunned, he fell to the floor and rolled onto his back. His mouth and nose throbbed and he could taste his own blood. He spat out a lump of blood, mucous, and his new crowns. He looked up in pained surprised at the ceiling of the departure lounge. Two heads popped into view and looked down at him.

"Mate, that looks painful," said Spock.

"Just lay there and we will go to get you some help," added Stu.

Just for the time being.

THE END

"Thank you for taking time to read 'Something to Read While Travelling: THAILAND'. If you enjoyed it, please consider telling your friends or posting a short review. Word of mouth is an author's best friend and much appreciated. Thanks a lot." Rob

Appendix

Siam has been known as Thailand since 1939.

'Khun is the polite way to address an older, or senior, Thai person; similar to Mr or Mrs.

The Temple of the Emerald Buddha

The 'Emerald Buddha' is a large gold coloured statue of a sitting Buddha approximately 50 feet high. On its head is an emerald, approximately 4 inches high has the effigy of Buddha carved into it. This is mounted in a small gold and glass case. The Thais regard this as the holiest Buddha in Thailand. It is open to the public, as are some other parts of the Imperial Palace.

Pitou is a long curved spike with eight slits around the point and a carved wood handle. It is a weapon that would be inserted into the back of the neck,.and pierce the base of the skull and go into the medulla oblongata, the part of the brain that controls all major bodily functions, including breathing and heartbeat. Once it reached its target, the bearer would press a catch on the handle, and eight blades would spring out of the slits. With a quick twist, the medulla oblongata was turned to mush; an instant death. Once the catch released, the blades would spring back and the pitou easily removed. Using one hand to cover the victim's mouth and one hand to operate the pitou, it is a silent, devastatingly efficient weapon and exclusively a Tinju weapon.

Glave is a small double-bladed weapon, with each blade crescent-shaped and razor sharp. At its centre, a handle wrapped with cotton; it was used like a dagger to slash or stab. It may be thrown. It is very deadly and accurate.

All Thais have ID cards, which stay with them throughout their lives. On these cards are names, date of birth etc. They are used in everyday life for many things, opening bank accounts, renting apartments etc. and crossing borders into Cambodia or Burma. They are carried at all times, and the Thai people are fined quite heavily or imprisoned if caught without them.

There are small villages in Thailand cut off from society, therefore don't have any need, or use, for ID cards, Salaburi being one.

Thai people cross over into Cambodia, to the east of Thailand or to Burma in the west, mainly for gambling, as gambling in Thailand is illegal. Cambodia and Burma have capitalised on this exodus, building many top-class casinos close to main border crossings, and mainly run by corrupt high-ranking police and organised crime syndicates with American or European investors. Beggars as young as five years old walk around outside these casino's in the scorching heat in their droves. They follow border crossers, shading them with umbrellas' to get one or two Bahts. Some of the children carry babies in shabby slings. These new-borns are usually brothers or sisters, used to get sympathy and to look desperate.

Poi pet on the Cambodian side and Aranyaprathet on the Thailand side are the main crossings, and the most visited border crossing, leading into the eastern heart of Thailand.

Cambodians are allowed to cross over the border into Thailand. These are usually the market traders, who sell their wares at Aranyaprathet, the Thailand-side market. These traders would go across with a small cart, piled high with their wares, many times higher than the cart, many people would push these barrows and people sit on top to stop the load from falling off. These traders don't require passports as they only set up at the border markets.

Thai people have forenames and surnames, their family also gave them nicknames at a very young age. These names were usually chosen by circumstances. For example, if it was raining when they

358

were born, their nickname could be Phon meaning 'falling rain'. If they are small, Noi or Lek, meaning 'small' or 'little' could be used. They could also use a portion of their first name if it has a meaning. Duengdao, for example, shortened to Dao, means 'Star'. They tend to be known by these short nicknames as opposed to long actual names throughout their lives. However, they revert to their real names on reaching middle-age or obtaining a higher status.

Thai boys are conscripted into a Buddhist temple at a young age, usually 12 years-old. These boys are selected by a town/village lottery. They are required to serve several years as a monk, to learn Buddhist teachings. A few stay on, making it their lifetime calling.

Thai Bar Girls. Some Thai girls go to the tourist areas to find bar work in bars and go with foreigners. Most leave their children with their grandparents. They usually came with hard luck stories of their child's father, who would have either been a drunk, taking drugs or a butterfly, someone who went from girl to girl. Many of these stories were untrue, but told to get a foreigner to send them money. Most girls would have several foreign men sending money, which they shared among their friends and current Thai boyfriend. This was again, the Thai way. Western society considered this as degrading and believed they were forced into this life, and were being exploited, and yes, probably some were. Nevertheless, as most bargirls would tell you, they earn good money, can take care of their family, party every night, get a shag, and are paid for it. To a Thai, sex is just another bodily function. However, they will not go with a man if they don't like him; it is their choice. When the girls first come to work the bar, until they have a few Farang under their belt, they are usually shy, until they learned the ropes from the more experienced girls and the 'mamasan'. At this stage, they have not been corrupted or brainwashed, so sometimes, the lucky ones marry a foreigner. This happened quite frequently; a Thai wife is a loving, loyal and usually beautiful partner. Not all Thai girls are bar girls; they are a minority. Most Thai women are usually the same as the western women, homemakers, doctors, students, teacher's etc. However, bar work is a

359

very accepted part of the Thai way of life, which is why many single and married men, come to tourist areas like Pattaya and Phuket

Thais require a visa to enter countries outside South East Asia. It is a well-known fact the United Kingdom is one of the most difficult to obtain. Most embassies just stamp the visa as routine. However, for the U.K., it is a strict interview with copies of guarantees and bank statements and funds available for the person's stay. The Thais also need to have a reason to return, Business, property etc. and a healthy bank account. Even then it's not guaranteed that they will obtain a visa, even just for a short holiday and marriage to a Thai does not guarantee a visa, which can be a long process obtaining.

THE KING OF THAILANDS RAIN

This little known or publicised fact is true. King Bhumipol Adulyadej of Thailand can make rainfall. He invests a lot of money in agriculture and development and although Thailand can have a lot of rain during the rainy season, some areas of Thailand can be dry if the season isn't too wet or long. With the Opium trade turned now by the King to fruit growing, these areas require more rain.

In 1956, the King formed the royal Rainmaking research and development project. Its task was to research into making artificial rain. They were successful and in 1969, the first artificial rain came down on the northern provinces of Thailand.

The process is relatively simple. Light aircraft locate a suitable cloud high up in the atmosphere over an area that requires rain. The cloud is then permeated with 'seeding chemicals' and the base of the cloud is sprayed with liquid Nitrogen, 'Dry ice', which, when mixed with the seeding chemicals produces precipitation and lowers the now rain filled cloud. As the cloud gets lower to the ground, it releases the rain. It is similar to natural clouds formation.

So, not only can they make rain, they can pretty much determine the area to receive the rain. King Bhumipol of Thailand holds the patent on this technique and three other patents in agricultural innovations. This is one reason why he has the title 'The Great' and one of the reasons why he is well loved and respected by his people.

Any sceptics amongst you, just ask any Thai person, or research for yourself on the World Wide Web about THE KING OF THAILANDS RAIN.

Koh Samet, like most Islands in Thailand, are jungle covered rocky outcrops or mountains. The larger islands have been developed to a stage were very little jungle remained, just sporadic spots. Large islands, such as Phuket and Samui have been modernised, with any spare piece of land turned into hotels, resorts, or other buildings to attract the hoards of foreign visitors and their money. The smaller islands remain relatively unscathed, with tourist developments only being around the flat areas around beaches, leaving the harder to develop hillsides untouched and still prime lush jungle.

Chantaburi, a town situated on the south end of the eastern seaboard of Thailand; is one of the world's leading coloured gemstone trading centres, dealing in both precious and semi precious stones. There are four stones classed as precious; Ruby, Sapphire, Emerald, and Diamond. These stones are classed as precious, by their scale of hardness and density. Ruby Sapphire and Emerald register between 9 - 9.5 and diamond, being the hardest, registers at 10. Every other gemstone, such as Amethyst, Garnet, etc register below 9 and classed as semi-precious.

Diamond and Emeralds are not usually found traded at Chantaburi. Diamonds are mainly traded in Africa and Amsterdam. Emeralds are usually traded in South America.

Chantaburi and its neighbour Trat, used to have large deposits of Ruby and Sapphires. The mines, although almost paid out, left a legacy of a highly lucrative trading centre. Millions of dollars changed hands every day in exchange for precious Rubies and multi-coloured Sapphires that would be set in jewellery and worn by people all over the world. Chantaburi bustled with activity on trading days and boosted the Thai economy. Most Rubies now though came from Africa or the nearby Burma and Sapphires from Sri Lanka. Chantaburi has the reputation for having some of the world's most skilful cutters of the stones, turning the drab, raw, dull stones into beautifully faceted gems. The Thai ruby is one of the rarest and most sought after, as it is Pigeon blood red with a tint of violet. The Thai blue sapphires are darker than the light sky blue colour of Sri Lanka sapphires and are very sought after. Both the Thai ruby and sapphire are now extremely rare.

Inclusions are small imperfections in gemstones. Inclusions lessen the stones value. No inclusions, the stone is classed as 'flawless'.

Durian is a tropical fruit that originates in Southeast Asia. It is also referred to as the "King of Fruits." Although it is a delicious fruit, it has a foul smell. The fruit has an oblong shape with a thick, greenish-brown thorny skin. It is one of the heaviest fruits available. Length of the fruit can extend to 18 inches with a weight of up to 15 pounds. It contains vitamins A, B1, B3, B6, C and folic acid. The fruit is rich in calcium, phosphorous, potassium and magnesium. Several trace minerals also occur in the fruit. It is a rich source of protein, phytonutrients and simple fats.

Pai-Non or sleeping sticks are an effective Tinju weapon, although death came slowly, it came peacefully. It was the easiest method for the monks in ancient times to dispatch their duties, because buying essence sticks from monks was considered lucky, a rumour spread by monks, possibly the Tinju.

The victim would light the stick. The top two or three inches would burn like normal essence stick and it gave off a pleasant fragrant aroma. The heat would then hit the mix and the aroma would change slightly, although remain pleasant and the victim would be unaware that they were slowly being murdered. After a few moments of the

362

mixture burning, the victim would fall asleep and, as they continued to inhale the poison-filled air, their muscles would become paralysed, lungs, heart, and finally, brain. The same effect as Thiopentone, used as an anaesthetic and Potassium Chloride, used to stop the heart. The mixture has to be carefully prepared, if there was too little Aroona and graphite; the victim would wake up paralysed, making for a very unpleasant death; nevertheless, sometimes requested by the ruler if he did not like someone. If there were too little skeet roots, the organ paralysis would not occur leaving the victim in a deep sleep for a few days.

Gnostic gospels are alleged documents written by Disciples of Christ, containing the actual words of Christ. It is rumoured they also claim that Mary Magdalene was married to, and had a child by, Jesus, and that a holy bloodline exists.

Sato is a Thai moonshine made from rice, cloudy yellow in colour and tastes similar to Sake, its Japanese, better known equivalent.

Urban whiskey or Loa Khaw is fermented tree bark, dark amber in colour, and the more aged vintage jar, tastes similar to port or sherry and is regarded as a natural 'Viagra'. Both drinks are very potent, going from 'sober' to 'wankered' in four or five small glasses.

Radiocarbon dating, or carbon dating 14, is a radiometric dating method that uses the naturally occurring radioisotope carbon-14 (14C) to determine the age of carbonaceous materials up to about 58,000 to 62,000 years. Raw, i.e. uncalibrated, radiocarbon ages are usually reported in radiocarbon years "Before Present" (BP), "Present" being defined as AD 1950. Such raw ages can be calibrated to give calendar dates

Robert A Webster

Novels

Siam Storm - A Thailand Adventure

A stolen holy relic from a secluded Thai Buddhist Monastery sends a combatant monk on a quest to retrieve the sacred item. Three English lads who are having the holiday experience of a lifetime in Thailand, become inadvertently embroiled in the deadly pursuit.

Enjoy the first adventure of Nick, Spock and Stu as they assist in the recovery of the relic and the subsequent voyage of discovery.

Chalice - Siam Storm 2 – A Cambodian Adventure

The discovery of a mysterious corpse leaves law enforcement agencies baffled. This adventure sees the lads join forces with their new friend, Pon, as they once again attempt to recover a holy relic, which has this time stolen for a completely new and sinister reason. The chase takes them into Cambodia, as they thwart plans that could affect the planet and change them into fruit based drinkers.

Bimat - Siam Storm 3 - A Vietnamese Adventure

A kidnap and ransom demand lead our hapless heroes into a pursuit through Vietnam. They encounter an old foe, driven by obsession in his revenge driven quest. This time they face many challenges in both their adventure and their personal circumstance and although they almost lose everything, they never lose hope.

Trilogy: All three Southeast Asia adventures.

Protector – Siam Storm 4 – The Final Adventure

The adventure continues in, Protector, the fourth book of the Siam Storm Series.

When descendants of Siddhartha Gautama arrive at the Royal Palace in Bangkok, it is Prime Master Pon's duty to discover who is responsible for the murder of the other descendants, along with their age-old protectors.

After capturing an assassin, Pon assembles a team of combatant monks to track down the leader of a rising savage group of terrorists. The fun begins when Spock and Stu join the team, and as usual, they find trouble. Even with Spock and Stu underfoot, the team uncovers evidence of a plot with worldwide implications.

Protector follows the hazardous journey through unfamiliar terrain as the team races the clock to stop further killings of their brethren, only to discover that things are not always as they seem.

Spice

Ben Bakewell is a master baker with a unique gift that made him the grand master of his culinary craft. More commonly known as 'Cake' he meets up with Ravuth, a Cambodian man residing in England ,who has spent the majority of his life trying to trace his long lost family.

Jed Culver is a disgraced D.E.A agent whose bitterness for his old employer and lust for revenge lead him along a deadly path, as he also pursues the plant, although for a far more sinister gain.

This thrilling, but yet sometimes hilarious quest, takes you from the glitz and glamour of the fashionable London restaurant scene, to the wild, untamed tropical forests surrounding the Cardamom mountains region of Southeast Asia, as the participants race to discover the whereabouts of a remarkable plant and locate a misplaced family.

Fossils

Enjoy the hilarious antics of an elderly four piece band as they embark on a whirlwind tour of several countries in Southeast Asia, unaware of their amazing worldwide success. Steve Baker (Strat) Elvin Stanley (Chippers) Charles Clark (Nobby) and Wayne Logan (Sticks) more famously known as 'Fossils,' are four musicians from varying background who are inadvertently united and form a band with a unique and exciting sound that filled an auditory hiatus that has been lacking for decades in the modern day music industry. Pursued and hounded by ruthless record producers, this unassuming rock band discover a new, exciting and carefree way of life, which they enjoy to the fullest, or at least what remains of it. Viagra, snuff, and Rock'n'roll.

P.A.T.H

A team of three psychics use their unique talents to provide a link between the mortal world and the celestial. Commissioned by lost souls; they find lost treasures for the troubled sprits, which they give to the mortal beneficiaries. One particular case finds the team caught up in a plot that had been conceived during world war two, which is instigated in the present day. The team has to solve a mystery that threatens to split the delicate fabric joining the two worlds.

The return of the Reich.

NEXT - PATH 2

With the fate of humankind resting on their shoulders, the PATH team, along with the mortal Keepers and Guides around the world, are sent on various quests. Each individual test will push them all to their limits as time slowly ticks down towards armageddon and their destiny.

Covenant of the Gods.

Non - Fiction

Help Safely Lower Your Blood Sugar with the Tree of Life

This book has been written by a collaboration of medically trained diabetics – not by Medical Practitioners, PhD professors or salespeople. – They are people who until recently struggled to control diabetes with diet, exercise and high levels of glycemic drugs alone. After learning about products made from the Moringa tree, they were able to dramatically lower their blood glucose levels within weeks and continue to do so. They did their research thoroughly and found the pods and leaves of this unique tree dramatically lowered their blood glucose levels quickly, and that continues to be the case. They now want to share their knowledge and extensive research in a simple to understand way, so you too can also benefit from their experience.

Something to Read While Travelling- THAILAND.

A travellers' companion that contains; useful information about Thailand, some of which you won't find in travel guidebooks. Thai Language Made Simple: Popular Thai Recipes: Fun Quizzes and Brainteasers: Hilarious Jokes: Short Stories: and the full comedy adventure novel, SIAM STORM – A Thailand Adventure.

Home Pages :

Amazon-http://www.amazon.com/Robert-A.-Webster/e/B004ZK975K

Kobo-https://store.kobobooks.com/en-CA/search?query=Robert%20A%20Webster&fcsearchfield=Author&fclanguages=all

itunes   -   https://itunes.apple.com/us/artist/robert-a.-webster/id376017369?mt=11

Websites:

http://www.buddhasauthor.com/

http://stormwriter.weebly.com/

connect:

Facebook - https://www.facebook.com/Buddhasauthor

Twitter - https://twitter.com/buddhasauthor

QUIZ ANSWERS

Thai Knowledge

1. Sawadee Khap 2. Sawadee Kah 3. Ho-ng naam Ti nai Khap? 4. Aw Pai Sanam bin Kah. 5. King Bhumipol Adulyadej 6. Bangkok 7. Never mind, no problem, don't mention it. 8. Siam 9. 26 December 2004 10. Thai Baht 11. Mai Kow Chai, Khap, 12. Aw Bia song co-at, Kah. 13. Yee sib et 14. Wan Jan 15. Suvarnabhumi Airport 16. Sabaii dee Khap/Kah or Mai Sabaii. depending how you feel. 17. My name is .... 18. Andaman Sea 19. Tow lie khap/ Kah 20, Song Roi 21. Koh 22. South China Sea. 23. Elephant 24. Roi haa sup haa. 25. 10 Baht 26. Muay Thai 27. Ruby and Sapphire 28 Cambodia 29. Neung Pan 30. Bangkok

General Knowledge

1 The Boy Scouts 2, Operation Sea Lion 3. Margaret Thatcher 4. Gateshead 5 Saws wood 6 Robert Maxwell 7. Woe 8 Turkey 9. The candela 10. The knees 11. Ugli Fruit 12. 42 13. 10 Feet 14 Single Lens Reflex 15. Who Dares Wins 16 Eire and Denmark 17, 27 Years 18. The Sun 19. Andromeda 20 Femur 21 Optic Nerve 22 Denmark 23 1923 24 Open Spaces 25 1000 26 July 4th 27 Rene Descartes 28 Italy 29 PC Plod 30 collar bone 31 Blue Peter 32 Franz Hals 33 Noah 34 Canada 35 Kenya 36 Mercury 37 Onions 38 Cob 39 Artist 40 Menorah

Brainteasers

1. The couple who married are called Mr and Mrs Not, so the boys are Not brothers
2. Tommy.
3. Mt. Everest...it just wasn't discovered yet.
4. There is no dirt in a hole.
5. Incorrectly (except when it is spelled incorrecktly).

6. You can't take a picture with a wooden leg. You need a camera (or iPad or cell phone) to take a picture.
7. You would be in 2nd place. You passed the person in second place, not first.
8. One. If he combines all his haystacks, they all become one big stack.
9. Nothing.
10. A coffin.
11. A stamp.
12. A watermelon.
13. SOS.
14. First mom and dad – 2 minutes. Dad comes back – 3 minutes, both children go to mom – 8 minutes. Mom comes to dad – 10 minutes and they both get to their children – 12 minutes.
15. None. Moses wasn't on the ark, Noah was.

Intelligence IQ Test

1. 22 and 24: there are two interwoven sequences. Starting at 19, alternate numbers progress +2, +3, +4, +5. Starting at 20, alternate numbers progress +2, +4, +6, +8.
2. 47632: all the others are three-digit numbers followed by their square root, eg 361 followed by its square root, 19.
3. parade, somnambulate. The keyword to insert is walk: parade on a cat-walk, sleepwalk is to somnambulate.
4. KP: there are two alternate sequences. Starting at A, - ABcDefGhijK; starting at Z, ZYxWvuTsrqP.
5. 112 pairs of shoes = 224 shoes. 224 ÷ 28 = 8.
6. derivative, archetypal
7. Synonyms: excuse, condone   -   Antonym: condemn
8. 1 apple costs £0.18 and 1 banana costs £0.14.
9. WNW, WSW, SSW, SSE, SE, ESE, ENE, NNE
10. 34826: each number is the sum of the last two digits of the previous number, preceded by the remaining numbers in reverse.
11. H
12. whimsical, eerie

13. Synonyms: console, assuage - Antonym: torment
14. 4.5 and 13.5 should be interchanged. The top sequence progresses +3, +3.5, +4, +4.5, +5. The bottom sequence progresses +5, +4.5, +4, +3.5.
15. Irritation

Rating	SCORE
Smart as a Rock	1 - 10
smart as amoeba	11 -20
Just smarter than the average Bear	21 -30
Now we're getting somewhere	31 - 40
Okay, so you're average	41 - 50
Cooking on gas	51 - 60
Smarty - pants	61 - 70
Now you're smokin'	71 - 80
Stephen Hawkins is now worried	81 - 90
Bloody hell! A Genius	91 - 100

QUIZ	SCORE
THAI	
GENERAL KNOWLEDGE	
BRAIN TEASER	
IQ	
TOTAL	

"Thank you for taking time to read 'Something to Read While Travelling: THAILAND'. If you enjoyed it, please consider telling your friends or posting a short review. Word of mouth is an author's best friend and much appreciated. Thanks a lot." Rob

Bibliography

Information and tips

http://bangkokthailandairportmap.blogspot.com/2013/06/detail-bangkok-map-for-travelers-guide.html

http://www.bangkok.com/most-popular-historical/

http://www.ixigo.com/travel-guide/koh-samui

http://www.pattaya.net/

http://www.phuket.net/things-to-do/

http://www.webmd.com/

http://www.kohjumresort.com/map_thai.html

http://www.thailand-immigration.org/

http://www.tourismthailand.org/

http://www.tourismthailand.org/Where-to-Go/Chiang-Mai

http://www.orangesmile.com/common/img_city_maps/pattaya-map-0.jpg

http://thailandholiday.org.uk/guide/phuket/

Thai Language

http://www.thai-language.com/lessons

http://pattaya-funtown.com/thai_vocabulary/

Popular Thai recipes

http://thai.food.com/

Jokes

http://www.laughfactory.com/jokes/popular-jokes

Quiz's brainteasers

http://www.freepubquiz.co.uk/general-knowledge-quiz-questions.html

https://cambomaths.files.wordpress.com/

Short Stories

http://www.thaifiction.com/book_view.php?id=58

http://www.world-english.org/stories.htm

https://en.wikipedia.org/wiki/Thai_folklore

DISCLAIMER

376

Memory By Than Yutthachaivodin: A Muay Thai Story By Derby Shaw

Printed in Great Britain
by Amazon.co.uk, Ltd.,
Marston Gate.